THE LITURGICAL YEAR

THE
LITURGICAL YEAR

Volume Three

THE PASCHAL TRIDUUM, THE EASTER SEASON

by

Adrian Nocent, O.S.B.

translated by

Matthew J. O'Connell

THE LITURGICAL PRESS

COLLEGEVILLE   **MINNESOTA**

Cover design by Clement Schmidt.

Available in four volumes, THE LITURGICAL YEAR is the authorized English version of *Célébrer Jésus-Christ, L'année Liturgique*, published by Jean-Pierre Delarge, 10, rue Mayet, 75006 Paris, France.

Nihil obstat: William G. Heidt, O.S.B., S.T.D., *Censor deputatus.*
Imprimatur: ✝ George H. Speltz, D.D., Bishop of St. Cloud, October 12, 1977.

Printed in the United States of America. ISBN 0-8146-0964-3

CONTENTS

THE PASCHAL TRIDUUM

THE EASTER SEASON

SOLEMNITIES OF THE LORD

THE LITURGICAL YEAR

THE PASCHAL TRIDUUM, THE EASTER SEASON

BIBLICO-LITURGICAL REFLECTIONS

ON THE PASCHAL TRIDUUM

The Climax of the Liturgical Year

Devotion to the paschal mystery is not optional for Christians, any more than its celebration is something exceptional in Catholic liturgy. The paschal mystery rather exemplifies and prescribes the law that must govern our lives: the law of death, and the law of life coming through death and by means of death. Therefore, the paschal mystery is really the very heart of the liturgy, and the entire liturgical year grows out of it.

The early generations of Christians were very conscious of the primordial place of the paschal mystery. They celebrated only the night of the "Pasch," which they understood as a "passage" through death to authentic life.

Even today the holy days are celebrated with great simplicity in some of the rites. In the Coptic Rite, for example, the celebration consists entirely of readings from the Old and New Testaments that enlighten us on the meaning of the paschal mystery, praise the Lord for it, render it present, and prepare the faithful for his return. This liturgy, with its monastic simplicity and essentially contemplative character, is especially notable during the Paschal Vigil, where, once again, it consists entirely of readings.

At Rome, the focus of celebration was the Paschal Vigil that ended with the Eucharistic sacrifice and soon came to include the administration of baptism as well. This primitive nucleus was quickly expanded. In fifth-century Africa, when St. Augustine speaks of the paschal celebration, he calls it "the triduum of Christ crucified, buried, and risen,"

3

and is referring to Good Friday, Holy Saturday, and Easter Sunday. The climax of the three days was the single Eucharistic celebration during the night between Saturday and Sunday.

At Jerusalem, however, where it was easier than elsewhere to follow the historical unfolding of the paschal mystery by visiting the holy places, the liturgy was already quite extensively developed. The travel diary of Egeria, a fourth-century widow, provides us with a detailed description of the Jerusalem liturgy, beginning with Palm Sunday.[1] The liturgy took the form of a deliberately accurate reconstruction of the final actions of Jesus' life; yet the liturgy celebrated the whole of the paschal mystery and did not break it up, even if each day was given over to one particular aspect of it.

In order to copy what was done at Jerusalem and to bring to life the details afforded by the evangelists, the Western liturgy expanded. A detailed celebration took up the whole of what we now call Holy Week, although the main concentration was on the last days of the week and on Easter Sunday.

The danger of such a detailed and anecdotal reconstruction of the sacred actions that make up the paschal mystery was that the faithful might break up the mystery into unconnected parts and might separate the celebration of Jesus' death too much from the celebration of his resurrection. The danger of fragmentation, of turning the whole into disparate aspects not seen in the context of the paschal mystery, was not always successfully avoided. In the Middle Ages Holy Week was referred to as the "Week of Sorrow," thus emphasizing the suffering of Jesus and the loving compassion of Christians for him, but insufficiently adverting to the aspect of triumph and victory.

The tendency to an anecdotal reading of the Gospel had important consequences, some of which are still with us. Toward the middle or end of the seventh century, a commemoration of the Last Supper was introduced at Rome, where Holy Thursday had hitherto been chiefly the day for the reconciliation of penitents. This caused a displacement: The paschal triduum now meant Holy Thursday, Good Friday, and Holy Saturday. We shall return to this later. The point to be made here is that this new triduum could turn the minds of the faithful from the full meaning of the paschal mystery, inasmuch as what we now call "the three holy days" do not perfectly coincide with what the Church of St. Augustine's time called the Holy Triduum. For Augustine, the three days were Friday, Saturday, and Sunday; for us they are Thursday, Friday, and Saturday.

The intention of people at that time was evidently to lend the liturgy a dramatic quality, but the quality was somewhat factitious; it could also be, and has in fact often been, misunderstood. The liturgy, after all, is not simply a play. We do not take part in the liturgy in order to recall past events in an atmosphere of spiritual emotion. We take part in it in order to celebrate a mystery that the liturgy itself renders present. The liturgical celebration makes present the spiritual efficacy of a moment that in its material anecdotal form is historically past. The historical event was complete in itself. For this reason it does not have to be repeated; what we want is that it should be present to each moment of history as a source of value.

We must keep these basic considerations in mind, for they are essential to the celebration of Holy Week, and indeed to every liturgical celebration.

1. A CRUCIFIED GOD

Three basic questions

The three holy days raise three closely related problems that are basic for Christian life and indeed for the life of the world at large: the problem of a crucified God; the problem of his resurrection; and the problem of the Eucharist as a sign that renders the other two saving events present and active in our midst.

We must repeat here what we had occasion to say early on in each of the two preceding volumes in this series, namely, that anyone who does not believe in the reality of this crucified God, his resurrection, and the Eucharist will be unable to accept or understand what follows upon them. At the same time, however, even if we do believe in them, we should ask ourselves what kind of faith we have in them and how they affect modern man's life and the difficulties he faces. To ask these questions is not to enter into apologetics. Our aim is more modest. We want simply to discover or rediscover these three realities. They are so basic that if the Church were no longer to acknowledge them as real, she would cease to exist.

Albert Camus wrote the following lines, which are truly fine, even if they are open to some valid criticism:

> Christ came to solve two problems: evil and death, both of which are problems of rebellion. His solution first consisted in taking them on himself. The God-man also suffers, and does so with patience. Evil cannot be as fully ascribed to him as death, as he too is shattered and dies. The night of Golgotha only has so much significance for man because in its darkness the Godhead, visibly renouncing all inherited privileges, endures to the end the anguish of death, including the depths of despair. This is the explanation of the *Lama sabachthani* and Christ's gruesome doubt in agony. The agony would have been easy if it could have been supported by eternal hope. But for God to be a man, he had to despair.[2]

Jürgen Moltmann, who quotes these lines from Camus, offers his own reflections on them. As he reads Camus, the latter does not really think that Christ has resolved evil and death as problems of rebellion.[3] We must not let ourselves be fooled by the excellence of Camus's writing here. He does emphasize the importance of what Christ did in accepting crucifixion; the crucifixion is asserted to be a solution for the world's problems; there is no denying that Christ experienced agony and abandonment on the Cross, as the evangelists insist. Nonetheless, there is something essential lacking in Camus's reflections. Moltmann puts his finger on it quite accurately: "He [Camus] saw God vanish on the cross, but he did not see Christ's death or the cross taken up into God. Yet only this change of perspective indicates why the night of Golgotha gained so much significance for mankind."[4]

We may recall here the simplicity and grandeur with which St. Paul describes this same change of perspective: "And being found in human form he humbled himself and became obedient unto death, even death on a cross. Therefore God has highly exalted him and bestowed on him the name which is above every name" (Phil. 2:8-9).

Camus's words undoubtedly could serve as a starting point for theological reflection, but it would be reflection closely allied to humanism and congenial to a contemporary vision of anthropology. Our concern, on the contrary, is with God's approach to reality. How does Scripture envisage the "crucified God"? If we want to understand the Cross and its efficacy, we must take as our starting point, not ourselves nor our rebellions in the face of suffering and death nor our ideas about God, but God's own plan as expressed in the Scriptures and in the Church's understanding of the Scriptures.

Jesus and his Cross

Let us begin by asking Jesus himself about the meaning and efficacy of the Cross. Who better than he can show us the way to a true understanding?

Christ draws his disciples' attention to this very same question: "How is it written of the Son of man, that he should suffer many things and be treated with contempt?" (Mark 9:12). He does not provide them with a direct answer to the question, but if we continue to search through the Gospels, we may be able to find an answer.

In many passages Jesus foretells his own violent death. St. Matthew records these significant words: "So will the Son of man be three days and three nights in the heart of the earth" (12:40). According to St. John, Christ says: "Destroy this temple, and in three days I will raise it up" (2:19). And there comes a point when Jesus begins to tell his disciples frequently that he must go up to Jerusalem and be put to death (Matthew 16:21, with the parallels: Mark 8:31; Luke 9:22; Mark 9:31; 10:32-34).

Later on, Jesus speaks of the "hour," which indicates not so much a point of time as his personal, free self-offering as obedient Victim to the Father. Thus, at the moment when Jesus' arrest is imminent, he says: "Behold, the hour is at hand, and the Son of man is betrayed into the hands of sinners" (Matthew 26:45). This idea of being "handed over" occurs frequently not only in Matthew but in the other Synoptics as well: "The Son of man will be delivered to the chief priests and scribes" (Matthew 20:18; Mark 10:33; cf. Luke 18:31). In Matthew's Gospel, Jesus continues the sentence just quoted: ". . . the chief priests and scribes, and they will condemn him to death, and deliver him to the Gentiles to be mocked and scourged and crucified" (Matthew 20:18-19). Yet the true disciple must share that death with Jesus: "He who loses his life for my sake will find it" (Matthew 10:39).

In St. Mark's Gospel, as we have already seen, Jesus makes the same prediction in the form of a question: "How is it written of the Son of man, that he should suffer many things and be treated with contempt?" (9:12). A little earlier, Mark reports the following incident:

> And he began to teach them that the Son of man must suffer many things, and be rejected by the elders and the chief priests and the scribes, and be killed, and after three days rise again. And he said this plainly. And Peter took him, and began to rebuke him. But turning and seeing his disciples, he rebuked Peter,

and said, "Get behind me, Satan! For you are not on the side of God, but of men" (8:31-33).

Christ is not giving the disciples an answer to his question, "Why the Cross?" but he does make the Cross something necessary, something the Father wills. The Cross is his response and justifies the words the Father spoke at the transfiguration: "This is my beloved Son; listen to him" (Mark 9:7).

And yet Jesus did feel a certain inward rebellion against what the Father was asking, for we see him praying that, if possible, this "hour" might pass him by (Mark 14:35; Matthew 26:39; Luke 22:42; John 12:27).

St. Luke develops the same themes as Matthew and Mark, and there is no point in going over all of them again. According to Luke, Jesus, in predicting his death, uses the image of baptism: "I have a baptism to be baptized with" (12:50). A little later, he says: "The third day I finish my course" (13:32). Not only does Jesus foretell his death (18:33; cf. Matthew 20:19; Mark 10:34), but the evangelist, speaking in his own name says: "When the days drew near for him to be received up . . ." (9:51).

A glorious Cross

In St. John's Gospel we find a more theological kind of reflection on the death of Jesus. As the reader is aware, the Synoptics supply historical details of the Passion that are not to be found in St. John. St. John, on the other hand, develops aspects of the Passion that in some instances are present in rudimentary form in the other Gospels but are not spelled out as they are in the Fourth Gospel. We have in mind especially the voluntary aspect of Christ's death. Jesus hands himself over, and does so with great dignity and on condition that his disciples are allowed to go free (John 18:6-8). Elsewhere, he himself chooses the "hour" when he will surrender to his executioners.

The theme of the "hour" is quite extensively developed in St. John. Christ uses the word himself: "My hour has not yet come" (2:4); "My time has not yet come" (7:6); "I have said this to you in figures; the hour is coming when I shall no longer speak to you in figures" (16:25); "The hour is coming, indeed it has come, when you will be scattered" (16:32). In two passages Jesus' use of the word is connected with a theology of his Passion and death: "The hour has come for the Son of man to be glorified" (12:23). But the glorification in no way lessens his burden of anguish: "'Now is my soul troubled. And what shall I say? "Father, save me from this hour"? No, for this purpose I have come to this hour. Father, glorify thy name.' Then a voice came from heaven, 'I have glorified it, and I will glorify it again'" (12:27-28).

For St. John, then, Christ's Cross and death are unintelligible unless they are seen as a sign of his glorification and exaltation. In this context, the evangelist twice uses the verb "lift up" with a double meaning. "Now is the judgment of this world, now shall the ruler of this world be cast out; and I, when I am lifted up from the earth, will draw all men to myself" (12:31-32). John then adds an explanation: "He said this to show by what death he was to die" (12:33). The Cross thus effects both Christ's own glorification and the unification of mankind.

As St. John sees it, the sacrifice of the Cross changed the course of history. The crucifixion is indeed a sign, but not a sign of death alone; it is also a sign of exaltation to glory. If Christ had simply died, history would only have witnessed one more man laid low. But Christ also rose from the dead; his resurrection is inseparable from his death and is but the other side of it.

Here John seems to be making his own a tradition that was already a vital one since the very first days of the Church. Thus he insists several times on the reality of Christ's resurrection. Inevitably, then, the Cross points not only to death but to glory, and is therefore an event that has forever changed the meaning of man's life in this world. It would doubtless be an exaggeration to say that the other New Testament writings present Jesus' death as a humiliation and then bring in the resurrection as the great corrective to the humiliation. But at least we must say that in St. John's Gospel, the Cross itself is presented as resurrection and glory no less than as death. John certainly depicts the crucifixion as a visible, sensibly real event, but he also insists that it be seen as a sign that contains what it signifies, namely, Christ's glorification. When Christ is dying, he is already going back to the Father (16:17; cf. 14:28; 16:10). We shall have further occasion to emphasize this point, which is so dear to John.[5]

The death-resurrection

It is impossible for us to present here the whole Johannine theology of Christ's death. Let us therefore pass on to the theology of St. Paul and recall its main characteristic lines.

As with John, so with Paul we must see death and resurrection as closely related if we are to understand the meaning and importance of the death itself. At the same time, however, it is legitimate for us to ask what the death on the Cross meant, as such, to St. Paul.

Again as with John, we find developed to some degree a theology of the Cross. In this regard Paul is aware of having inherited a firm tradition, as the First Letter to the Corinthians shows. He tells us there that the death and resurrection of Jesus are the principal object of Christian preaching and that if a person is converted to the faith, his belief in the death-resurrection of the Lord is decisive (1 Cor. 15:1-11).

There is also a close link between the Eucharist and the death-resurrection of Christ. Thus we see Paul, in the First Letter to the Corinthians, telling us how a very summary account of the death of Christ is part of the Eucharistic celebration (11:23-25). In this he is but following a tradition he himself has received. The Supper also contains the true theology of the Cross. When Christ celebrates the Supper, he does so in order that the memorial of his covenant sacrifice may be celebrated, that is, rendered always present and active. The death thus rendered present is the new covenant in Christ's blood; it is his death for the forgiveness of sins.

The Cross and love

When Paul speaks of the death of Christ, the factor on which he lays the greatest emphasis is love. Theologians have often tended to see in the Cross of Christ a kind of divine vengeance, with Christ as the necessary Victim. What Paul sees in it is above all a proof of love: Christ's love for men, and the Father's love for Christ and for men. It is out of love that Christ handed himself over to death (1 Cor. 8:11-13; Rom. 14:15; Gal. 11:20; Eph. 5:1-2, 25). St. John says the same (13:1). But in Christ's love for men we glimpse the Father's love for them too, and we can grasp something of the depth of the Father's love for us precisely from the fact that when we were still sinners, Christ died for us (Rom. 5:8). God did not spare his own Son but handed him over for us (Rom. 8:32).

The Cross and sin

The death of Christ must also be seen in relation to sin. It is a central motif of the Letters of Paul that Christ died for our sins: "Jesus . . . was put to death for our trespasses" (Rom. 4:25); "Christ, who died for us" (1 Thess. 5:10); "one has died for all" (2 Cor. 5:14); "While we were yet helpless, at the right time Christ died for the ungodly" (Rom. 5:6); "While we were yet sinners Christ died for us" (Rom. 5:8); "One [the brother] for whom Christ died" (Rom. 14:15; cf. 1 Cor. 8:11). We should note, too, that Paul often speaks of "sin" rather than "sins." In other words, he concentrates on an attitude taken by man rather than on the many actions that flow from the basic attitude which is "sin."

The death of Christ liberates man from this state of sin. St. Paul likes antitheses, especially the antithesis of slavery and freedom. On the one hand, "you were slaves of sin" (Rom. 6:20; cf. 6:6, 16); "making me captive to the law of sin which dwells in my members" (Rom. 7:23); "as sin reigned in death" (Rom. 5:21; cf. 6:14); "both Jews and Greeks are under the power of sin" (Rom. 3:9). On the other hand, "we . . . died to sin" (Rom. 6:2); "Our old self was crucified with him so that the sinful body might be destroyed, and we might no longer be enslaved to sin" (Rom. 6:6); "now . . . you have been set free from sin" (Rom. 6:22); "For the law of the Spirit of life in Christ Jesus has set me free from the law of sin and death" (Rom. 8:2).

The death of Christ ransoms us — although there is no need, when we use a word like "ransom," to insist on the metaphor; the real point is that his death makes us free. We were "sold" to sin (Rom. 7:14), but now we have been bought back at a great price (1 Cor. 6:20; 7:23); we have been ransomed from the curse of the law (Gal. 3:13). Our liberation was effected by the Cross: "Christ redeemed us from the curse of the law, having become a curse for us — for it is written, 'Cursed be every one who hangs on a tree' — that in Christ Jesus the blessing of Abraham might come upon the Gentiles, that we might receive the promise of the Spirit through faith" (Gal. 3:13-14). We are now justified by the redemption wrought for us in Christ Jesus (Rom. 3:24-25); he is our ransom (1 Cor. 1:30). "In him we have redemption through his blood, the forgiveness of our trespasses according to the riches of his grace which he lavished upon us" (Eph. 1:7-8).

To be freed from sin is simultaneously to be reunited to God: "For if while we were enemies we were reconciled to God by the death of his Son, much more, now that we are reconciled, shall we be saved by his life" (Rom. 5:10); "that he might . . . reconcile us both to God in one body through the cross, thereby bringing the hostility to an end" (Eph. 2:16; cf. Col. 1:21-22). The initiative in this reconciliation comes from God himself: "All this is from God, who through Christ reconciled us to himself and gave us the ministry of reconciliation; that is, God was in Christ reconciling the world to himself, not counting their trespasses against them, and entrusting to us the message of reconciliation" (2 Cor. 5:18-19).[6]

The Cross, a sacrifice of expiation

The Cross also brings us forgiveness. When dealing with this aspect of redemption, St. Paul often cites texts from the Old Testament, as in Romans 4:7-8, where he cites Psalm 32:1-2: "Blessed is he whose transgression is forgiven, whose sin is covered. Blessed is the man to whom the Lord imputes no iniquity." We obtain redemption, the forgiveness of our sins, through the Son (Col. 1:13).

Furthermore, Paul thinks of the Cross of Christ as being a sacrifice; it is as a sacrifice that it forgives sins. He writes, in his Letter to the Romans: "Since all have sinned and fall short of the glory of God, they are justified by his grace as a gift, through the redemption which is in Christ Jesus, whom God put forward as an expiation by his blood, to be received by faith" (3:23-25). If we are now able to "enter" the promised land, we can do so thanks to the Lamb who was sacrificed: "Christ, our paschal lamb, has been sacrificed" (1 Cor. 5:7). Jesus offered himself as a sacrifice for us: "Christ loved us and gave himself up for us, a fragrant offering and sacrifice to God" (Eph. 5:2) We must bear in mind, however, that Christ redeemed not only us but the entire world through his Cross: "He [God] disarmed the principalities and powers and made a public example of them, triumphing over them in him [Christ]" (Col. 2:15).

St. Paul, like the rest of us, finds it difficult to describe, in the terms elaborated by human wisdom, the meaning of the Son's death. In fact, for us that death is foolishness; only God could have imagined saving mankind through the Cross. The First Letter to the Corinthians is quite hard on those who attempt to explain this extraordinary action of the Father and the Son by human reasoning (1 Cor. 1:17-25). All we can really do is grasp the fact, without fully understanding it: "Christ Jesus . . . though he was in the form of God, did not count equality with God a thing to be grasped, but emptied himself, taking the form of a servant, being born in the likeness of men. And being found in human form he humbled himself and became obedient unto death, even death on a cross" (Phil. 2:6-8). There can be no explanation in human terms for such a gesture. The only hint given us is: "Therefore God has highly exalted him" (Phil. 2:9).

Knowing God through the Cross

"The new converging trends in theological thought today concentrate the question and the knowledge of God on the death of Christ on the cross, and attempt to understand God's being from the death of Jesus."[7] Only the study of Scripture can get us anywhere in this area. If we do look into the Scriptures, we find that they see Christ as the sign of encounter with God. In fact, "the scriptural basis for Christian belief in the triune God is . . . the thoroughgoing, unitary testimony of the cross; and the shortest expression of the Trinity is the divine act of the cross, in which the Father allows the Son to sacrifice himself through the Spirit."[8]

Some years back, a Jewish writer spoke of the problem of God. The way in which he does so brings home to us the problem of the Cross:

> The SS hanged two Jewish men and a youth in front of the whole camp. The men died quickly, but the death throes of the youth lasted for half an hour. "Where is God? Where is he?" someone asked behind me. As the youth still hung in torment in the noose after a long time, I heard the man call again, "Where is God now?" And I heard a voice in myself answer: "Where is he? He is here. He is hanging there on the gallows."[9]

Carrying the Cross of Christ is not something reducible to

mere metaphor. Yet, heavy though the Cross is, God carries it with us, although this is a fact that faith alone can grasp. The Church preaches the Cross no less than she preaches the resurrection. We can and must affirm that the Cross was raised for our sake and that it manifests God's love for us, now and always. How can a God suffer? How could Christ, fully God as well as fully man, suffer? These are questions we shall not tackle, important though they are. They contain a mystery that St. Paul says is foolishness to men and impossible for their wisdom to deal with.

2. THE GLORIOUS CHRIST, VICTOR OVER DEATH

Reality of the resurrection

It is a notable fact that the Church has never celebrated the death of Christ without at the same time celebrating his resurrection. This conjunction is exceptionally important. It means that the living tradition of the Church has always kept in view the ultimate purpose of the Cross, namely, a life that lasts until, and beyond, the reconstruction of the created world and the parousia of Christ. Despite interpretations claiming the contrary, at no time or place in her history has the Church ever celebrated the death of Christ in isolation; at all times that death is linked to his resurrection. It could not be otherwise, since the Scriptures look at the death and resurrection as one complete action.

It is common knowledge that the objective reality of the resurrection is under attack today. But

> to reduce the *fact* of the Resurrection to nothing but the birth of the Apostles' *faith* is . . . to contradict the Gospel, by presenting their *evidence* on the Resurrection as the *only* historically certain *content* of the Resurrection. What the Apostles intended to bear

witness to was not a faith which governed the existence of a fact, but rather a fact which gave birth to
their faith.[10]

The anthropology of the resurrection has to be studied
first of all in Scripture. We cannot expect to find there a
theological reflection on the resurrection, nor shall we attempt to supply for the lack; but we do find a concrete experience of the resurrection. The apostles experienced it,
or, more accurately, "in the *Risen* they . . . as it were
grasped the ungraspable character of the *Resurrection*."
Yet, the fact and objective reality of the resurrection are not
reducible to the faith and experience of the apostles, because their experience "is not for us the *only reality* of that
resurrection; it is the *historical* approach to that supreme
event, which cannot be reduced to the experience; for what
the Apostles *experienced* concerns *something in existence*,
which, now that it exists, *is binding* on us."[11]

The evangelists are very discreet when it comes to the
resurrection, so much so that we are tempted to think they
could have dwelt a good deal more on it. After all, would
not the resurrection have provided an extraordinarily effective apologetic argument for the divinity of Christ and the
redemptive value of his activity? In answer, we must point
out that, unlike those theologians who have a rather narrow
view of the resurrection, the evangelists never thought of it
in apologetic terms but as a sign of life's victory over death,
a victory now shared by all believers. Once we start looking
for the passages concerning the resurrection, we find that
they are relatively few in the Gospels. Matthew speaks of it
in four places (12:39-41; 17:22-23; 26:32; 28:2); Mark in
three (8:31; 9:31; 16:1-20); Luke in six (9:22; 11:30; 18:33;
24:1-52 [vv. 5, 24, 31]). John dwells on it more often and in
a more "theological" fashion (seven places: 2:19; 7:33-34;
7:39; 12:16; 13:31-32; 14:18-19; 20:1-10).

If we summarize what we are told in these passages, we
are left with three points: the assertion of the resurrection
on the third day; the empty tomb; the glorification of Christ

and the action of the Spirit. None of the evangelists is interested in the "how" of the resurrection; they simply describe a fact: the empty tomb. But, given that fact, they — especially St. John — dwell on the reality of Christ's human body after his resurrection, despite the fact that some great change has also taken place in his body. This is why the accounts of the apparitions are so important.

Christ behaves quite differently than he did before his death: he suddenly appears and disappears; he is no longer subject to the restrictions of space and the resistances of matter; he enters rooms even while the doors are, and remain, closed. And yet it is indeed he; his body is truly his body, for he eats like other men. Again, we are not given theological reflections on the nature of a glorified body; what the evangelists, especially St. John, want to communicate to us is their experience of Christ's glorified body. The faith of the apostles is built on facts, and what they want us to share is not a theology of the resurrection but their own experience of the fact. The risen Christ appears within historical time after his death. He is evidently no longer subject to the conditions of space and time, and yet, though no longer the same, he continues to be the same Jesus. *That* is the point of the apparition stories; no explanation of any kind is being offered.

The glory of the resurrection

The difficulties we have in adapting ourselves to the evangelists' approach are due entirely to our modern mentality. The fact of the resurrection stirs what we might call our "medical" curiosity. But such is not the apostles' viewpoint. They feel no need of knowing how it all happened. They know for a fact that they laid Jesus' body in the tomb, that the tomb is now empty, and that everyone saw Jesus later on. That is enough for them.

We, on the contrary, find it difficult not to wonder about how all this happened. How can a corpse come back to life? The apostolic writings will not satisfy our curiosity.

Their only concern is that Christ was crucified and died and is now in his glory; that he sends us the Spirit who raised him up, and thereby gives us a share in his glorified life. Since that is their only concern, the evangelists leave us with a kind of negative vision: the empty tomb, and a distinct positive vision: the apparitions and the apostolic experience of the real but glorified body of Christ.

Let us dwell for a moment on St. John's presentation of the mystery. In the farewell discourse of Christ we find a dialogue on the departure and return of the Lord (13:31–14:31). The whole passage speaks simply of departure and return, but it is not difficult to see that Christ is telling the disciples of his death and resurrection. The dialogue begins with a vision of glory: "Now is the Son of man glorified, and in him God is glorified; if God is glorified in him, God will also glorify him in himself, and glorify him at once" (13:31-32). The disciples cannot understand this, so Jesus repeats it in more concrete terms: "Yet a little while I am with you. . . . 'Where I am going you cannot come'" (13:33).

The glory that Jesus already has and will increasingly have is going to be shared by others. That sharing is the purpose of his death and resurrection: "And when I go and prepare a place for you, I will come again and will take you to myself, that where I am you may be also. And you know the way where I am going" (14:3-4).

All this will take place in order to transform the disciples' life. Here Christ grows more specific. If the disciple keeps Christ's word, "my Father will love him, and we will come to him and make our home with him" (14:23). Jesus tells them this while he is still with them, and they must believe. The Holy Spirit whom the Father will send in Jesus' name will instruct them fully and remind them of everything Jesus had said (14:25-26). Finally, Jesus returns to his opening theme: "You heard me say to you, 'I go away, and I will come to you.' . . . And now I have told you before it takes place, so that when it does take place, you may believe" (14:28-29).

Chapters 15 and 16 go back over the same themes but

add new revelations that are extremely important for the life of the disciples and the future Church. In 15:1-17 Jesus speaks of the union between Father, Son, and Church (that is, the first disciples who were to spread the Church throughout the world). A deeply moved Christ uses the language of love for these disciples whom he himself has chosen and who are now his friends. He is going to give his life for them; they must abide in his love and must love one another. In 15:18–16:33 the disciples see themselves confronting a world that does not understand them. But the Spirit will come and lead them to the truth, despite all opposition.

In these chapters we see how John thinks of the death and resurrection of Jesus. He does not think in our categories, nor do the difficulties felt by our contemporaries occur to him. For him, all difficulties are lost from sight in the glory of the *Kyrios* and his close union with his Church, which he now protects and which the Spirit guides.

The experience of St. Paul

St. Paul, too, tells us of his experience of Christ as risen. In fact, his very first Christian experience is a vision of the risen Christ, given him at the moment of his conversion. He takes this vision as comparable to that enjoyed by the apostles; like them, he has seen the risen Christ and is a witness to him:

> For I delivered to you as of first importance what I also received, that Christ died for our sins in accordance with the scriptures, that he was buried, that he was raised on the third day in accordance with the scriptures, and that he appeared to Cephas, then to the twelve. Then he appeared to more than five hundred brethren at one time, most of whom are still alive, though some have fallen asleep. Then he appeared to James, then to all the apostles. Last of all, as to one untimely born, he appeared also to me (1 Cor. 15:3-8).

Since he has seen the risen Christ, Paul is an apostle: "Am I not an apostle? Have I not seen Jesus our Lord?" (1 Cor. 9:1).

We must turn to Paul's discourse at Antioch in Pisidia (Acts 13:16-41) if we want to see how, in writing about the resurrection, he refers to the Scriptures and to the way the Christian community thought of the event. In his discourse Paul recalls Old Testament history down to the sending of Jesus. Then, after reminding his hearers of Jesus' death and descent into the tomb, in accordance with the Scriptures, Paul says: "But God raised him from the dead; and for many days he appeared to those who came up with him from Galilee to Jerusalem, who are now his witnesses to the people" (Acts 13:30-31).

Finally, Paul comes to the essential point in his message:

> And we bring you the good news that what God promised to the fathers, this he has fulfilled to us their children by raising Jesus; as also it is written in the second psalm, "Thou art my Son, today I have begotten thee." And as for the fact that he raised him from the deed, no more to return to corruption, he spoke in this way, "I will give you the holy and sure blessings of David." Therefore he says also in another psalm, "Thou wilt not let thy Holy One see corruption" (Acts 13:32-35).

Paul goes on to point to the effect of Christ's death and resurrection: "Through this man forgiveness of sins is proclaimed to you" (v. 38).

Elsewhere, though less extensively, Paul continues to rely on the Scriptures. He tells us that the prophets had proclaimed Christ's resurrection (Rom. 1:2-4), and that Psalm 110, which sings of exaltation at God's right hand, was already foretelling Christ's glorification (Eph. 1:20; Col. 3:1).

Resurrection: Revival of a dead man?

Objections to the resurrection existed even in St. Paul's day. Since the Greek philosophers regarded the body as a burden upon the soul, they hoped the day would come when the soul would be completely freed of the material body. Why raise the body? An all-powerful God can undoubtedly restore life to a corpse, but why should he do so? Why should he restore life to that which is inferior and only brings humiliation on man?[12]

In answer, Paul repeats, but in more precise and concrete terms, what he had already taught in this First Letter to the Thessalonians. In the First Letter to the Corinthians he writes: "What is sown is perishable, what is raised is imperishable. It is sown in dishonor, it is raised in glory. It is sown in weakness, it is raised in power. It is sown a physical body, it is raised a spiritual body" (1 Cor. 15:42-44). The Apostle is here attempting to give a kind of definition of a glorified body; its qualities, such as they are, are possessed in a supreme degree by the body of the risen Christ.

Flesh and blood, then, cannot possess the kingdom of God. The Christ, the Lord of glory, does possess a risen body, but it is heavenly and incorruptible. Christ is one and the same; he whom the apostles saw and touched before his death is the one whom they saw and whom Thomas touched after the resurrection. The body they saw and touched after the resurrection is, however, a glorious body that is no longer subject to space and time or to the material condition proper to things of our world.

Risen in Christ

The resurrection of Christ has two consequences for us, or rather a single consequence that can be seen as possessing two stages: Christ's resurrection guarantees ours, and ours has in a way already begun. That is a legitimate way of summing up St. Paul's thought on the matter. In his view, there is not only the resurrection at the parousia but also a kind of resurrection that is already ours and marks, as it were, the beginning of the parousia. If we believe in the final resurrection of each of us, in virtue of Christ's resurrection, then we ought also to believe that this resurrection has already begun for each of us.

The resurrection is linked to the *eschaton*, the messianic age. Numerous texts thus connect our resurrection at the end of time with the resurrection of Christ: "For as by a man came death, by a man has come also the resurrection of the dead. For as in Adam all die, so also in Christ shall all be made alive" (1 Cor. 15:21-22), and our resurrection will make us like the risen Christ (1 Cor. 15:49). Earlier in this same letter Paul writes: "God raised the Lord and will also raise us up by his power" (1 Cor. 6:14).

This change in us will not have its source totally outside us: "For if while we were enemies we were reconciled to God by the death of his Son, much more, now that we are reconciled, shall we be saved by his life. Not only so, but we also rejoice in God through our Lord Jesus Christ, through whom we have now received our reconciliation" (Rom. 5:10-11). We are truly assimilated to Christ in his risen state (Rom. 6:8) and truly share in his glory (Rom. 8:17), and the agent of this resurrection is the Spirit who now dwells within us: "If the Spirit of him who raised Jesus from the dead dwells in you, he who raised Christ Jesus from the dead will give life to your mortal bodies also through his Spirit who dwells in you" (Rom. 8:11).

More than this, we have already in a way been raised from the dead, and our bodies already possess a certain glory, since they are the temple of the Spirit (1 Cor. 6:19). We experience the presence of the Spirit in us (2 Cor. 5:1-19); we already possess the riches of heaven (1 Cor. 4:8). The risen Christ is thus the source of all life (Rom. 1:4; 1 Cor. 15:45).

We shall find that all these consequences of the resurrection are given concrete expression in the celebrations of the holy days.

3. THE RESURRECTION AND
THE EUCHARIST

As we shall be asserting again later on, the most important Eucharistic celebration in this last part of Holy Week is not that of Holy Thursday, which is rather commemorative in character, but that of the Paschal Vigil. The celebration during the Vigil is the culmination of all the celebrations during Holy Week, and the latter should be steps toward this climax.

The central importance of the Vigil Eucharist is not yet fully understood by many people. In a good number of locales, people set a higher value on the Christmas Midnight Mass, with its folklore and familial spirit, than on the Paschal Vigil. As a result, we find them tending to push the Vigil service back into the early evening of Saturday.

The ceremonies of the Vigil, moreover, are strange to people and a bit complicated. The attention of the faithful thus tends to be drawn to what is in fact peripheral rather than to what is the real heart of the celebration, namely, the Eucharist of the risen Christ.

For these various reasons, we must stop for a moment and show at least in broad outline the connection between the resurrection and the Eucharist.

During his earthly life, Jesus was the instrument of our salvation because in him we could touch and see the Father. Christ says as much in his rather impatient answer to Philip's request, "Show us the Father": "Philip, . . . he who has seen me has seen the Father" (John 14:8-9). Conversely, the reason why the Father sent Jesus was that in Jesus we might encounter the Father. For in encountering the man Jesus in a personal way, every man has access to the Father, the one who determined that the Son should be his instrument in saving the world.

At this point, however, a difficulty arises, for the post-resurrection situation of Christ seems to contradict the Father's plan. The Father sent his Son in human form in order that we might see his real bodily self and thus be in contact with a person who, though divine, is also truly a man. Yet now Jesus tells us: "It is to your advantage that I go away" (John 16:7)! How can this be so, since it means that during the time between the Passover and resurrection of the Lord, at one end, and his parousia or return, at the other, we shall no longer be able to be in contact with the instrument of our salvation, the very one whom the Father sent that he might save us and reunite us with the Sender. Are we then to encounter Christ only through memory, by recalling what he did, as we recall the deeds of the human beings who gave us life and helped us on our earthly journey?

But there is another side to the same problem, and it provides us with an answer. We can get at this other side by recalling what John and Paul and early Christian tradition thought about the resurrection of Christ. What good would the Incarnation have been if it had ended with the expiatory death of Jesus on the Cross? Such a death would indeed have been a great and magnificent thing, but if it had also marked the end of Christ's incarnation, we would be left with a highly juridical view of his coming, as though his whole purpose was to pay a debt that man owed. That aspect of it is part of the picture, but is it the whole picture? Must we not look beyond the death to the glorification and the glorified body if we want to see the full meaning and scope of the Incarnation? The risen Christ has a glorified body that is not subject to the conditions of time and space. Cannot this body be in contact with us through signs?

It can indeed, and this is exactly what happens through the mediation of the Church and its sacraments, each of which can be regarded as being in its own way an earthly extension of the glorified body of Christ. Now the condition for such a possible contact with Christ, the absolutely necessary condition of his further presence to us as incarnate, was his resurrection in a glorified body and his departure. Once he was risen and had withdrawn his visible presence, he could send the Spirit who gives life. The flesh of itself has no value here. The Spirit enables us to be always and everywhere in contact with the glorified body of the risen Lord.

Christ's presence among us is thus in no sense something abstract. Through faith we can touch him by touching the Church and celebrating the sacraments. We understand the word "sacraments" here in a broad sense, since we also touch Christ present among us by listening to his word and by contact with the Church in our various dealings with her.

Christ, then, wanted to retain the possibility of encountering us as a man. This possibility he has by reason of his glorified body. On our side, our possibility of having some concrete contact with him depends on the Incarnation being prolonged somehow in our midst; in other words, the heavenly body of Christ has to be made visible here on earth. Christ creates this visibility through earthly realities that function as signs. A sacrament makes it possible for us to enter into contact, through visible things, with the invisible but real, glorified body of Christ. The sacraments are thus earthly extensions of the glorified humanity of Christ, and each sacramental action embodies his presence when and where it is celebrated.

This presence has its highest form in the Eucharist. By virtue of transubstantiation, Christ is really present (he is also really present in the other sacraments) and in a special way that involves changing the very substance of the sign that points to his presence. He is present in the Eucharist both as sacrificing Priest and as Victim. Consequently, through the Eucharistic sign he is in contact with today's world just as he was in contact with the world of his time on earth.

It would have been impossible, however, to repeat the Supper as anything more than an outward gesture if Christ had not been raised from the dead and given the glorified body that is now in contact with us through the Eucharistic sign.[14] He touches us, therefore, as the Lord who is Master of death. The entire world is now "changed" and "assumed" by the glorified Christ; it is in contact with his person. When he appeared to people after his resurrection, he appeared in his visible body. In the Eucharistic sign the presence is the same but the manner is not. Christ remains invisible, and we touch him through the sign that is truly life-giving by reason of the resurrection and ascension of Christ and the sending of the Spirit. We possess what we love but we do not see it, and we wait for the time of signs to end so that we may enter into direct contact with the Christ of glory.

The resurrection of Christ, therefore, is essential if the Church is to have her deeper meaning as sacrament and as basis for all the individual sacraments, especially the Eucharist. How could we speak of the "real" Eucharistic presence if Christ were not risen and in possession of a real, glorified body? Evidently, then, the life of every Christian is centered on the resurrection and glorious body of the Lord.

At the same time, however, every celebration of the Eucharist looks forward to the day when Christ returns to do away with signs and we can see him directly, as the apostles did when he appeared in their midst. To celebrate the Eucharist, then, is to celebrate our own resurrection and to wait with active hope and love for the day when our own bodies will be made glorious like that of the Lord whom we "put on" in baptism.

STRUCTURE AND THEMES
OF THE THREE HOLY DAYS

A. THE MEMORIAL OF THE LORD
Holy Thursday Evening

4. CELEBRATIONS ANCIENT
AND MODERN

The Christian faith has always found its essential statement in the affirmation: "On the third day he rose again from the dead." Two fourth-century Fathers of the Church tell us in straightforward language what they consider to be the meaning of the paschal triduum. St. Ambrose, bishop of Milan, writes:

> We must observe not only the day of the Passion but the day of the resurrection as well. Thus we will have a day of bitterness and a day of joy; on the one, let us fast, on the other let us seek refreshment. . . . During this sacred triduum. . . . [Christ] suffered, rested, and rose from the dead. Of that three-day period he himself says: "Destroy this temple, and in three days I will raise it up." [15]

St. Ambrose here bases his argument on the biblical typology of the temple that is destroyed and then rebuilt in three days. Christ's words also show that his death and his resurrection are inseparable from each other:

> It is one and the same temple that is destroyed and then raised up in three days' time, one and the same Lord who dies and then is raised up in the mystery of

a single Pasch, that is, his passage from this world to the Father. St. Ambrose emphasizes the fact that this Pasch or passage of the dead and risen Christ is celebrated by the Church in a single process that includes the fasting and mourning of Friday and Saturday and the joy of the Eucharistic celebration during the Paschal Vigil. The fasting stands in contrast to the joy, yet it also prepares for it and forms with it a single whole. The three-day celebration of the Pasch means for the Church a passage from repentance to joy, from mourning to new life.[16]

The other fourth-century Father to whom we refer is St. Augustine. He concentrates especially on the typology of Jonas and its application to Christ, and on Jesus' words in speaking of his resurrection on the third day. Thus Augustine speaks of "the triduum in which the Lord died and rose,"[17] and of "the most holy triduum of the crucified, buried, and risen [Lord]."[18]

There can be no doubt that the triduum of which Augustine and Ambrose speak begins on Friday and ends on Easter Sunday evening.

The paschal mystery includes both the Passion and the resurrection of Jesus Christ, the two being inseparable. Not only is the resurrection inseparably connected with the Passion, but it also springs from the Passion as it were: life springs from death, and redemption from sin has its roots in the suffering that is the consequence of sin.[19]

This is not the place to explain at length what the paschal mystery is. In any case, we can best come to understand this mystery by living through these holy days. What we have been saying will be enough to show that the early Church, by celebrating the paschal triduum from Good Friday to Easter Sunday evening, was really respecting the true theological nature of the mystery. In view of the new grasp that the Christian people have of the value and meaning of the paschal mystery, the liturgical reform, especially since Vatican Council II, might well have returned to ancient practice by celebrating a paschal triduum that runs from Friday morning to Sunday evening.

If we adopt the ancient perspective, Holy Thursday marks the end of the Lenten fast. The day begins with the reconciliation of penitents, who are thereby readmitted to the Eucharistic table; then, in the evening, the Church solemnly celebrates the institution of the Eucharist as something intimately linked to the paschal mystery.

In the Roman Church down to the seventh century, Holy Thursday was simply the day for the reconciliation of penitents; there was no trace of a commemoration of the Last Supper. The Eucharist to which the penitents were readmitted was the paschal Eucharist that was celebrated during the Easter Vigil as the climax of the whole liturgical year.

In the middle of the sixth century we find two Masses being celebrated on Holy Thursday, one in the morning, the other in the evening.[20] At Rome, however, we find no Eucharistic celebration on Holy Thursday during this period; as we just said, Holy Thursday at Rome was given over to the reconciliation of penitents. We have plenty of evidence for this. For example, in a letter to Bishop Decentius of Gubbio (beginning of fifth century), Pope Innocent I says that the Roman custom is to reconcile penitents on the Thursday before Easter.[21] Various Church writers have left us descriptions of public penance and of the reconciliation of sinners on Holy Thursday. St. Jerome, for example, describes the penance that Fabiola had undergone fifteen or twenty years earlier at the Lateran Basilica, prior to Easter.[22]

Elsewhere, the Council of Carthage in 397 shows that the Eucharist was being celebrated on Holy Thursday.[23] From a well-known letter of St. Augustine to Januarius, we can see that the Eucharist might be celebrated twice on that day — once in the morning for those who wanted to end their fast sooner, the other in the evening.[24]

According to Egeria's travel diary, the same custom was followed at Jerusalem:

> When all the people have assembled [at the eighth hour], the prescribed rites are celebrated. On that day the sacrifice is offered at the Martyrium, and the dismissal from there is given around the tenth hour. Before the dismissal is given, however, the archdeacon raises his voice, saying: "At the first hour of the night [7 p.m.] let us assemble at the church which is on the Eleona, for much toil lies ahead of us on this day's night." Following the dismissal from the Martyrium everyone proceeds behind the Cross, where, after a hymn is sung and a prayer is said, the bishop offers the sacrifice and everyone receives Communion.[25]

It is possible to follow the development of the Roman liturgy for Holy Thursday from the seventh century on, although the liturgists do not agree on all points of historical interpretation.[26] It seems that beginning at that time there were three Masses at Rome — one in the morning, a second at midday, at which the holy oils were consecrated, and a third in the evening. The Mass for the consecration of the oils and the Mass in the evening contained no liturgy of the word but began immediately with the offertory. The absence of a liturgy of the word, though unusual in the seventh century, was nothing new in the Roman liturgy. We know, for example, from St. Justin's description of the baptismal Mass in 150, that when baptisms were held, the Mass after them began directly with the offertory.[27] Later, in 215, the *Apostolic Tradition* of St. Hippolytus of Rome shows that the same practice was followed in the Mass after a baptism and in the Mass for the consecration of a bishop.[28]

As we have already insisted, Holy Thursday at Rome was first and foremost the day for the reconciliation of penitents.

The *mandatum*, or washing of feet, was already part of the ritual at Jerusalem in the middle of the fifth century.[29] The rite then spread throughout the East, and from there into the West.

The Romano-Germanic Pontifical of the tenth century shows only the chrismal Mass in the morning and the evening Mass.[30] The first morning Mass, therefore, was no longer being celebrated; on the other hand, the evening Mass now contained a liturgy of the word.

The Holy Thursday liturgy later received two further additions. The first was the solemn transfer of the reserved Sacrament to the repository, where it awaited the ceremonies of Good Friday. This rite developed during the period from the thirteenth to the fifteenth centuries; we shall come back to it later and see the different stages of this development.

The other addition was the stripping of the altars. In the seventh century this was still a simple utilitarian action, since the cloths were left on the altars only for the celebration of the Eucharist, but with the passage of time the rite came to symbolize the stripping of Christ for his crucifixion.

In the post-Vatican II liturgical reform, the Holy Thursday celebrations have been restored to their original, very simple forms. It might perhaps have been preferable to eliminate Holy Thursday from the paschal triduum, thus returning to the early tradition as found in the Fathers. Such a move, however, would probably have been an exercise in archaism and would have disturbed many of the faithful. In any event, there is a danger of expending greater attention and devotion on the Holy Thursday Eucharist than on the Eucharist during the Paschal Vigil, the Eucharist that is the climax of the triduum.

The Church of today wants the Holy Thursday Eucharist to be for priests a celebration and commemoration of their priesthood and of their union with their bishop. Moreover, concelebration is strongly recommended on this day. In this regard, we should note that the Church in our day has courageously adapted to new situations. The fifth-century Church at Rome would doubtless never have even thought of concelebration; she saw Christ in the bishop and preferred to have him be the sole celebrant on this day of days when the institution of the Eucharist is commemorated.

The Church in our day sees Holy Thursday as commemorating rather the priesthood shared by every priest in union with his bishop.

The ritual has been very much simplified, and secondary matters have been put in their proper place. For example, anything suggesting sadness or sorrow has been eliminated from the celebration of the Eucharist; the procession to the repository has, like the repository itself, been simplified; the stripping of the altar is done without accompanying ceremony. The washing of the feet has been retained but is not obligatory; it is left to the discretion of the one responsible for the community in which it is to be celebrated, and he must judge whether or not the gesture will have the ring of authenticity.

SCRIPTURE READINGS IN THE LITURGY OF THE HOURS

Holy Thursday	Jesus, the High Priest Heb. 4:14–5:10
Good Friday	Jesus enters the sanctuary Heb. 9:11-28
Holy Saturday	The Lord's rest Heb. 4:1-13

5. THE PASCH AND UNITY

Glorying in the Cross of the Lord

In anticipation of the Eucharistic celebration that will be the climax of the Paschal Vigil, the Church reminds us on Holy Thursday evening of the institution of the Eucharist at the Last Supper.

Even in the entrance antiphon of the Mass, as the Church invites us to share in the meal, she also lets us know what

READINGS IN THE EUCHARISTIC LITURGY

	Old Testament	Apostle	Gospel
Holy Thursday	The Passover of the Jews Exod. 12:1-8, 11-14	Proclaim the Lord's death by eating the bread and drinking the cup 1 Cor. 11:23-26	Love that is faithful even to death John 13:1-15
Good Friday	The Servant mistreated because of our sins Is. 52:13–53:12	The obedient Jesus, cause of our salvation Heb. 4:14-16; 5:7-9	Passion of the Lord John 18:1–19:42
Easter Vigil	1) Creation Gen. 1:1–2:2 2) Sacrifice of Isaac Gen. 22:1-18 3) Crossing of Red Sea Exod. 14:15–15:1 4) The new Jerusalem Is. 54:5-14 5 An eternal covenant Is. 55:1-11 6) Wisdom has come to earth Bar. 3:9-15, 32–4:4 7) A new heart Ezek. 36:16-17a, 18-28	The risen Christ dies no more Rom. 6:3-11	Christ is risen A. Matthew 28:1-10 B. Mark 16:1-8 C. Luke 24:1-12

the meal really means: "We should glory in the cross of our Lord Jesus Christ, for he is our salvation, our life and our resurrection; through him we are saved and made free."

When we hear the word "glory," and when we recall what was said earlier about the true meaning of the Cross, especially in St. John's Gospel, namely, that the Cross glorifies the risen Christ and glorifies us as well, we may well be inclined to ask: Should we not rather say in the antiphon that we are glorified by the Cross of Christ? Christ and his Cross, after all, are the source of our salvation, life, and resurrection. Biblically and theologically, such a rephrasing would say a great deal more than is expressed in the simple statement that "we should glory in the cross." When we repeatedly celebrate the sign of the Supper, we make really present in time and space the one sacrifice of Christ on Calvary and the victory over death that brought him to his glory. We then share in that sacrifice and, in consequence, some of Christ's glory is reflected in us.

The opening prayer of the Mass is a brief recall of what the rite that we are about to celebrate means: "Let us pray. God our Father, we are gathered here to share in the supper which your only Son left to his Church to reveal his love. He gave it to us when he was about to die and commanded us to celebrate it as the new and eternal sacrifice. We pray that in this eucharist we may find the fullness of love and life."

One phrase in the prayer creates a problem. It is the phrase "when he was about to die," which is paralleled by another in the words of consecration: the blood that "will be shed" (*effundetur*). Both verbs refer to the future and confront us with something very mysterious. Christ is already celebrating, at the Last Supper, something that will take place only later on. Does the celebration, then, have a real content, or does it simply image forth what will be in the future?

By reason of our faith, we believe that the Supper was truly a rendering present of what was going to happen later on. We should note, moreover, that the Greek text of the words of consecration uses a participle that functions with either a present or a future sense: "which is *or* will be poured out," while the Vulgate translation in Latin uses a simple future: "which will be poured out"; we are therefore dealing with words whose exact meaning must be carefully established. In any event, what Christ does at the Supper is an actualization of something that, as a historical event, will take place the next day, Good Friday.

On the other hand, what we do at Mass and what Christ has entrusted his Church with doing is to repeat the Supper and thereby actualize that same Good Friday event, an event that is now past and no longer in the future, as it was at the Last Supper. Thus the Last Supper and our celebration of the Eucharist are alike in that they actualize the Good Friday event; they differ in that the Supper actualized what was yet to come, while our Eucharist actualizes an event now past.

Can we not go a step further and lift at least a corner of the veil that hides the mystery? The actualization of an historical event, whether future or past, is possible because Jesus is both God and man. As man, Christ was subject to the limitations of space and time; as God, however, he exists outside the conditions of time and space. He can, as God, anticipate his human death and the glorification of his body, and can render present the coming sacrifice and establish a sign of his glorified body. Similarly, he can entrust to the Church the command to celebrate the Supper again and render present the now past sacrifice, using the sign of the presence of his glorified body. In this sense, we may say that the Church "renews" the sacrifice of the Cross. The statement does not mean that the sacrifice is repeated in its historical reality; it was a once-and-for-all sacrifice and cannot be repeated. It can, however, be rendered present and be a here-and-now offering that Christ, as Head of the Church, makes to the Father's glory for the forgiveness of sins.

The Exodus meal

The first reading at the Holy Thursday evening Mass describes the Jewish Passover ritual. The reading is very appropriate and should remind us that Jesus had a reason for instituting his Eucharist in the context of a meal that commemorated the Exodus. In fact, if we look closely, we will find that chapter 6 of St. John, the account of the multiplication of the loaves (a prefiguring of the Eucharist), is developed in a manner strikingly parallel to the account in the Book of Exodus. In the present reading, however, the emphasis is on the ritual and its meaning as a memorial.

Without going into too much detail, we think it useful to give here some information on the ritual according to which the Jews celebrated the Passover. The ritual used today has undoubtedly been often revised since the time of Christ, and yet it may also be said to have preserved a substantial identity. We should note, to begin with, that the celebration of Passover is a domestic affair; it takes place in a family's home, with the head of the house presiding, and not in the temple or synagogue.

The *Seder*, or supper service, for the first two evenings of Passover goes back to the time of the Exodus from Egypt. The Torah (Exod. 12:8) prescribes that at the beginning of the fifteenth day of Nisan the Jews are to eat the *Korban pesaḥ*, the lamb slain earlier that afternoon; with it they are to eat unleavened bread and bitter herbs. The same passage orders that the children of the family are to be told of the events being commemorated. This part of the ceremony is so important that the verb *hagged*, "to narrate," has given rise to the noun *haggadah*, the commemorative story told during the meal. Since the destruction of Jerusalem and the Temple, the lamb cannot of course be sacrificed. The Jews have continued, however, to eat the bitter herbs, the unleavened bread, and a substitute leg of lamb; they also continue to tell the story of the Exodus. Here are the general components of the service:

A. First, there are prayers and blessings taken from the

psalms used in the synagogal liturgy or in the domestic liturgy for weekdays. Among these prayers we find the *Kiddush* (introductory prayers); the *Hallel*, consisting of Psalms 112 and 113; the *Birkat ha-mazon*, or thanksgiving prayers for the liberation from Egypt; the *Hallel ha-gadol*, or Psalms 114–117 and, in some communities, Psalm 135; the *Nismat* or *Birkat ha-shir*, which are the concluding prayers.

B. Second, there is the *haggadah*, or story of the Exodus: the persecutions, the punishment of the Egyptians, and the liberation. This story is meant for the children of the family.

C. In a sort of appendix come hymns of more recent origin; some of these have a liturgical character, others are of a more popular kind.

We have no intention of describing the ritual in all its detail, but it is important for us to be aware at least of its broad outline.[31]

1) The Kiddush is recited over a first cup of wine; the blessing varies according to whether or not the feast falls on a Sabbath.

2) The guests wash their hands in silence.

3) The master of the house dips the bitter herbs in vinegar and distributes them; before eating them, all recite a blessing: "Blessed art Thou, Eternal our God, Ruler of the universe, Creator of the fruit of the earth."

4) On the table before the master of the house are three matzoth; he breaks the middle one of the three and puts one half aside to be eaten after the supper, while the other half he places between the two unbroken matzoth.

5) He uncovers the matzah and lifts up the plate for all to see; he then begins the recital of the Haggadah with these words: "This is the bread of affliction which our forefathers ate in the land of Egypt. All who are hungry — let them come and eat. All who are needy — let them come and celebrate the Passover with us. Now we are here; next year may we be in the land of Israel. Now we are slaves; next year may we be free men." He then puts down the plate and covers the matzah; the second cup of wine is filled.

6) The youngest present asks the four questions about why this night is different from all others; the rest of the Haggadah is a response to these questions. It recounts the sufferings of the Israelites in Egypt and the punishments the Lord inflicted on the Egyptians; the way the Lord rescued them from Egypt, and the reason why the Passover lamb is eaten. (See the reading from the Book of Exodus, chapter 12, in the Holy Thursday evening Mass.)

7) The narrator points to the matzah and explains its meaning (Exod. 12:39).

8) He points to the bitter herbs and explains their meaning (Exod. 12:14).

9) He then sings the first part of the Hallel (Pss. 113–114); he raises the cup of wine and says:

> Blessed art Thou, Eternal our God, Ruler of the universe, Who redeemed us and redeemed our forefathers from Egypt, and brought us to this night to eat thereon matzah and bitter herbs. Thus may the Eternal our God and God of our fathers bring us to future feasts and festivals in peace; and to the up-building of Your city Jerusalem, and to the happiness of Your service, so that we may partake there of the ancient offerings. We shall then offer unto You a new song for our redemption and salvation. Blessed art Thou, Eternal, Who redeemed Israel.

> Blessed art Thou, Eternal our God, Ruler of the universe, Creator of the fruit of the vine.

Those present drink the second cup of wine.

10) The guests wash their hands to the accompaniment of a blessing.

11) The master of the house then says the two blessings over the matzah: "Blessed art Thou, Eternal our God, Ruler of the universe, Who brings forth bread from the earth," and "Blessed art Thou, Eternal our God, Ruler of the universe, Who made us holy with His commandments, and commanded us concerning the eating of matzah." The matzah are eaten.

12) The bitter herbs are dipped in the *haroseth* (a compote of nuts, fruit, and wine) to the accompaniment of a blessing, and are then eaten.

13) The festival meal begins.

14) After the meal, the *afikoman*, or half of a matzah that was set aside at the beginning of the meal, is distributed and eaten.

15) The third cup of wine is poured; this is the "cup of blessing" or thanksgiving. Psalms are sung and prayers are said; these may differ from country to country, but all strike the note of thanksgiving. The third cup is drunk.

16) The fourth cup is poured and drunk to the accompaniment of a blessing:

> Blessed art Thou, Eternal our God, Ruler of the Universe, for the vine, and for the fruit of the vine, for the produce of the field and for that precious, good and spacious land which You gave to our ancestors, to eat of its fruit, and to enjoy its goodness. Have compassion, O Eternal our God, upon us, upon Israel your people, upon Jerusalem your city, on Zion the abode of Your glory, and upon Your altar and Your temple. Rebuild Jerusalem, Your holy city, speedily in our days. Bring us there, and cheer us with her rebuilding; may we eat of her fruit and enjoy her blessings; and we will bless you for this in holiness and purity. Grant us joy on this Festival of Matzoth, for You, O God, are good and beneficent to all; and we therefore give thanks unto You for the land and the fruit of the vine. Blessed are Thou, Eternal, for the land and the fruit of the vine.

After the rest of the Hallel (Pss. 115–118) has been sung, other hymns may be added that differ according to country.

The New Testament and the Jewish Passover ritual

The ritual whose broad outline we have just sketched can help us understand the actions of Christ at the Last Supper.

Though the ritual has developed over the centuries, its main lines have remained the same. We can see from the accounts given us in the Gospels that the narrators present what they actually experienced, even if their descriptions of the Supper also reflect the liturgy of the very early Church.

With the Jewish Passover ritual in mind, we will be struck by a word that both Matthew and Mark use in describing Jesus' consecration of the bread. Just as a prayer of "blessing" is said over the bread in the Passover meal, so, according to these two evangelists, Jesus "says a prayer of blessing" before he breaks the bread. Similarly, and still with the Passover ritual as a point of reference, they tell us that when Jesus took the cup, he "said a prayer of thanks" before passing it around. In the Passover ritual, as described above, there is a similar distinction between the prayer of blessing over the bread and the prayer of thanksgiving over the cup at the end of the meal (*eulogēsas* in Matthew 26:26 and Mark 14:22; *eucharistēsas* in Matthew 26:27 and Mark 14:23).

St. Luke and St. Paul likewise tell us that when the meal was finished, Christ gave thanks over the cup (Luke 22:20; 1 Cor. 11:25). What we have, therefore, in all these writings is a liturgical narrative relating to the Supper. The Passover context is still discernible, but now the meal proper has been eliminated, and the liturgical account brings into immediate proximity the two key moments of the "consecration" of the bread and the wine.

A sacrificial meal

The second reading of the Holy Thursday evening Mass brings us to the heart of today's celebration. St. Paul avoids any possible confusion at the very outset by telling us that the Eucharist is not an ordinary meal but a commemoration of something very special:

> The Lord Jesus on the night when he was betrayed took bread, and when he had given thanks, he broke it, and said, "This is my body which is for you. Do

this in remembrance of me." In the same way also the
cup, after supper, saying, "This cup is the new covenant in my blood. Do this, as often as you drink it, in
remembrance of me." For as often as you eat this
bread and drink the cup, you proclaim the Lord's
death until he comes (1 Cor. 11:23-26).

This meal is inseparably connected with the Lord's Cross
and is therefore a sacrificial meal and the sign of the new
covenant.

Many writers have reminded us of the fact in the past, but
we must remind ourselves once again that the Lord's Supper was a Jewish meal in the course of which a prayer of
blessing was spoken. It is important for us to realize that
our Lord, consistently applying a pedagogy dear to him, did
not introduce strange new practices into the world. He was
anxious to meet man on ground familiar to him, and so he
tried to convey the realities of salvation in the form of practices already in use. For this reason we will be unable to
understand the Mass unless we start with the everyday sign
Christ used: the meal.

Recent books on the date of the Last Supper have given
us some new information but have not dissipated all
obscurity. The problem is too complicated for us to go into
it here, and, in any case, such a discussion would be out of
place for us.[32]

Christ's words, "Do this in remembrance of me" (Luke
22:19; cf. 1 Cor. 11:24-25), invite us to inquire into the nature of this memorial meal. As soon as we ask the question,
we see that the Last Supper is no ordinary meal but stands
apart. The material elements are those of the usual repast,
but the meal as such is not an everyday affair.

The Book of Leviticus, in describing how the showbread
is to be made, uses the term "memorial":

And you shall take fine flour, and bake twelve cakes of
it; two tenths of an ephah shall be in each cake. And
you shall set them in two rows, six in a row, upon the
table of pure gold. And you shall put pure frankin-

cense with each row, that it may go with the bread as
a memorial portion to be offered by fire to the Lord.
Every sabbath day Aaron shall set it in order before
the Lord continually on behalf of the people of Israel
as a covenant for ever. And it shall be for Aaron and
his sons, and they shall eat it in a holy place, since it
is for him a most holy portion out of the offerings by
fire to the Lord, a perpetual due (Lev. 24:5-9).

This text speaks of three things that are evidently related:
the showbread, the memorial, and the covenant. The meaning is quite clear. The showbread recalls the covenant between God and his people, and the offering of it reminds
God that he has bound himself to the nation of Israel. There
is no slightest doubt of Yahweh's fidelity; nonetheless the
people need to persuade themselves that he cannot forget,
that in fact he does not forget, and that whenever he remembers, that is, at every point of time, he acts in their
behalf.

By this cultic action, then, the people voice their persua-
sion that Yahweh keeps his promises with utmost fidelity. It
is by no means unusual in the Old Testament to find men
offering prayers or other cultic actions as a reminder to the
Lord of his covenant with them. Even things that are quite
external can recall the fidelity of God, for example, the
adornments of the high priest (Exod. 28:6-14; 39:2-7; 28:29,
35) or the feast of Passover (Exod. 12:14) or an offering
(Lev. 2:1-2).[33] But we already have a good example from the
time of the Exodus itself, and what we are told of the sacrifice offered at Sinai is extremely valuable to us.

And he sent young men of the people of Israel, who
offered burnt offerings and sacrificed peace offerings
of oxen to the Lord. And Moses took half of the blood
and put it in basins, and half of the blood he threw
against the altar. Then he took the book of the covenant, and read it in the hearing of the people; and
they said, "All that the Lord has spoken we will do,
and we will be obedient." And Moses took the blood

and threw it upon the people, and said, "Behold the blood of the covenant which the Lord has made with you in accordance with all these words" (Exod. 24:5-8).

The Book of Leviticus (2:1) shows that part of the sacrifice was offered to Yahweh, while the rest was eaten.

When St. Paul relates Christ's words, "Do this in remembrance of me" (1 Cor. 11:24-25), he could not have failed to remember, any more than Christ himself could have, the scene in Exodus. In reporting the Lord's words, then, Paul knows that he is describing a covenant rite that reminds God to be faithful. Paul's remarks to the Corinthians make it clear enough that this covenant rite involved eating part of the offering as a sign of the union between God and his people. There is, however, an essential difference between the rite in Exodus and the rite at the Last Supper. It is indicated by Christ's words, "This is my body," "This is my blood." Christ himself is the Victim of sacrifice, which is now eaten by all. This in turn presupposes, not a new immolation, but the presence throughout time and space of the one sacrifice of the Lord upon the Cross of Calvary.

The Passover meal was itself a memorial meal. But how did the Jew conceive of this memorial?

> In the course of the commemorations of events now past, the Jew voices his view, his belief, that he is a contemporary of what once was. To commemorate is not to stand off from what had once taken place; on the contrary, it means eliminating the distance that separates. It means bringing the past to life again; it means thinking that each and all of us are contemporaries of the historical events whose consequences we still endure or whose effects are still real in us. Nothing could be more illuminating in this respect than something that is said during the Jewish Passover meal, which commemorates the departure from Egypt; a verse in the Haggadah for the Seder says that on this feastday each Jew must think of himself as

having been personally brought out of Egypt. What is meant is not a symbolical or allegorical liberation, not a liberation whose reality would be an idea or a burst of feeling. By the fact that our forebears were liberated from Egypt, we ourselves will be liberated from all the new Egypts that can exist either within our hearts or around our religious community.[34]

Here we have the spiritual context within which Christ could institute his own memorial meal — a memorial within a memorial! The Passover ritual has often been described. We would like here to concentrate for a moment on the prayers said during the meal as an accompaniment to the ritual action. They are a type of prayer that goes back to the earliest times depicted in the Bible.[35]

In Genesis 24 we are told how the servant of Abraham returns to Nahor in Aram Naharaim looking for a wife for his master's son. In the account we are given an example of the characteristic Jewish prayer, the "blessing." The servant, not knowing how to proceed, asks the Lord for a sign. When he receives the sign, he bows in worship and says: "Blessed be the Lord, the God of my master Abraham, who has not forsaken his steadfast love and his faithfulness toward my master" (Gen. 24:27). The prayer is not a liturgical prayer, but how well and spontaneously it expresses what the moment calls for! First there is an exclamation of praise, then a statement of the reason for the exclamation. This kind of prayer, so dear to the Jewish people, must early have become a liturgical form, a function for which it was well suited. In private prayer we find it still being used in the New Testament; recall the *Benedictus*: "Blessed be the Lord God of Israel, for he has visited and redeemed his people" (Luke 1:68), and the *Magnificat*: "My soul magnifies the Lord, . . . for he has regarded the low estate of his handmaiden" (Luke 1:46-48).

In its liturgical use, the statement of the motives for the exclamation "Blessed be you, Yahweh" was quite naturally expanded; the result was the special literary genre of the "anamnesis."[36] At the end of a sometimes lengthy list of motives, there would be a return to the initial exclamation of praise, in the form of a doxology, for example, "To you be glory through the ages. Amen."

The Jewish blessing clearly influenced Judeo-Christian prayer. A good example of the latter is the prayers found in the *Didache*, a document that dates perhaps from the end of the first century A.D. In these prayers we will note that after recalling what the Lord has done, the one praying makes God's past goodness the basis for petitions regarding the future. This element must also have been present in the Jewish blessing.

What we have, then, is a blessing or prayer with four parts: an exclamation to the Lord, "Blessed be you, Yahweh"; the enumeration of motives for the exclamation; a petition inspired by God's past manifestations of his power and goodness; a final brief hymn of praise, or doxology. Not all four elements are present in every instance, nor is the order of components always the same; sometimes a petition is enclosed between two doxologies. Here is a passage from the *Didache*:

> After you have eaten enough, give thanks thus: "We thank you, holy Father, for your holy name which you have made to dwell in our hearts, and for the knowledge and faith and immortality you have revealed to us through Jesus your Servant. Glory be yours through all ages! Amen. All-powerful Master, you created all things for your name's sake, and you gave food and drink to the children of men for their enjoyment so that they might thank you. On us, however, you have bestowed a spiritual food and drink that leads to eternal life, through Jesus your Servant. Above all, we thank you because you are mighty. Glory be yours through all ages! Amen. Remember, Lord, your Church and deliver it from all evil; make it perfect in love of you, and gather it from the four winds, this sanctified Church, into your kingdom

which you have prepared for it, for power and glory is yours through all ages. Amen." [37]

At the Last Supper, then, Christ was using a traditional prayer formula when he spoke his "blessing." After "blessing" the Father, he enumerated all the extraordinary things the Father had done in saving Israel, especially the liberation from Egypt and the crossing of the Red Sea. But then he went on and added a remembrance or anamnesis of his own sacrifice: "Here is the body broken for you; here is the blood shed for you." This anamnesis rendered present the one all-important sacrifice of the new covenant. Having mentioned the various covenants that God had made with Israel, Christ designated the sacrifice he was rendering present as the sacrifice of the new and eternal covenant in his blood.

Here the memorial embodied in the Supper departed radically from the memorial proper to the Old Testament. At the Supper a sacrifice offered once and for all is made present, and the very Victim of that sacrifice is eaten by the guests as a sign that they accept the Lord's covenant. The Fathers of the Church liked to apply Psalm 110 (111):5 to the Supper: "He provides food for those who fear him; he is ever mindful of his covenant."

By sharing in the meal as a sign, we enter into the mystery of the Eucharistic celebration. For in this sacrificial meal, which can be repeated over and over, the one sacrifice meal, which can be repeated over and over, the one sacrifice offered by Christ alone is made present. Consequently, in the Mass the whole Church can associate itself with the action that brought the new covenant into being. Before his Passion, Christ celebrated the Supper as an anticipatory sacrifice. Now that the Cross is in the past, the sacrifice of the Cross is made present. It cannot be repeated, for it was a historical action; it need not be repeated, for it was of infinite value. It is, however, made present, and the Church now joins Christ in offering it.

Proclaiming the death of the Lord

To recall the "wonderful deeds" the Lord has done is to proclaim his power and work. So too, when the Church gives thanks and in her anamnesis mentions the death, resurrection, and glorious ascension of Christ, she proclaims these to the world. This proclaiming is the basic form her message takes, and it is also the basic form of Christian witnessing, an effective witness given by the entire Church as it gathers and proclaims the death of the Lord by eating the bread and drinking the cup. Thus, in the great prayer of blessing that is called the "Canon" in the Roman Latin liturgy, the Church is constantly recalling and proclaiming the Lord's death. She does so and will continue to do so until the Lord returns. For the Supper is only a prefigurement of the covenant meal at the end of time. Christ himself says that a day will come when he will drink new wine with his disciples (Luke 22:18; Mark 14:25; Matthew 26:29).

The unity of God's people

What the Gospel for Holy Thursday has to tell us is closely connected with St. Paul's teaching on the Eucharist. According to Paul, Christ has given us a double gift: he handed himself over to be slain for our salvation, and he gave us the rite wherein we celebrate the mystery of his body and blood. Love was evidently the motive that led to this twofold gift, and love plays an essential role in the Holy Thursday liturgy, as indeed it does in every liturgy. It was love that Christ came to reveal to the world: the love of the Father in which we all share, having received it from Christ, and which we must pass on to others. For this reason the Church at an early date introduced into the Holy Thursday liturgy a solemn and moving rite in which she imitates the action of Jesus as recorded in the Gospel.

In the time of St. Augustine the washing of feet in imitation of Christ was a common Holy Thursday practice.[38] In monasteries (in St. Benedict's time, for example) it was the custom to wash the feet of a guest simply as a sign of hospitality.[39] In addition, those assigned to serve table for the week washed the feet of their brothers as a sign of humility when their period of service ended on Saturday.[40] At Rome, in the seventh century, the Pope washed his chamberlains' feet on Holy Thursday.[41]

The third canon of the seventeenth Council of Toledo speaks of the washing of feet and offers some instruction on it; we are now in the year 694. The washing of feet on Holy Thursday became increasingly widespread in the Carolingian period. It was practiced in cathedrals, where a distinction was made between the washing of the clerics' feet and the washing of the feet of the poor; it was also practiced in monasteries, where, again, there were two distinct ceremonies. From the end of the Middle Ages on, only the washing of the feet of the clerics or monks was practiced in cathedrals and monasteries.

The *mandatum* is to be found on Holy Thursday at Jerusalem as early as the fifth century.[42] In many regions the feet of the newly baptized were also washed as they came from the font. For St. Caesarius, in Gaul, this was a gesture of welcome and hospitality. For St. Ambrose, at Milan, it was more than a simple act of humility; it brought with it a special grace, and he calls it a "sanctifying" action.[43] A number of exegetes have asked "whether we should not relate the Gospel account of the washing of the feet to baptism or the Eucharist."[44]

In the Syrian and Byzantine Rites the washing of the feet comes during the Gospel, not after it.[45] This ceremony, however, takes place after the celebration of the Eucharist, as it did in the Roman liturgy down to the reform of 1955. In fact, the rite was not used at all except after the morning Mass on Holy Thursday. The recent reform has followed the Coptic usage and put the washing of the feet before the liturgy of the Eucharist in the Mass.[46]

The Byzantine practice of washing the feet during the reading of the *mandatum* Gospel after the Mass offers us the example of an Eastern rite celebration. Several personages take part in it: the priest, who reads the Gospel; the superior of the monastery, who represents Christ; the porter, who plays Judas; and the steward of the house, who plays Peter.

The superior rises and prepares to imitate the actions of the Lord as each is told in the Gospel:

Jesus, knowing that the Father had given all things into his hands, and that he had come from God and was going to God, rose from supper, laid aside his garments [*the superior lays aside his mandhyas* [47]], and girt himself with a towel [*the superior puts on a savvanon* [48]]. Then he poured water into a basin [*the superior pours warm water into a basin*] and began to wash the disciples' feet, and to wipe them with the towel with which he was girded [*the superior begins to wash the feet of the assigned brothers, who are seated on benches on both sides; he begins with the porter, who represents Judas, and comes finally to the steward, who represents Peter. He dries and kisses the feet of each. Meanwhile the priest repeats the relevant words of the sacred text as often as is needed — eleven times in fact. When the superior comes to the steward, the reader continues with the sacred text. The superior speaks the words of Christ, the steward those of Peter, and the priest the connecting narrative*]. He came to Simon Peter; and Peter said to him, "Lord, do you wash my feet?" Jesus answered him, "What I am doing you do not know now, but afterward you will understand." Peter said to him, "You shall never wash my feet." Jesus answered him, "If I do not wash you, you have no part in me." Simon Peter said to him, "Lord, not my feet only but also my hands and my head!" Jesus said to him, "He who has bathed does not need to wash, except for his feet, but he is clean all over; and you are clean, but not all of you." [*As the superior says these words, he turns slightly toward the porter or even points to him.*

Then he washes the steward's feet. Meanwhile the priest finishes the reading of the Gospel.][49]

Modern exegetes have seen in the washing of the feet more than a simple gesture of humility. When Christ thus took the part of a servant, he must inevitably have reminded his disciples of the prophecy concerning the Servant of Yahweh in the Book of Isaiah: "By his knowledge shall the righteous one, my servant, make many to be accounted righteous; and he shall bear their iniquities" (53:11). Against this background, the gesture of washing the feet can be seen to be rich in teaching concerning salvation: concerning the blood of the covenant, the union of love between all the redeemed, the significance of mutual loving service. What real meaning does baptism have, after all, if it is not ordered (together with confirmation, which brings out all the priestly implications of baptism) to the celebration of the Eucharist within the unity of a new people?

When the *Asperges* was introduced into the Sunday service in the West (about the ninth century), it carried many of the same overtones. The verse (7) from Psalm 51, "Purge me with hyssop, and I shall be clean; wash me, and I shall be whiter than snow," was soon taken as alluding to baptism. It has been pointed out, moreover, that this verse at times showed an interesting variant: "You will sprinkle me with hyssop through the blood of the Cross."[50] During the Easter season the antiphon for the *Asperges* was taken from Ezekiel (47:1); it sang of the water that flowed from the right side of the temple. It is thought that the application of this verse to Christ is what led some artists to paint the crucified Christ with the wound from the lance in his right side rather than in his left.[51]

The passage from St. Paul that is read at this Holy Thursday evening Mass (1 Cor. 11:23-26) reminds the Christians of Corinth that they must be united in love, especially at the celebration of the Supper. The Eucharistic celebration presupposes unity; the Church has always taken this as obvious, since the Lord himself had given very pointed instructions on the matter: "So if you are offering your gift at the altar, and there remember that your brother has something against you, leave your gift there before the altar and go; first be reconciled to your brother, and then come and offer your gift" (Matthew 5:23-24).

St. Paul insists on this necessary union of the members of the community, although he is well aware how difficult it is to maintain: "Because there is one bread, we who are many are one body, for we all partake of the one bread" (1 Cor. 10:17).

In the Letter of St. James we find the same concern for the character of the Christian assembly; the concern is given more concrete expression than in St. Paul:

> My brethren, show no partiality as you hold the faith of our Lord Jesus Christ, the Lord of glory. For if a man with gold rings and in fine clothing comes into your assembly, and a poor man in shabby clothing also comes in, and you pay attention to the one who wears the fine clothing and say, "Have a seat here, please," while you say to the poor man, "Stand there," or, "Sit at my feet," have you not made distinctions among yourselves, and become judges with evil thoughts? (James 2:1-4).

The third-century *Didascalia Apostolorum* (a Greek original that we now have only in a Syriac and a fragmentary Latin version) gives very clear instructions on the point St. James raised. The instructions are all the more notable in that they are directed to the bishop himself, in whom the *Didascalia* sees Christ. We read in chapter 12.

> But if, as you are sitting, some one else should come, whether a man or a woman, who has some worldly honour, either of the same district or of another congregation: thou, O bishop, if thou art speaking the word of God, or hearing, or reading, shalt not respect persons and leave the ministry of thy word and appoint them a place; but do thou remain still as thou art

and not interrupt thy word, and let the brethren themselves receive them. And if there be no place, let one
of the brethren who is full of charity and loves his
brethren, and is one fitted to do an honour, rise and
give them place, and himself stand up. . . . But if a
poor man or woman should come, whether of the
same district or of another congregation, and especially if they are stricken in years, and there be no
place for such, do thou, O bishop, with all thy heart
provide a place for them, even if thou have to sit upon
the ground; that thou be not as one who respects the
persons of men, but that thy ministry may be acceptable to God.[52]

The Church is thus strong on the concrete manifestation
of Christian brotherhood, especially in the celebration of
the Eucharist. St. John has preserved for us the marvelous
discourses of the Savior after the Last Supper, and it is from
his thirteenth chapter, in which the Lord gives his disciples
a "new commandment" (*mandatum novum*) that we derive
the ritual of the washing of feet, which is a gesture pointing
to the love that is at the core of all Christian action. The rite
itself was given the name *mandatum* in the Church, for it
symbolizes that new commandment that is to be a distinctive sign of the Christian. "By this all men will know that
you are my disciples, if you have love for one another"
(John 13:35). To obey this new commandment is simply to
imitate the loving Christ: "Love one another; even as I
have loved you, that you also love one another" (John
13:34).

The antiphons sung during the washing of the feet repeat
these last two texts, along with others from the Gospel of
the Mass. During the procession that follows upon the
mandatum, a song is sung that combines texts from St. Paul
with other texts:

Where charity and love are found, there is God. The
love of Christ has gathered us together into one. Let
us rejoice and be glad in him. Let us fear and love the

living God, and love each other from the depths of our hearts.

Where charity and love are found, there is God. Therefore when we are together, let us take heed not to be divided in mind. Let there be an end to bitterness and quarrels, an end to strife, and in our midst be Christ our God.

The sixth of the antiphons sung during the *mandatum* recalls the three theological virtues and reminds us that love is the first and most important of them: "Faith, hope, and love, let these endure among you; and the greatest of these is love" (1 Cor. 13:13).

6. THE LORD'S SUPPER

The Lord's twofold gift of himself

The Eucharistic celebration on Holy Thursday evening, and indeed every Eucharistic celebration, is a memorial of the Lord's twofold gift of himself: his death for our salvation and his institution of the Eucharist. The first preface of the Holy Eucharist brings out the double gift: "He is the true and eternal priest who established this unending sacrifice. He offered himself as a victim for our deliverance and taught us to make this offering in his memory."

The "night when he was betrayed" (1 Cor. 11:23) is what the Church is commemorating on this day. She has already been commemorating it in the Liturgy of the Word, where a number of read or sung texts recall this "betrayal," this "handing over" of the Lord to his death. By means of these texts in the liturgy of the word, the Church has already been celebrating a genuine "memorial." We should not think of the songs and readings as simply an exhortation or a reminder of the great moment in the Lord's life when he seals his covenant and becomes a part of men's lives. No, the proclamation is already an "objective memorial" of God's acts, and a way of making the Savior and his saving actions present again in his Church. As the *Constitution on the Sacred Liturgy* (no. 7) says: "Christ is always present in his Church, especially in her liturgical celebrations. . . . He is present in his word since it is he himself who speaks when the Holy Scriptures are read in the Church" (Flannery, pp. 4–5).

Just as the readings are not simply a record of the past, neither is the celebration of the Eucharist intended merely to remind us of past events. The Eucharistic action is a present action of Christ, although one that depends for its redemptive value on a past action of Christ that was accomplished once and for all.

It is that past action of the Christ who was handed over and who gave himself to his Father that we commemorate by rendering it present. In the Garden of Gethsemani, Christ — and we — become aware of the dramatic conflict that the Gospel of Mark sums up in a few words: "Yet not what I will, but what thou wilt" (14:36). The outcome of the struggle in Christ is completely in keeping with his mission, for he, the completely just man, came into the world to do God's will (see Heb. 10:5-9). In the Acts of the Apostles, St. Paul quotes Psalm 89:21, which refers to David but is far more applicable to Christ: "I have found in David the son of Jesse a man after my heart, who will do all my will" (Acts 13:22).

Christ was betrayed and handed over to death, yet there is no contradiction when we sing in the entrance antiphon of the Holy Thursday evening Mass: "We should glory in the cross of our Lord Jesus Christ, for he is our salvation, our life and our resurrection; through him we are saved and made free." Why is there no contradiction? Because while Christ was indeed handed over, this happened because he himself freely chose that it should be so. We have adverted to this truth already in saying that Christ's "hour" designates not so much a point of time but an action deliberately taken. The hour in which Jesus is handed over and which seems to mark the victory of his enemies is also the hour when Jesus asks the Father to glorify him: "Father, the hour has come; glorify thy Son that the Son may glorify thee" (John 17:1). Elsewhere, Jesus is careful to point out that his "being handed over" is in fact his own voluntary giving of his life to the Father for the sake of those whom he loves: "For this reason the Father loves me, because I lay down my life, that I may take it again. No one takes it from me, but I lay it down of my own accord. I have power to lay it down, and I have power to take it again; this charge I have received from my Father" (John 10:17-18).

Later on, when he is being questioned, Jesus says to Pilate: "You would have no power over me unless it had been given you from above" (John 19:11).

The heart of Christ's redemptive act is the voluntary offering he makes of himself and of the human race he represents. What effects our redemption is not strictly the death of Christ nor the shedding of his blood, but the interior act that these signify, that is, the voluntary and total gift Jesus makes of himself to his Father. But we must properly understand this statement.

The philosophies to which we are accustomed distinguish between a sign and the reality it signifies. The Semite is hardly aware of any distinction of this kind; for him, the sign already contains in a way the reality signified. From the Semite's point of view, then, we can rightly say that the bloodshed and death of Christ redeem us. These signs, in the Semite's view, contain, and cannot but contain, the reality to which they point, namely, Christ's unreserved gift of himself to his Father, an act that more than makes up for the first man's refusal to serve.

If, moreover, it is accurate to say that Christ's shedding of blood and his death could not, simply by themselves, have redeemed us, it is also accurate to say that we could not have been redeemed without them, that is, if his self-giving had not involved the shedding of his blood and his death. The reason is that the sign is closely bound up with the reality it signifies. In addition, we who are creatures composed of body and soul need a sensible sign through which we can touch the realities of our salvation.

It is this voluntary self-giving of Christ to his Father that the Eucharistic celebration makes present to us. When Christ says, "This is my body which is for you" (1 Cor. 11:24, with variant reading), the substance of the bread is no longer there, and we are in the presence of his body. We are thereby also in the presence of all the mysteries of Christ and are even in a position to relive them with him for the rebuilding of the world. The past mysteries of Christ thus become truly present in the liturgy. It is *now* that Christ is handed over for our sake; were this not so, the Mass would be almost emptied of meaning.

At the same time, however, we cannot believe that the past begins all over again. St. Leo writes: "This state of infancy, which the Son of God did not judge unworthy of his majesty, became with age the state of perfect man. Once he had achieved the victory of his suffering and resurrection, all the actions he did for us in lowliness passed away." [53] But the Saint also writes: "All that the Son of God did and taught for the reconciliation of the world we not only know from the history of the past but we experience in virtue of his present works." [54]

The singleness of Christ's redemptive sacrifice is taught clearly in the Letter to the Hebrews: "He did this [offered sacrifice] once for all when he offered himself" (7:27). St. Paul says the same: "For we know that Christ being raised from the dead will never die again; death no longer has dominion over him. The death he died he died to sin, once for all, but the life he lives he lives to God" (Rom. 6:9-10).

Despite this undeniable truth, we must admit that the Christ who is really present in the Eucharist brings with him the real presence of all his mysteries. These mysteries are not repeated, any more than his death is, but they are made present so that we can actively participate in them. We cannot claim that the mysteries of the Lord continue to act on us and that we have an obligation of participating in them with him unless they are in some way rendered present. The Mass, then, makes present the self-giving of Christ to his Father and draws us to give ourselves along with our Head.

Christ, then, was given over to death, but he also gave us the mysteries of his body and blood. The Holy Thursday evening Mass says as much in the *Hanc igitur* prayer: "Father, accept this offering from your whole family in memory of the day when Jesus Christ, our Lord, gave the mysteries of his body and blood for his disciples to celebrate."

All this means that the Eucharist offered by any priest must be regarded as the Eucharist offered by Christ himself. What is the Eucharist, after all? If we examine it closely, we see that it is simply a response of man to God's plan for him and for mankind. It is thanksgiving, in response to the God who calls and who distributes to men the wonders of his salvation. Yet this response was in fact impossible for man, and it would continue to be impossible if Christ himself were not making that response by celebrating the Eucharist through a priest's agency. No longer is the response made to God by an isolated Christ; it is made by Christ and the Church that he won as his Spouse through the Cross. This brings us back once again to the need of unity as a condition for properly celebrating the Eucharistic mystery, since it is on the mystery of unity that the possibility of a genuine response to God depends, both for the individual and for the people of God as a whole.

Christ's prayer after the Supper tells us why this unity is so basic:

> I do not pray for these only, but also for those who believe in me through their word, that they may all be one; even as thou, Father, art in me, and I in thee, that they also may be in us, so that the world may believe that thou hast sent me. The glory which thou hast given me I have given to them, that they may be one even as we are one, I in them and thou in me,

that they may become perfectly one, so that the world
may know that thou hast sent me and hast loved them
even as thou hast loved me (John 17:20-23).

What Jesus' sacrifice effected was his own perfect unity
with the Father. We can share in that mysterious unity only
if we are completely one with Christ. All of us, therefore,
must be caught up in the one Eucharist that Christ offers.
That in turn is possible, however, only if Christ continues
unceasingly to celebrate for us his one Eucharist that makes
the entire Church one. It was to this end that Christ "gave
the mysteries of his body and blood for his disciples to
celebrate." Not any and every individual can thus render
present the Lord's one Eucharist (to say so would be to
think in terms of magic), but only those to whom the Lord
handed over the mysteries of his body and blood.

When the Second Vatican Council voted to restore
Eucharistic concelebration in the modern Latin Church, it
proposed Holy Thursday as one occasion for it (*Const. on
the Liturgy*, no. 57; Flannery, p. 19). Concelebration makes
manifest the point we have just been emphasizing about
Christ's one Eucharist, namely, that there is really only one
celebrant, Christ himself. So true is this that the multiplication of celebrations does not mean a multiplication of
Christ's Eucharist or thanksgiving. In all the Eucharists of
all the earthly priests there is but a single Eucharist: that
which Christ is offering through the mediation of those
whom he appoints and to whom he has entrusted the mysteries of his body and blood. Thus, when new priests celebrate the Eucharist on the day of their ordination with the
bishop who has just ordained them, there is really only a
single celebration.

It seems we must say that concelebration as practiced today, in which all the priests pronounce at least the words of
consecration, was not the practice of the early Church.
Since there is in reality only one celebrant, namely, Christ
who offers his Eucharist through his Church, we can understand why, in the early Church, only the bishop spoke

the Eucharistic Prayer, while the other priests shared in the celebration simply by receiving the consecrated bread and wine. That was their way of concelebrating.

In the Roman Church, as far back as we can go, we find concelebration in the modern manner in only two cases. One was the consecration of a bishop; on this occasion the consecrating bishops all joined the newly consecrated bishop in imposing hands on the offerings.[55] The other was the ordination of priests; on this occasion the new priests joined the bishop in performing the rite of the Eucharist. The point in both cases was to emphasize the sharing of power and to bring out a kind of collegiality.

Apart from these cases, a priest celebrated the Eucharist (i.e., pronounced the prayers of the liturgy) only in the service of a community and when the bishop could not be there to do it himself. On these occasions he celebrated the Eucharist as the bishop's delegate, a fact brought out by means of the *fermentum* (literally, "leaven"). The *fermentum* was a piece of consecrated bread that the bishop sent from his altar to a priest whom he had appointed to celebrate the Eucharist elsewhere. The priest showed that he was celebrating only as a delegate, and in union with the bishop, by putting the *fermentum* in his own chalice. There was therefore, at the human level, only one celebrant, in a sense; this oneness pointed in turn to the one Christ who celebrates his Eucharist in every earthly Eucharist.

From this we can see that concelebration should not be thought of simply as a pragmatic way of easing the burden of a sacristan when "private" Masses are multiplied. Nor is it meant merely to satisfy the desire of the individual priest not to have to say Mass by himself. Concelebration of the modern type should be reserved for certain occasions when it is desirable to manifest the unity of priesthood and Eucharist. We are not saying, of course, that the "private" Mass is invalid; we do say, however, that its meaningfulness is lessened by the absence of a congregation. The early Church thought of the Mass in terms of a service to the Christian community; it was in the service of the community that a priest, representing Christ in his one sacrifice, repeated the gestures and words of the Supper.

Until the recent reform, a single priest said the Eucharistic Prayer at the Holy Thursday Mass; other priests associated themselves with the rite by receiving Communion. Such was the normal practice of the Latin Church in the first centuries, except on days of episcopal consecration or priestly ordination. The practice highlighted the unicity of the priest, namely, Christ. The modern practice of having all the priests say the Eucharistic Prayer together emphasizes something else, namely, the unity of the priesthood, and was hitherto reserved, as we have indicated, for two occasions: episcopal consecration and ordination to the priesthood.

The Second Vatican Council has opened the way for more frequent concelebration (in the modern form), and there is no reason for renouncing the possibility. Moreover, there exists the alternative, for those priests who wish it and who have no obligation to celebrate for a community, of participating in the Sacrifice by receiving under both species.

They recognized him in the breaking of the bread

The phrase "breaking of bread" was for a long time an accepted synonym for "celebrating the Eucharist," in accordance with the well-known text in St. Luke: "Then they told . . . how he was known to them in the breaking of the bread" (Luke 24:35).[56] Full participation in the covenant requires the eating of the bread, since the covenant rite consists in the eating of a sacrificial meal. As we observed earlier, there is something strikingly new about the covenant meal of Christ: that what we eat is not simply bread but the very Victim of the historical sacrifice offered once and for all for the world's redemption.

Communion is not, however, to be thought of as being simply an extension of the sacrifice. The distinction between the priestly consecratory prayer and the Communion is required in exposition because our minds cannot grasp and express wholes all at once. As a matter of fact, we cannot conceive of the Eucharist apart from the eating that is required under pain of eliminating its character as covenant sign and thus entirely destroying it. We must be fully incorporated into Christ if we are to share in his covenant, and we must therefore eat the bread if full expression is to be given to our solidarity with him and our entry into the unity with the Father that he has restored.

Given this truth, we can see why we really offer nothing (ritually) in the sacrifice of the Mass; instead, Christ takes our gifts and offers them himself to the Father, and then gives us a share in the covenant unity established by his blood. This is why the word "offertory" as a description of the preparation of the matter for the sacrifice in the Roman liturgy is so ill-chosen. There are not two moments of "offering" in the Mass — one when the faithful come with their gifts, the other when Christ offers himself to the Father. No, there is only one real offerer, Christ; with him we are closely associated, to the point of sharing in his body and blood.

The sharing in the body of Christ and in the covenant sealed by his blood is our pledge of eternal life. To understand this, we need only read St. John, chapter 6, and meditate on the Lord's words:

> I am the bread of life. Your fathers ate the manna in the wilderness, and they died. This is the bread which comes down from heaven, that a man may eat of it and not die. I am the living bread which came down from heaven; if anyone eats of this bread, he will live for ever; and the bread which I shall give for the life of the world is my flesh. . . . He who eats my flesh and drinks my blood has eternal life, and I will raise him up at the last day (John 6:48-51, 54).

After Mass on Holy Thursday, the Eucharistic species are carried with some solemnity to a chapel prepared for reservation; these species will be distributed the next day. In the older Roman liturgy, the remains of the consecrated bread were placed in a small box and deposited in a drawer in the sacristy, without any special outward signs of honor. At the next Mass, the box was brought to the altar at the moment of the fraction, and its contents were placed in the chalice. At the beginning of that Mass, when the pontiff entered the Church, the box had been presented to him open, and he had venerated the sacred species for a moment.[57] Once devotion to the Blessed Sacrament began to develop, the reserved species also began to receive special honor. In some churches during the eighth century the ciboria were placed near the reliquaries on the altar; in the eleventh century, tabernacles set in the wall began to appear.

The cult of the Blessed Sacrament developed gradually; the process was speeded up in the second half of the thirteenth century, once Pope Urban IV extended to the whole Church the feast of Corpus Christi (August 11, 1264). The Holy Thursday repository then became a place for manifesting devotion to the Eucharist on the anniversary of the Last Supper. Once the Holy Thursday liturgy took over some customs that were signs of sadness (no playing of the organ; use of a clapper or rattle instead of bells; etc.), the repository came to be regarded in some places as a symbolic tomb for Christ.

The solemn stripping of the altar seems to have been simply a ritualization of an older utilitarian action, since the altarcloths had always been removed once the Mass was over. An age in quest of (often artificial) symbolisms needed no special prodding to see in the stripping of the altars the stripping of Christ's garments from him in preparation for crucifixion. The altarcloths were left off the altar until Saturday evening, simply because no Mass was celebrated until the Easter Vigil. Here again, however, symbolism came into play. The end result was that Holy Thursday acquired an atmosphere of sadness that the new Holy Week ritual has deliberately removed.

In some monasteries and churches, the altars are washed on Holy Thursday, but it is done without special solemnity.

Clerics in surplices first wash the altar with water and wine, then dry it. In the Byzantine Rite, however, there is a solemn washing of the altar; while psalms are sung, the patriarch, prelates, and priests wash the altar with water.

B. THE THREE HOLY DAYS OF CHRIST DEAD, BURIED, AND RISEN

Good Friday, Holy Saturday, Easter Sunday

7. THE UNITY OF THE THREE HOLY DAYS

In the early centuries the paschal triduum comprised Good Friday, Holy Saturday, and Easter Sunday. It was known simply as the triduum of Christ dead, buried, and risen. The penitential fast of Lent ended on Holy Thursday; on Good Friday there began a festive, intra-paschal fast that ended with Communion during the Paschal Vigil.

In Tertullian's time, the paschal fast began on Good Friday and lasted through Holy Saturday until the celebration of the Eucharist during the night between Saturday and Sunday. Friday and Saturday were days of fast for all. At that time people had a very realistic conception of the Eucharist; it was regarded as the most real of all foods, to the point that to receive the Eucharist was to break one's fast. When Tertullian wanted to persuade Christians to celebrate the Eucharist on a fast day, he did not challenge their belief that it would break their fast; he simply argued that to celebrate the Eucharist is more important than to fast.

The fast on Good Friday and Holy Saturday did not mean that there were special celebrations on these days. We remarked earlier that the Church of the first centuries did not think of breaking up the paschal mysteries into stages and celebrating these one by one. The simple structure of the paschal liturgy in the early Church showed, and was meant to show, the real unity of Christ's death and resurrection. Life came from death.

By a normal and inevitable development, the Church gradually came to celebrate the stages of the one mystery; she did not separate the stages, but she did focus her attention on each in turn, while remaining always aware that they formed a unity. In a now classic text St. Ambrose is a witness to the evolution that had already occurred: "We must observe not only the day of the Passion but the day of the resurrection as well. Thus we have a day of bitterness and a day of joy; on the one, let us fast; on the other, let us seek refreshment." A few lines further on, he presents us with the ancient idea of the paschal triduum: "the sacred triduum . . . during which he suffered, rested, and rose, and of which he says, 'Destroy this temple, and in three days I will raise it up.'"[58]

We have already pointed out how the triduum was organized in the early Church (St. Augustine's "most holy triduum of the crucified, buried, and risen [Christ]"[59]), and we need not insist further on it. It is clear, however, that this apparent breaking up of the one mystery could lead to the faithful fragmenting the mystery in their own minds and forgetting its basic unity. Yet if we but read the liturgical texts for the three days, we will find the Roman liturgy insisting that the death and resurrection of Christ form a single indivisible mystery.

C. THE GLORIOUS PASSION OF CHRIST OUR LORD

Good Friday

8. CELEBRATIONS ANCIENT AND MODERN

Celebration of the word

The liturgy of the day comprises three actions, among which there is no very clear connection. The three are the celebration of the word, the veneration of the cross, and Communion.

The celebration of the word is the basic element, and it is found everywhere in the Good Friday liturgy. It is especially interesting as far as the history of the Roman liturgy is concerned. This is because we still find in it the simple, rather elementary structure that characterized the liturgy of the word is described by St. Justin in his *First Apology* (ca. 150). St. Justin tells us that on Sundays "the memoirs of the apostles or the writings of the prophets are read, as far as time allows; then, when the reader is finished, he who presides admonishes and exhorts those present to imitate the splendid things they have heard."[60] The celebration of the word ended with solemn prayers offered by the whole assembly.

The Gospel of St. Luke shows us Christ reading Isaiah (61:1-2) and then explaining what he had read (Luke 4:16-22). The liturgy of the word as described by St. Justin was really still the Jewish morning liturgy on the Sabbath. This office consisted of a reading of the Law and the Prophets and of ensuing acclamations. Prayers were then offered by the congregation for all the needs of the community, and a final blessing marked the end of the liturgy. The first Christian liturgies all followed the pattern of the Jewish synagogal liturgy. As late as the time of St. Augustine, we find liturgical meetings in which the word was proclaimed but no Eucharist was celebrated. That was the Roman custom on Wednesdays and Fridays.

The first part of the Good Friday office still reflects this early liturgical pattern and, apart from a few variations, is marked by the ancient simplicity: readings and chants, homily, solemn general intercessions. That is the nucleus of the liturgy of the word. As all are aware, the conciliar *Constitution on the Sacred Liturgy* has restored the more frequent use of Bible services that are not followed by the celebration of the Eucharist (*Const. on the Liturgy*, no. 35; Flannery, p. 13).

The precise order followed in this ancient Good Friday liturgy of the word has, however, varied in details from period to period and even from place to place. In ancient Roman practice the service began with the bishop prostrating himself and praying in silence; then there was a first reading followed by a tract, a second reading followed by another tract, the singing of the Passion, and the solemn intercessions. These last were the only prayers said during the service.[61]

In some liturgical books, however, when the celebrant had reached the altar, he invited the congregation to pray, and the deacon told the faithful to kneel down. When all had stood up again, the celebrant read the prayer *Deus a quo et Iudas* ("O God, who punished Judas . . ."). There was then a first reading, followed by a tract and the prayer *Deus, qui peccati veteris* ("O God, through the Passion of your Christ . . ."); a second reading, with its tract; the singing of the Passion; and the solemn intercessions.[62]

Still another organization of the ceremony was as follows: prostration of the celebrant, who prays silently; a first lesson followed by a tract and the prayer *Deus, a quo et Iudas*; a second reading and tract; the singing of the Passion; the solemn intercessions.

Finally, there is the organization we find in the new Holy Week ritual: silent prostration, followed by a prayer; first reading and responsorial psalm; second reading and verse before the Gospel; singing of the Passion; solemn intercessions. There is no entrance song and no *Gloria*; there is no *Kyrie* because it is replaced by the solemn intercessions.

The "prayer of the faithful" was part of the Roman Mass liturgy down to the time of Pope Gelasius I (492–96). In the Eastern liturgy it has been preserved down to our time, but in the Roman liturgy, except for its rather archaic use in the Good Friday liturgy, it vanished completely from view. Vestiges of it, such as the prayers of the prone in some countries, would not have reminded anyone but a few specialists of the original prayer of the faithful. But this is not the place to sketch the history of this prayer.

We should point out, however, that since the time (about the fourth century) when the Eastern and Western rites began to be differentiated, the Good Friday prayer of the faithful took on a different form in East and West. In the Western rite, the celebrant announces the intention; everyone prays silently; then the celebrant says a prayer in which the congregation joins with its "Amen." In the East, the deacon proclaims the intentions and the faithful answer each with a *Kyrie eleison* or similar response; only at the end of the litany does the celebrant say a prayer to which the faithful answer "Amen." In Egeria's account of the Jerusalem liturgy, we see the children chanting *Kyrie eleison* in answer to intentions proclaimed by the deacon at the end of Vespers.[63] The *Kyrie* seems to have been introduced into the Roman liturgy at least before 529,[64] and to have been sung in response to an intention.

With regard to the *Kyrie*, we still possess an important document that has been attributed to Pope Gelasius. The "prayer which Pope Gelasius determined should be sung throughout the Church" consists of nineteen intentions, each answered with a *Kyrie eleison* or a *Christe eleison*.[65] The ancient prayer of the faithful, in the form of the solemn intercessions, thus took on a new shape and became like the prayer of the faithful as found in the Eastern liturgy. Its greater simplicity and directness undoubtedly helped it replace the older solemn intercessions. It is difficult, however, to determine whether the displacement of the prayer of the faithful occurred at the same time as its form changed (from solemn intercessions to litanic prayer) or whether, on the contrary, there were two stages: introduction of the litanic form and then the shift of the prayer of the faithful to a position before the readings. In any case, by the time the first Roman *Ordines* were composed (around the middle of the seventh century), the offertory rite comes immediately after the Gospel and homily, leaving no place for a litanic prayer.[66]

The chanted solemn intercessions of Good Friday are ten in number. We should be aware of the theology implied in putting these solemn intercessions after the proclamation of the word. The faithful are first penetrated by the word that the Lord himself addresses to them; then, as men and women transformed by that word, they join in prayer for the important intentions of the Church.

Adoration of the Cross

Egeria, the fourth-century traveler, is our first witness to this liturgical custom:

> A throne is set up for the bishop on Golgotha behind the Cross, which now stands there. The bishop sits on his throne, a table covered with a linen cloth is set before him, and the deacons stand around the table. The gilded silver casket containing the sacred wood of the Cross is brought in and opened. Both the wood of the Cross and the inscription are taken out and placed on the table. As soon as they have been placed on the table, the bishop, remaining seated, grips the ends of the sacred wood with his hands, while the deacons, who are standing about, keep watch over it. There is a reason why it is guarded in this manner. It is the practice here for all the people to come forth one by one, the faithful as well as the catechumens, to bow down before the table, kiss the holy wood, and

then move on. It is said that someone (I do not know when) took a bite and stole a piece of the holy Cross. Therefore, it is now guarded by the deacons standing around, lest there be anyone who would dare come and do that again.

All the people pass through one by one; all of them bow down, touching the Cross and the inscription, first with their foreheads, then with their eyes; and, after kissing the Cross, they move on. No one, however, puts out his hand to touch the Cross.[67]

At Rome, where a piece of the wood of the Cross was preserved, a ritual of veneration similar to the one described by Egeria was introduced.[68] But, though the seventh-century Mozarabic liturgy has a service of adoration of the Cross that it seems to have gotten from Jerusalem,[69] the Roman liturgy did not derive its ritual from Spain. Only in *Ordo* 23 (700–50) do we find a lengthy description (the work of a pilgrim) of the rite of adoration of the Cross; the description is quite close to Egeria's,[70] and the ritual undoubtedly did come from Jerusalem. The Eastern influence is evident. For example, the Pope himself carries the smoking censer in the procession, something found nowhere else in the Roman liturgy. It has been noted by historians that just at the period when the Good Friday veneration of the Cross appears in the Roman liturgy, the See of Peter was occupied by Eastern popes, from John V (685–86) to Zachary (741–52).[71]

The procession starts at the Lateran and moves to Santa Croce de Gerusalemme; the Pope, barefooted, carries the censer, while a deacon follows him with the box containing a relic of the Cross. The box is placed on the altar and the Pope opens it; he then prostrates himself in prayer before the altar, rises, kisses the relic, and goes to his throne. At a signal from him, the bishops, priests, deacons, and sub-deacons come up to kiss the cross on the altar; they are followed by the faithful. After the adoration of the Cross, a deacon goes into the pulpit and begins the reading from the prophet Osee. This whole ritual precedes the liturgy of the word, and that is exactly the custom of which we learn in Egeria's journal.[72] Neither in *Ordo* 23 nor in Egeria's account is anything said of singing during the adoration; the whole ceremony was probably conducted in profound silence.

From the eighth and ninth centuries on, the procession of the faithful to the altar to adore the Cross (a ceremony that took place in the evening) was accompanied by the singing of the antiphon *Ecce lignum crucis* ("Behold the wood of the Cross, on which hung the salvation of the world") and Psalm 118 (119), "Blessed are those whose way is blameless, who walk in the law of the Lord."[73] Later on, other antiphons were added to the psalmody, for example, *Salva nos, Christe* ("Save us, O Christ") and especially *Crucem tuam adoramus, Domine* ("We adore your Cross, O Lord, and we praise and glorify your holy resurrection . . ."). This last is Byzantine in origin[74] and was already known to Amalarius.[75]

According to *Ordo* 31 (850–900), after the Pope has communicated, the cross is carried from behind the altar to the front of the altar, while the *Trisagion* is sung, another composition that came to Rome from the Eastern liturgy by way of Gaul.[76] During the adoration of the Cross by the lower clergy and the faithful, not only the *Ecce lignum crucis* and Psalm 118 (119) are sung, but also the hymn *Pange lingua* ("Sing, my tongue . . . ," composed by Venantius Fortunatus, who died in 600), along with the antiphon *Crux fidelis* ("O faithful Cross . . .").[77] According to this same *Ordo*, the *Ecce lignum crucis* was sung while the cross was being shown to the faithful.

Nothing is said in these various *Ordines* about unveiling the cross, a ceremony that makes its appearance only in the twelfth century[78] but thenceforth acquires an ever greater importance. With the Roman Pontifical of the twelfth century, the ceremony undergoes a kind of dramatization.[79]

Later on, during the adoration of the Cross, the *Improperia* ("Reproaches") are joined to the *Trisagion*; the practice can be found as early as the end of the ninth century.[80]

In the new Holy Week rite, two ways of showing the cross are provided. The cross may be brought veiled to the altar, where the celebrant uncovers it in stages, singing at each stage the antiphon, "This is the wood of the cross, on which hung the Savior of the world." Or else the celebrant or deacon may carry the cross, unveiled, from the back of the church, stopping to sing the antiphon three times on the way. During the adoration of the Cross, the antiphon *Crucem tuam adoramus, Domine*, and the *Improperia* are sung.

According to the old *Ordo* 31, the faithful kissed the cross immediately before receiving Communion. The adoration of the Cross and the reception of Communion were thus brought into close proximity and became in effect a single action.

Reception of Communion

The reception of Communion on Good Friday was not practiced at Rome before the seventh century. In his Letter to Decentius, Pope Innocent I (401–17) wrote: "It is clear that during these two days the apostles were filled with grief and even hid themselves out of fear of the Jews. Nor is there any doubt that they fasted during that time; consequently, it is the tradition of the Church that the mysteries not be celebrated on these two days."[81] We saw above that in Tertullian's time reception of the Eucharist was considered to break the fast. The same view prevailed in the time of Innocent I.

In *Ordo* 23 (700–750) we find an interesting rubric to the effect that neither the Pope nor the deacons communicate on Good Friday; anyone wishing to communicate may go to some other church of Rome and there receive the Eucharist that had been reserved after the Holy Thursday Mass.[82] Here we have divergent customs existing side by side at Rome. The papal liturgy had no Communion rite, while the other churches of the city did have one in which the Eucharist reserved from Holy Thursday was distributed. The introduction of Communion on Good Friday presupposed a mitigation of the intra-paschal fast.

In the present Byzantine liturgy, the liturgy of the presanctified is not celebrated on Good Friday (therefore, no Communion that day), unless the day happens to fall on March 25, the feast of the Annunciation, which is not transferrable. During Lent, Mass is not celebrated in the Byzantine Rite except on Saturdays and Sundays; on the other days of the week, however, a liturgy of the presanctified is celebrated after Vespers. The Romans may have been led to their Good Friday practice of a liturgy of the presanctified by observing the Lenten custom of the Byzantine colony at Rome.

In the Roman liturgy of that period, the people received Communion under both species. The oldest documents expressly mention the reservation of both the consecrated bread and the consecrated wine. Later documents, which seem to reflect Gallican usage, mention only the reservation of the consecrated bread, but, in the same context, they mention that the consecrated bread is silently placed in a chalice of unconsecrated wine. This practice was based on a theological opinion that arose around 800.

It was not an easy matter, of course, to reserve for Friday enough of the precious blood that had been consecrated at the Thursday Mass. Consequently, it had been customary to pour some of the precious blood into a chalice of unconsecrated wine and to use the mixture for the Communion of the faithful on Friday. But around 800 there arose the opinion that by mingling consecrated bread with unconsecrated wine, a consecration of the wine was effected. This was due not to any combining of molecules, but simply to contact with the consecrated bread. Amalarius is a witness to the resultant liturgical usage.[83] The Romano-Germanic Pontifical of the tenth century explicitly accepts the belief in consecration by contact: "The unconsecrated wine is sanctified by the consecrated bread."[84]

This, then, was how Communion was celebrated. The

bread consecrated the day before was brought to the altar, along with unconsecrated wine. They were incensed; then the celebrant sang the Our Father; the *Pax Domini* was not sung. The host was divided into three parts, one of which was silently placed in the chalice. The Roman Pontifical of the twelfth century still attested to the now longstanding belief: "The unconsecrated wine is sanctified by the mingling with the body of the Lord."[85]

At the beginning of the thirteenth century, however, the theologians, with Peter Cantor (d. 1197) at their head, rejected the theory of consecration by contact. As a result, we find the Pope alone receiving Communion at his Mass.[86] From that time on, down to the reform of 1955, only the celebrant communicated at the Good Friday liturgy, but the rite of commingling continued in use. The 1955 reform suppressed the commingling and restored the practice of Communion for all, the first traces of which we saw in the non-papal Roman liturgy of the seventh century. After Communion there is now a closing prayer, and, by way of dismissal, another that the celebrant says with his hands extended toward the congregation.

9. THE BLOOD OF THE LAMB

The primary concern of the Office of Readings in the Liturgy of the Hours on Good Friday is to situate the Passion in its proper messianic context.

The psalms

Psalm 2 has always been regarded as messianic by both the Jewish and the Christian traditions. It shows men rebelling against God: "The kings of the earth set themselves, and the rulers take counsel together, against the Lord and his anointed" (v. 2). But "he who sits in the heavens laughs;

the Lord has them in derision" (v. 4). Then we are told the role of the Messiah: "The Lord . . . said to me, 'You are my son, today I have begotten you. Ask of me, and I will make the nations your heritage, and the ends of the earth your possession. You shall break them with a rod of iron, and dash them in pieces like a potter's vessel'" (vv. 7-9).

The perspective here is already paschal, since the Son, begotten according to the flesh, will shatter his enemies as though they were a potter's dish and will receive the nations as his inheritance.

In Psalm 22 we hear Christ lamenting and praying. A lover of the psalms, he will utter aloud the opening words of this psalm as he hangs on the Cross: "My God, my God, why hast thou forsaken me? Why art thou so far from helping me, from the words of my groaning? O my God, I cry by day, but thou dost not answer; and by night, but find no rest" (vv. 2-3).

Verses 7 and 8 of this psalm remind us of the fourth song of the Suffering Servant (Is. 52:13–53:12), and the evangelists took the psalm as a description of the Lord's Passion. St. Matthew (27:46), for example, puts verse 2 of the psalm on Christ's lips at the ninth hour when he utters his loud cry, *"Eli, Eli, lema sabachthani?"* In thus verbalizing the Savior's cry, Matthew does not mean that Christ is expressing despair; on the contrary, Matthew has in mind the later part of the psalm in which the psalmist voices his certainty of final victory. At the beginning of the crucifixion scene, Matthew and John allude to (Matthew) or quote (John) verse 18 of Psalm 22, "They parted my garments among them, and for my clothing they cast lots" (John 19:24).

Psalm 38, the third psalm in the Office of Readings, likewise expresses distress. Once again we find the accents of the fourth song of the Suffering Servant (Is. 53:7), "But I am like a deaf man, I do not hear, like a dumb man who does not open his mouth. Yea, I am like a man who does not hear, and in whose mouth are no rebukes" (Ps. 38:13-14). The distress of Christ, weighted down as he is with the sins of the world, finds voice in even more violent words in verses 17-18, "For I am ready to fall, and my pain is ever with me. I confess my iniquity, I am sorry for my sin."

The antiphons are chosen in order to convey the same thoughts and feelings. Thus the antiphon for the first psalm emphasizes the violence used by the enemy: "Earthly kings rise up, in revolt; princes conspire together against the Lord and his anointed." The second antiphon, taken from Psalm 22 itself, reminds us of Calvary: "They divided my garments among them; they cast lots for my clothing."

Christ the Priest enters the sanctuary

The atmosphere in the first reading, from the Letter to the Hebrews, is quite different, as it shows us Christ the High Priest entering once and for all into the Holy of Holies (Heb. 9:11-28). The passage gives us a theological vision of the Lamb who is sacrificed. It is not with the blood of goats or calves but with his own blood that Christ enters once and for all into the sanctuary and wins eternal redemption for us (v. 12). He is the mediator of a new covenant (v. 15), but in establishing it he shed his blood only once. Unlike the priests of the Old Testament, he does not have to shed blood over and over, but has appeared at the end of the ages to take away sin once and for all (v. 26). Now he has entered heaven in person so that he might appear before God on our behalf (v. 24).

The passage ends with the expression of a great hope of salvation; it is a hope whose reality we already possess in germ: "So Christ, having been offered once to bear the sins of many, will appear a second time, not to deal with sin but to save those who are eagerly waiting for him" (v. 28).

The covenant in the blood of Christ

The language and imagery of the Letter to the Hebrews should not prevent us from seeing that it is speaking of a true sacrifice and that blood is required by the covenant.

In the Eucharistic liturgy, when the celebrant shows the consecrated bread to the faithful he says: "This is the Lamb of God who takes away the sins of the world." These words sum up the whole paschal mystery, the life of the Church, and our individual lives. In the Fourth Gospel, John the Baptist already speaks of Christ in the same way: "Behold, the Lamb of God, who takes away the sin of the world!" (1:29).

When the Baptist used the title "Lamb of God," he was undoubtedly making his own a current image. But the image was in fact a double image. It could refer either to the Passover lamb of the Book of Exodus (ch. 12) or the lamb led to slaughter in the Book of Isaiah (ch. 53). In the Book of Exodus, the Lord gives instructions to Moses and Aaron: "You shall keep it [the lamb] until the fourteenth day of this month, when the whole assembly of the congregation of Israel shall kill their lambs in the evening. Then they shall take some of the blood, and put it on the two doorposts and the lintel of the houses in which they eat them" (Exod. 12:6-7). The lamb here is a lamb sacrificed; its blood is shed. Later in the chapter we are told that "the Lord will pass through to slay the Egyptians; and when he sees the blood on the lintel and on the two doorposts, the Lord will pass over the door, and will not allow the destroyer to enter your houses to slay you" (v. 23).

Blood thus played a part in Israelite religion as it did in other religions of antiquity. The blood represented the being's life. The Book of Deuteronomy, for example, commands: "Only be sure that you do not eat the blood [of the animals slaughtered for food]; for the blood is the life" (12:23). The life in question depends directly on God: "I kill and I make alive; I wound and I heal" (32:39). The use made of blood in worship thus reflected the outlook of a people that had a sense both of life and of God. They realized that the blood of a being, like the life it supported, belonged to God alone and must be reserved for him in the form of sacrifice (Lev. 3:17).

Blood could be used only for expiation (Lev. 17:18). It

was natural for Israelites to assign blood a redemptive value. It was through the blood of the lamb, after all, that the Hebrews had won freedom from Egypt. The blood shed in circumcision had already served as blood that sealed a covenant (Exod. 4:26), but in Egypt the blood of the lamb also liberated the Hebrews and thus bound them to God in an even firmer covenant, for under this covenant they would become a kingdom of priests and a holy nation (Exod. 19:6).

The covenant would later be concluded by means of a communion sacrifice in which blood once again played an essential role:

> And he sent young men of the people of Israel, who offered burnt offerings and sacrificed peace offerings of oxen to the Lord. And Moses took half of the blood and put it in basins, and half of the blood he threw against the altar. Then he took the book of the covenant, and read it in the hearing of the people; and they said, "All that the Lord has spoken we will do, and we will be obedient." And Moses took the blood and threw it upon the people, and said, "Behold the blood of the covenant which the Lord has made with you in accordance with all these words" (Exod. 24:5-8).

The role of the young men is not clear, but the text as a whole conveys valuable information, namely, that part of the blood is poured on the altar, which represents God, and the other part is sprinkled on the people. First the altar is splashed; then the conditions of the covenant are announced; finally the people give their assent, and the rest of the blood is sprinkled on them. There is a point here to which commentators rarely advert. It is that the blood is splashed on the altar before the law is read out. This means that it is primarily the people who commit themselves. Yahweh is not the prisoner of his own covenant; on the contrary, it is he who takes the initiative and offers an unmerited gift. "There are here no reciprocal rights and duties as in human covenants."[87]

Once we realize that blood symbolizes the life over which Yahweh has full rights and which no one but he can dispose of, we can understand that the blood ritual in the covenant signifies a genuine community between God and his people. Yahweh "gives the people a share in what is his by divine right."[88] This is of the utmost importance. We can see that, above and beyond a covenant at the juridical level, this covenant in blood manifests Yahweh's desire to have Israel for a son to whom he will be attached by ties of blood. Then the threat to Pharaoh makes sense: "And you shall say to Pharaoh, 'Thus says the Lord, Israel is my first-born son, and I say to you, "Let my son go that he may serve me"; if you refuse to let him go, behold, I will slay your first-born son'" (Exod. 4:22-23). Later on, the Book of Wisdom will say that "when their first-born were destroyed, they [the Egyptians] acknowledged thy people to be God's son" (18:13).

The point of the rite of sprinkling thus seems to be to show that the vital bond linking Israel to its God is no less strong than the bond created by flesh and blood sonship.[89] The blood of the covenant is not only the blood that ransoms; it is also, and even more, the blood binding God to his people.

Christ the Lamb

The whole Christian tradition has seen in Christ the lamb, even the only true Lamb, as the first preface for Easter puts it.

By the very manner in which he relates the events of the Passion, St. John tells the world that Christ is the true Lamb. Jesus is put to death on the eve of the Feast of Unleavened Bread, as John several times reminds us (18:28; 19:14, 31). In other words, he dies on the day when the Passover lambs are sacrificed in the Temple. After his death, as John carefully notes, his legs are not broken, and the evangelist quotes the ritual prescription concerning the paschal lamb: "You shall not break a bone of it" (Exod. 12:46; cf. John 19:36).

Writing to the Christians of Corinth, St. Paul urges them to live like unleavened loaves, as it were, for "Christ, our paschal lamb, has been sacrificed" (1 Cor. 5:7). In his teaching, the Apostle also emphasized the value of blood in expiation; blood suggests sacrifice as well as ransom and justification.[90]

The First Letter of St. Peter, which is generally regarded as a baptismal catechesis, speaks of Jesus as the Lamb without sin (1:19) whose blood has ransomed mankind (1:18-19). This redemption by the blood of the Lamb means that men are freed from idols (1:14-18). Since they have been set free by the blood of the Lamb, Christians must be holy in all they do. They are now members of a royal and priestly people, and have been called from darkness into the light (2:9).

For St. John, too, Christ is the sinless Lamb (1:29 and 8:48; 1 John 3:5), who takes away the sin of mankind (1:29). It is especially in the Apocalypse, however, that St. John exalts Christ as the Lamb who has triumphed. Jesus is the Lamb (5:6) who buys mankind back with his blood (5:9). Christians have been ransomed from the world (14:3) and are now a kingly and priestly people (5:10). Thanks to the blood of the Lamb, they have overcome Satan (12:1). Now they can sing the canticle of Moses and the canticle of the Lamb (15:3).

In the Apocalypse we are given the basic theology that underlies the paschal mystery, for the Lamb who is slain is also "the Lion of the tribe of Judah, the Root of David" who "has conquered, so that he can open the scroll and its seven seals" (5:5). The Lamb has taken possession of his kingdom and now celebrates his wedding with his Bride, who has beautified herself for this day; she, the Church, joins the Lamb in inviting us to the wedding feast (19:6-9).

In this vision the Lamb is he who "takes away" the sins of the world. But it is also possible to regard the Lamb as the suffering Messiah who "bears" or "carries" the sins of the world. It has often been remarked that at a number of points in the Gospel of St. John words are used that can have two meanings. Thus the Greek verb *airein* can mean either "lift up and take away" or "carry." Given the latter of the two meanings, the word suggests the Servant song in the Book of Isaiah (ch. 53). Under heavy persecution a devout person could liken himself to a lamb led to slaughter (Jer. 11:19). Isaiah, in fact, applied the image to the Servant: "He was oppressed, and he was afflicted, yet he opened not his mouth; like a lamb that is led to the slaughter, and like a sheep that before its shearers is dumb, so he opened not his mouth" (53:7).

When the Ethiopian eunuch invited Philip into his carriage, the passage he had been reading and puzzling over was from the fourth Servant song: "As a sheep led to the slaughter or a lamb before its shearer is dumb, so he opens not his mouth" (Acts 8:33). With this passage as his starting point, Philip told the eunuch the good news of Jesus. Faith in this Lamb who was silent was the condition required for receiving the baptism Philip would administer. Philip thus linked up the two aspects of the Lamb that sum up the whole of the Good News: the mute Lamb led to slaughter and the spotless lamb whose blood is shed for the salvation of the multitude, those whom he draws with him in his victory over the powers of evil.

The Office of Readings in the Liturgy of the Hours has for its second reading a passage from a catechesis of St. John Chrysostom. In it the Saint is praising the power of Christ's blood.[91]

"Do you wish to know the power of Christ's blood?" To make his point, Chrysostom has recourse to typology, reminding his readers of the blood that the Israelites smeared on their doorposts. If the angel of death did not dare enter when he saw the blood that was in fact only a prefiguration, much more will he be afraid when he sees the real blood of Christ. The preacher then turns to the water and blood that flowed from the side of the crucified Christ. The water symbolizes baptism, the blood is the blood of the Eucharistic sacrament. The water comes first, because we are first washed clean in baptism; only then are we sanctified by the Eucharist.

The Jews immolated a lamb; we have come to know the fruit that Christ's sacrifice has produced. For from the pierced side of Christ the Church was born, just as Eve was born from the side of Adam. Chrysostom has St. Paul's teaching in mind when he says, "We spring from his body and blood," alluding to the fruitful side of Christ. Christ made the Church one with himself, and he nourishes us. It is by means of this food that we are both born and fed. As a woman nurtures her child with her blood and her milk, so Christ gives us a new birth through his blood and then feeds us with that same blood.

10. THE SERVANT PIERCED AND VICTORIOUS

The liturgy of the word on Good Friday is marked by a notable restraint. The severity, which also shows in the outward decor (the altar is completely bare, without cross, candlesticks, or cloths), could be misleading; it might induce a dramatic sense of sadness and make us forget that the death of Christ is in fact a triumph. In reality, bare altars were common in the early Church whenever the altar as such was to play no part. In any case, the prayer that follows the moment of recollection at the beginning of the service expresses in a balanced way the meaning of all that is to follow: "Lord, by shedding his blood for us, your Son, Jesus Christ, established the paschal mystery. In your goodness, make us holy and watch over us always." The alternate prayer conveys the same essential message: "Lord, by the suffering of Christ your Son you have saved us all from the death we inherited from sinful Adam. By the law of nature we have borne the likeness of his manhood. May the sanctifying power of grace help us to put on the likeness of our Lord in heaven, who lives and reigns for ever and ever."

The two prayers, taking as their point of the departure the mission and death of the Son, focus our attention on the mystery of the victorious Passover that is the source of our new life. The whole history of salvation is thus summed up in a few words at the moment when the Church is ready to celebrate the death of her Christ, something she cannot do without at the same time celebrating his triumph and ours.

The Servant pierced for our sins

In the first reading we meet the Suffering Servant. The description Isaiah gives of him cannot but be deeply moving when read on Good Friday (Is. 52:13–53:12). And yet the very first verse of the reading evokes the true spirit that should pervade us on this day: "Behold, my servant shall prosper, he shall be exalted and lifted up" (52:13).

The description that follows reveals its full meaning only in the light of that first verse. The Servant's lot is really a passage through suffering and death, a journey through death to exaltation and glory. For this reason the text became classic from the very first days of the Church as a way of describing the death and victorious resurrection of the Lord.

St. Matthew quotes a verse from it: "He took our infirmities and bore our diseases" (Matthew 8:17; Is. 53:4). In St. Luke, not long before the end, Christ predicts the fulfillment of what the prophets had said: "Behold, we are going up to Jerusalem, and everything that is written of the Son of man by the prophets will be accomplished" (Luke 18:31); he is referring here to the prophecies concerning the suffering of the Son of Man. In the Acts of the Apostles, when Philip meets the Ethiopian court official who is returning home from Jerusalem, the latter is reading the Book of Isaiah, chapter 53, verses 7-8, "Like a lamb that is led to the slaughter, and like a sheep that before its shearers is dumb, so he opened not his mouth. . . ." Philip uses the passage as his starting point in explaining the gospel of Jesus to the man (Acts 8:26-35).

The First Letter of Peter has a passage (2:22-24) that contains several implicit quotations from the fourth of the Servant songs: "He committed no sin; no guile was found on his lips" (cf. Is. 53:9); "He himself bore our sins in his body on the tree" (cf. Is. 53:12); "By his wounds you have been healed" (cf. Is. 53:5-6).

The exegetes do not agree on the identity of the servant described by Isaiah. Some believe it to be the prophet himself; others think Israel is meant. It is not easy, however, to apply the description to Israel, for, literary arguments aside, it would be surprising indeed to see Israel declared upright or to liken it to an innocent man being condemned, when everyone knew of its infidelities. It would seem rather that the servant is a prophetic figure.

In any case, when the Church reads this text, we see in it a moving description of the Christ who is laid low and accepts death as an expiatory sacrifice that will bring life to the nations. From our standpoint as Christians, the interpretation given the text by the New Testament is decisive: the Servant is Christ. We admit that by the rules of exegesis the servant may be interpreted as being either an individual or a people. Yet it is impossible for us to hear the poem read on Good Friday and not see in it the image of him whose victorious death the Church is celebrating. There is no need of our commenting on the text here; read it in the Lectionary or in the Bible, and it is perfectly clear.

Psalm 31, which serves as the response to the proclamation of Isaiah's picture of Christ, has a refrain that puts the whole into the context of the Cross: "Father, I put my life in your hands." The psalm is especially appropriate, since some of its verses are like an echo of the passage from Isaiah.

| I am the scorn of all my adversaries, a horror to | He was despised and rejected by men . . . one |

my neighbors, an object
of dread to my acquaint-
ances; those who see me
in the street flee from me
(Ps. 31:11).

from whom men hide
their faces (Is. 53:3).

Let thy face shine on
thy servant (Ps. 31:16).

He shall prolong his days
(Is. 53:10).

"A great priest over the house of God"

In St. John's Gospel, Jesus says: "And I, when I am lifted
up from the earth, will draw all men to myself" (12:32).
Through and because of the sacrifice of the Cross, we now
have "a great priest over the house of God" (Heb. 10:21).
To understand this, we must reread the passage from the
Letter to the Hebrews in which the author explains the
priesthood of Christ; the passage supplies the second reading for Good Friday. The key verses are these:

> Since we have a great high priest who has passed
> through the heavens, Jesus, the Son of God, let us
> hold fast our confession. For we have not a high priest
> who is unable to sympathize with our weaknesses,
> but one who in every respect has been tempted as we
> are, yet without sinning. Let us then with confidence
> draw near to the throne of grace, that we may receive
> mercy and find grace to help in time of need. For
> every high priest chosen from among men is ap-
> pointed to act on behalf of men in relation to God, to
> offer gifts and sacrifices for sins (Heb. 4:14-16; 5:1).

Someone — and that Someone is Christ, the all-powerful
Intercessor — can now understand our needs and present
them to the Father. The Church wants us to relive the Passion of Christ on Good Friday. For when the Church, which
is God's household, contemplates his suffering and the
power of the Christ who overcame suffering so victoriously,
she remembers that that she has at her head a great Priest.
Remembering it, she begins to invoke his aid, or, more ac-

curately, she prays with him for the important intentions of
his Body, which she is.

The glorious Passion

At this point, then, the Church proclaims to her believing
members, her catechumens, and mankind at large the death
of her Lord, as she has done in the past and will continue to
do until he comes again. Yet we will not properly understand what she proclaims unless we see it in its context,
and for this we must go back even beyond the Last Supper
in the Gospel of St. John, whose account of the Passion is
the one read on this day.

In chapter 12, just before Passover, Jesus announces his
death, but also his glorification through and by means of his
death: "The hour has come for the Son of man to be glorified. Truly, truly, I say to you, unless a grain of wheat falls
into the earth and dies, it remains alone; but if it dies, it
bears much fruit" (12:23-24).

A few moments later, a troubled Christ asks himself
whether or not he should pray to the Father to save him
from this hour. But he immediately answers his question:
"'No, for this purpose I have come to this hour. Father,
glorify thy name.' Then a voice came from heaven, 'I have
glorified it, and I will glorify it again'" (12:27-28). Then
Christ goes a step further in foretelling his glorious death:
"Now this is the judgment of this world, now shall the ruler
of this world be cast out; and I, when I am *lifted up* from
the earth, will draw all men to myself" (12:31-32). Earlier,
in chapter 8, he had said: "When you have *lifted up* the Son
of man, then you will know that I am he" (8:28).

In chapter 12, the word "lift up" reveals its double meaning, as the evangelist explicitly says: "He said this to show
by what death he was to die" (12:33). The contexts in which
the term is used leaves no doubt as to the two meanings of
"lift up": it means the crucifixion, but it also means the
glorious ascension that will follow.

The announcement during the Supper of Judas's betrayal links the Supper to the sacrifice of the Cross. In other words, the successive moments in which Christ hands himself over as food and is handed over to death belong together. When Judas eats the morsel and goes out into the night, Jesus says: "Now is the Son of man glorified, and in him God is glorified; if God is glorified in him, God will also glorify him in himself, and glorify him at once" (13:31-32). Thus, even at the very moment when the betrayal is assured and the Passion is imminent, Jesus speaks of his glorification.

In his farewell discourse, Jesus tells his disciples of his departure through death and of his resurrection, but he also tells them that only his disciples will realize his triumph: "Yet a little while, and the world will see me no more, but you will see me; because I live, you will live also. In that day you will know that I am in my Father, and you in me, and I in you" (14:19-20). The world will no longer be even thinking about the man who was crucified, but the disciples will see him alive, risen, and glorious. Then, when the disciples are nonetheless saddened, Jesus assures them: "Be of good cheer, I have overcome the world" (16:33).

We must also keep in mind the passages in which Jesus speaks of going to his Father and of sending the Spirit who will glorify him and communicate to the disciples the truth that is in Jesus (16:14).

The priestly prayer, in which Jesus offers himself to his Father and intercedes for the disciples, also emphasizes the glorious side of the coming Passion: "Father, the hour has come; glorify thy Son that the Son may glorify thee, since thou hast given him power over all flesh, to give eternal life to all whom thou hast given him. . . . Now, Father, glorify thou me in thy own presence with the glory which I had with thee before the world was made" (17:1-2, 5).

In his tenth sermon on the Passion, St. Leo the Great comments on this exaltation of Christ. In doing so, he shows how Christ's glorification resulted from his death;

more accurately, he shows that there is really no succession of steps here, but that Christ's death is already his glorification:

> When, then, Christ Jesus was raised up on the Cross, he brought death to the author of death and broke the power of all the Principalities and Powers ranged against him, by exposing to them his flesh in which he could suffer. He allowed the ancient enemy to assail him insolently; the latter unleashed his rage against a nature that was subject to his attacks, and dared demand tribute from one in whom there was in fact no slightest trace of sin. In consequence, the deadly bond under which we were all sold was rendered void, and the contract that enslaved us now passed into the Redeemer's hands. The nails that pierced the Lord's hands and feet inflicted everlasting wounds on the devil, and the pain which the sacred limbs experienced proved deadly to the hostile powers. Thus Christ won his victory, and in such a way that in and through him all who believed in him likewise triumphed.
>
> When the Lord, glorified by having his crucified body raised aloft, was effecting the reconciliation of the world from his high place of torment and was calling the converted thief to a home in paradise, you, the leaders of the Jews and the teachers of the law, were not touched by the evil you had done, nor softened at seeing the effect of your crime. No, to the sharp nails you added piercing words. . . .[92]

Death and exaltation

On Palm Sunday the Passion is read, with the Synoptics supplying the text in a three-year cycle. On Good Friday, the Gospel of John is read, in accordance with very ancient tradition. We have already had occasion to characterize briefly each of the synoptic accounts of the passion.[93] St. John's account is shorter and less anecdotal. It contains, nonetheless, a vibrant theology, the essential points of which we shall briefly note here.

First of all — and this is true from the very beginning of the account — John emphasizes Jesus' obedience to the Father's will. The theme is, of course, a favorite one with him. In the Garden of Olives, for example, we do not find Jesus praying to be relieved from drinking the cup of suffering; on the contrary, his words indicate that he accepts the cup as a duty and even as a gift that will lead him to his glory: "Shall I not drink the cup which the Father has given me?" (18:11).

Though John usually avoids the anecdotal, he does emphasize many of the details in the scene of Jesus' questioning by Pilate (18:28–19:16). He points out that the kind of death to which Jesus is sentenced is a fulfillment of his own prediction: "This was to fulfill the word which Jesus had spoken to show by what death he was to die" (18:32). Especially, however, John wants to emphasize the kingship of Christ. Jesus asserts that his coming into this world was motivated by the desire to proclaim the mystery of salvation; that is why his words are so important — because anyone who belongs to the truth hears his voice. But Jesus goes beyond hints of his kingship; he states it openly: "My kingship is not of this world. . . . You say that I am a king. For this I was born, and for this I have come into the world, to bear witness to the truth" (18:36-37). Here again we have a favorite theme of St. John's. Pilate even hands Jesus over to the Jews with the words, "Here is your King!" (19:14); it is not clear whether he is speaking ironically or whether he is half convinced.

The kingship of Jesus will be asserted even by the instrument of his death, for the inscription on the Cross read: "Jesus of Nazareth, the King of the Jews." The text was written in three languages and proclaimed a fact that has transformed the history of mankind. Here, once again, in a new guise, we find the theme of glorification: of the crucifixion that is also a victory, the hour of death that is also the hour of triumph.

The prayer of the Church

After having listened to the account of Christ's victorious death, the Church now recollects herself for prayer, in accordance with the ancient custom that every liturgy of the word should end with a prayer of the faithful. This is a custom that has now been happily restored.

On Good Friday, the general intercessions are of the kind used in the Roman Church down to the time of Pope Gelasius. The order of the intentions has been changed in the liturgical reform, and some intentions have been added. Ten intentions are proclaimed; each proclamation is followed by a moment of silent prayer, and then the celebrant utters a prayer in the name of all.

It will be enough here simply to list the intentions; they instruct us as to the concerns that should be ours as we recall the permanent presence of Christ's Passion. We pray for the Church, for the Pope, for the clergy and laity, for catechumens, for the unity of Christians, for the Jews, for those who do not believe in Christ, for those who do not believe in God, for those in public office, and for all men in their special needs.

It is good to realize that at the moment when the Church is celebrating the high point in the history of salvation, she does not lose interest in any individual but, on the contrary, seeks to bring into her celebration all things spiritual and human, all the situations men find themselves in, all their anxieties, all their divergent viewpoints.

"This is the wood of the Cross"

Communion should have immediately followed on the liturgy of the word, but the ceremony of the veneration of the Cross was inserted at this point, as an action called for by the proclamation of the Passion. The cross is lifted up and shown to the world; here is Christ crucified, and men must choose. The elevation, and the adoration that follows, are also an assertion of the decisive victory Christ has won over the powers of evil that are active in the world. He is "lifted up," and the lifting up means that mankind which had been dispersed has been gathered into unity once again.

The elevation of the cross thus points to the most important act in the history of salvation. The faithful respond by singing "Come, let us worship" and bending their knee in a rite that acknowledges a true victory. We have already spoken of the glorious aspect of the Lord's death and of how the Lamb slain on the Cross is also the Lamb of St. John's apocalyptic vision of triumph. What more does Christianity have to show to the world? The triumphant Cross is the source of all Christian meaning; the sign of the Cross, which this world regards as foolishness, is what distinguishes the Christian from unbelievers.

In his second sermon on the Passion, St. Leo the Great suggests what our thoughts should be as we gaze upon the Cross:

> We, then, beloved, to whom our Lord Jesus Christ crucified is not a stumbling block or folly but the power of God and the wisdom of God; we who are the spiritual seed of Abraham, not begotten of a slave but reborn into a free family; we who were rescued by God's mighty hand and outstretched arm from oppression and tyranny in Egypt and for whom the true and spotless Lamb, Jesus Christ, was sacrificed — let us embrace this marvelous and saving paschal mystery and be remade in the image of him who became like us in our deformity. Let us rise up to him who turned our lowly dust into his glorious body; and in order that we may merit a share in his resurrection, let us be thoroughly like him in his humility and patience. Great is the name of him whose service we have entered, and great the profession whose discipline we have accepted. Christ's followers may not abandon the royal road.[94]

The Church shows us the Cross and we adore it. It is difficult not to think of John and the words he cites from the prophet Zechariah: "They shall look on him whom they have pierced" (John 19:37; Zech. 12:10).

To "look on" means to know and understand the mystery of the Cross. The liturgy of the adoration of the Cross presupposes that we have this kind of concrete knowledge.

It might be said that the term "adoration" is out of place here, since we do not adore the Cross or, for that matter, the death of Christ. We adore his Person and what his Person means to us, symbolizing as it does the love of the Son for the Father and of the Father and the Son for us.

The Reproaches that are sung during the veneration of the Cross have to do with the exchange of love between God and man in Christ. They are a dialogue in which God, through his Christ, tells us of his love and forces us to admit what he has done for us and the world out of love.

The Reproaches developed in the course of time. The first part comprises the first three strophes (the third begins: "What more could I have done for you?") and seems to have been composed in the West. The "My people, what have I done for you?" appears for the first time in the seventh-century Spanish liturgical book, the *Liber ordinum*.[95] Scripture has evidently provided the inspiration for these stanzas.

The second part contains nine stanzas (with a refrain repeated after each), likewise inspired by Scripture, but in a much freer fashion. Each stanza contrasts what God has done and what the people have done in return. This second section seems to date from the eleventh century.

The responses (refrains) throughout are either the *Trisagion* or the words: "My people, what have I done to you? How have I offended you? Answer me!"

The Reproaches are an especially moving experience in the Good Friday liturgy. The first three stanzas, to which the *Trisagion* is the response, express the divine initiatives and the hardening of the people whom God wanted for his own. The second part goes into greater detail on God's initiatives on behalf of his people: the liberation from Egypt, the crossing of the Red Sea, the column of cloud, the manna, the water from the rock, the conquest of the kings of Canaan, and the royal house. How stirring a description of God's loving attentions to a people that responded by abandoning and betraying him!

The opening antiphon at the veneration of the Cross sums up the real meaning of the ceremony: "We worship you, Lord, we venerate your cross, we praise your resurrection. Through the cross you brought joy to the world."

The Body and Blood of the Lord

Once the veneration of the Cross is completed, the reserved Sacrament is brought to the altar. As usual, the celebrant recites the Our Father with the congregation. The words "Thy will be done on earth as it is in heaven" take on a special depth of meaning after the reading of the Passion, where we saw Christ bowing to the will he had come to do and obeying it with a love that would win him exaltation and a name above every other name.

All the faithful then receive the Body of Christ. It is possible to regret this custom, which was introduced at the most recent reform of Holy Week. The reason for the regret is that the practice may distract attention from the climactic point of the sacred triduum, the reception of the Eucharist during the Easter Vigil. Perhaps we should have followed the practice of the early Church by fasting even from the Eucharist until the Vigil. On the other hand, the reception of Christ's Body, which is the sign of his immolation and glorious Passion, is also an especially meaningful act on Good Friday. It is at least understandable that a rite should have been introduced that for a very long time was excluded from the papal liturgy.

D. THE LORD RESTS IN THE TOMB

Holy Saturday

11. CELEBRATIONS ANCIENT AND MODERN

Holy Saturday has a special character. Apart from such Hours as were chiefly monastic in origin (such as Matins), the day used to have no special Office of its own. On this day a fast was observed until into the night, but it was a festive fast, a fast marked by expectation of the Lord's return.

In the early centuries the only ceremony held at Rome on Holy Saturday morning was the "handing back" of the Creed by the catechumens and the final exorcism before the solemn renunciation of Satan.

In our volume on Lent, we followed the progress of the catechumen and observed his gradual transformation. On this Saturday the Church of Rome gave special attention to these catechumens, since that very night they were to become her children.

The old liturgical books have preserved a record for us of how the ceremony was conducted.[96] During Lent the catechumens had undergone three scrutinies, or, at a later period, six; the last scrutiny, a more solemn one, took place on Holy Saturday. Moreover, during Lent the Creed had been presented to the catechumens, along with a short explanation of its articles; now, on Holy Saturday, the catechumens were to recite the Creed, which they had learned by heart. The recital was not really a profession of faith. These individuals undoubtedly had an incipient faith, but faith in its fullness would be a gift received through baptism itself. Their profession of faith would in fact be part of the sacramental rite, since the officiating priest would ask them three questions: "Do you believe in the

Father . . . ," "Do you believe in the Son . . . ," and "Do you believe in the Holy Spirit . . . ," and to each the candidate would answer "I do." He would be immersed in the water of the font three times, once after each question.

The point, therefore, of the Holy Saturday morning ceremony was to gain assurance that the candidates knew the Creed and that they were disposed to profess their faith at the moment of baptism.

Still more impressive was the solemn renunciation of Satan by the catechumens. It was preceded by an imposition of hands by the bishop, the rite of the *Ephpheta*, and an anointing.

After this the catechumen renounced Satan and all his works and "pomps." In the interests of clarity, the word "pomps" has now been replaced by "empty promises."[97] It must be admitted, however, that this and other translations do not really capture the meaning of the original word. A *pompa* was a solemn public procession, and in this context the word called to mind the worship of pagan divinities, the games at the Circus, and all the extravagant display of a civilization characterized, and undermined, by wealth and conspicuous consumption. In short, the catechumen was renouncing the paganism around him.

Sometimes the ceremony became even more expressive, as, for example, in the East, where the catechumen spat in the direction of the West (the place of sunset and darkness), where the powers of evil dwelt. The Fathers of the Church enjoyed describing this solemn renunciation in which the catechumen rejected the "world" and pledged his fidelity.

In continuity with the ancient solemn scrutiny, the Church now asks all the baptized (at the renewal of the baptismal promises) to renew their rejection of Satan and the "world."

12. HIS BODY REPOSES IN HOPE

The reform of Holy Week has restored to Holy Saturday its authentic meaning and its ancient form. On this day the Church celebrates Christ resting in his tomb, but she also awaits his resurrection, for she knows that "his body reposes in hope" (Ps. 16:9).

The holy women remained sitting by the tomb

With the holy women, the Church sits by the tomb and meditates on the Lord as he rests there in peace.

This is the theme of the first antiphon in the Office of Readings: "In peace, I will lie down and sleep," and it strikes the keynote for the whole of the Office: repose in the expectation of a glorious resurrection. The thoughts of the praying Church are concentrated on the event that has just taken place, that is, the suffering and death of Christ, but the Church is also constantly aware that Jesus died certain of ultimate victory. Even as she meditates on the Lord's death and repose, she is, therefore, impatient to proclaim the coming resurrection. In the alternate responsory after the psalms of Lauds, she cannot help breaking out into the words: "For our sake Christ was obedient, accepting even death, death on a cross. Therefore God raised him on high and gave him the name above all other names."

Psalm 4 in the Office of Readings ends with words that tell us of the joy Christ already has, even before the resurrection, for he sees that his mission is completed and he tastes the victory:

> You have put into my heart a greater joy than they have from abundance of corn and new wine. I will lie down in peace and sleep comes at once for you alone, Lord, make me dwell in safety.

Psalm 16 reminds us of the resurrection and of Christ's entry into his inheritance:

O Lord, it is you who are my portion and cup;
it is you yourself who are my prize.
The lot marked out for me is my delight:
welcome indeed the heritage that falls to me!

And so my heart rejoices, my soul is glad;
even my body shall rest in safety.
For you will not leave my soul among the dead,
nor let your beloved know decay.

You will show me the path of life,
the fullness of joy in your presence,
at your right hand happiness for ever (Ps. 16:5-6,
9-11).

Psalm 24 expresses similar sentiments:

Who shall climb the mountain of the Lord?
Who shall stand in his holy place?
The man with clean hands and pure heart. . . .

He shall receive blessings from the Lord
and reward from the God who saves him. . . .

O gates, lift high your heads;
grow higher, ancient doors.
Let him enter, the king of glory!

Who is he, the king of glory?
He, the Lord of armies,
he is the king of glory (Ps. 24:3-5, 7-8).

The psalm is describing the victory of the risen Christ, who,
after conquering in battle, returns to his Father's house.

The repose of Christ

The reading from the Letter to the Hebrews bids us
strive to enter into Christ's rest (4:1-13). The reading de-

serves our attention, for the theme of the Lord's rest or repose suggests in turn a whole series of themes of which we, the baptized, should be aware.

The beginning of the passage may mislead us into thinking that the author of the Letter to the Hebrews is indulging in a bit of moralizing. In fact, however, he is simply urging us to learn from what happened to the Hebrews, who received the good news but did not accept it with faith nor profit by it.

Like the Hebrews, we too are invited to enter into rest. What rest is meant? The Letter reminds us that on the seventh day God rested from his work of creating. In like manner, a sabbath rest awaits those who hear the voice of the Lord and do not harden their hearts against it. "Whoever enters God's rest also ceases from his labors as God did from his. Let us therefore strive to enter that rest, that no one fall by the same sort of disobedience" (4:10-11).

The rest of Christ in the tomb thus leads the Church's thoughts to the Creator's rest on the seventh day, to the rest promised the Hebrews but not obtained because they lacked faith and disobeyed, and to the sabbath rest at the end of time for all who believe.

The death and rest of Christ are realities that make claims on us today. Entry into rest supposes obedient faith and a laborious effort to attain life in the Promised Land.

E. CHRIST OUR PASSOVER
Easter Vigil

13. CELEBRATIONS ANCIENT AND MODERN

A special feast of Easter does not seem to have been celebrated at Rome before the second half of the second century. Elsewhere, if we can trust Eusebius of Caesarea, the celebration of Easter had begun in the early second century.[98] This did not mean, of course, that the early Church did not live by the mystery of the Lord's death and resurrection. Quite the contrary. But every Sunday was a commemoration of the paschal mystery in the form of the Eucharistic celebration. Finally a single Sunday was chosen as a special day for the feast of Christ's resurrection and became the most solemn of Sundays, the Sunday *par excellence*, the Sunday of Sundays.

In acting thus, the Church was, as on other occasions, christianizing a Jewish feast. Since Easter is the feast of the Lord's resurrection and an anticipation of his second coming, St. Jerome writes that our Passover, like the Jewish, is marked by expectation of the Messiah's coming in power: "It was a tradition among the Jews that the Messiah would come during the night, at the hour when the Passover had been celebrated in Egypt. . . . That, I think, is why we have the tradition from the apostles that the congregation is not to be dismissed before midnight during the Easter Vigil, since they await the coming of Christ at that hour."[99]

Jewish Passover and Christian Easter

No one would deny that there are similarities between our Paschal Vigil and the Jewish Passover feast. We think, however, that what should be emphasized is not outward likenesses but the theology of expectation that underlies both. The Passover of the Bible is "a religious movement that inspires the entire people of God."[100] A dynamic sense of liberation dominates the Jewish Passover of the Bible, and the idea of "passage" is essential and central to it, as it is to the Christian Pasch. We should be aware, moreover, that in celebrating the Passover the Jews were not simply commemorating a past event. Rather, they were celebrating an event they regarded as a present reality: "To commemorate is not to stand off from what had once taken place; on the contrary, it means eliminating the distance that separates. It means bringing the past to life again."[101]

There are also, however, important differences between the Jewish Passover and the Christian Pasch. The Jewish Passover liturgy is a domestic affair; the Christian paschal liturgy is a community celebration with the Eucharist as its center. Moreover, the Jewish feast was only the starting point for the Christian feast, and the latter represents a goal reached, even if it also looks forward to a definitive fulfillment at the end of time.

In his *Ecclesiastical History*, Eusebius of Caesarea tells us that Christians saw their own Easter as so much like the Jewish Passover feast which they had christianized that they wanted to celebrate Easter on the fourteenth day of the month Nisan, that is, on the day when the Jews immolated the Passover lamb. We must qualify Eusebius's statement, however, since it was only the Christians of Asia Minor who insisted on this date. The other Churches, on the contrary, appealed to apostolic tradition and celebrated the feast on a Sunday, which had been the day of the Lord's resurrection. The controversy was quite a lively one, as the reader may know; Pope Victor I (ca. 189–ca. 198) put an end to it by decreeing that the celebration of Easter should take place on the Sunday following the fourteenth day of Nisan.[102]

In any event, the Passover that Christians celebrated had been perfectly described by St. Paul when he wrote: "Let us, therefore, celebrate the festival, not with the old leaven, the leaven of malice and evil, but with the unleavened bread of sincerity and truth" (1 Cor. 5:8).

The Easter Vigil in earlier times

Some of the components of the later Vigil are discernible even in Christian antiquity. There was a fast, followed by a nighttime prayer service that concluded with the celebration of the Eucharist. In the third-century Syrian *Didascalia Apostolorum*, these two — the fast and the prayer service culminating in the Eucharist — are the sole observances attested.[103] But one thing is clear: the Vigil service was already a well-established practice.

The *Apostolic Tradition* (ca. 215) of St. Hippolytus of Rome shows, however, that the administration of baptism had already been linked with the Vigil and was celebrated during the night.[104] Tertullian would write that Easter Sunday was the natural time for baptism.[105] The celebration of baptism during the Vigil became widespread, however, only in the fourth century.

The practice of singing a hymn of blessing at the lighting of the lamp in the home at evening is very ancient. St. Hippolytus gives a prayer for blessing the lamp at the community meal.[106] Nonetheless, what we now call the *Exsultet* made its appearance only in the fourth century, and in various forms. Moreover, although the blessing of the paschal candle became the practice almost everywhere, even in the churches of Rome (fifth century), it is still missing from the papal liturgy as late as the eleventh century.[107]

For the blessing of the fire there is no official formulary before the twelfth century. It then appears in the Roman Pontifical of the twelfth century, which describes the procession in which the acclamation "Light of Christ!" is sung.[108] The use of new fire (the old fires had been extinguished on Holy Thursday evening) is attested as a Good Friday usage at Rome in the ninth century.[109]

After this quick glance at the broad development of the liturgy of the Paschal Vigil, let us now retrace our steps and look at the various parts of the rite in greater detail.

The blessing of the new fire

The blessing of the new fire, as we just indicated, originated in a practical need. And yet the problem is really not that clear, for questions were being raised about the blessing as early as the eighth and ninth centuries.[110] Various traditions have to be considered.

At Rome it was the custom to flood the celebration of the Paschal Vigil with light, in order to impress on the participants the idea of Christ as the Light. The lamps were lit even before the Vigil began, and the light only intensified as the rite continued.

From the beginning of the Vigil there were two man-high candles on the scene. They were to be seen at either side of the altar, of the celebrant, and of the baptismal font. Originally these were not blessed. Then, in *Ordo* 16 (680–775) a blessing of the candles appears. According to *Ordo* 23 (700–750), the light for these candles is taken from the light "that was hidden away on Good Friday." In *Ordo* 17 there is a "blessing" of the candle that is lit at the fire hidden on Good Friday. *Ordo* 26 (750–775) provides new details.

According to *Ordo* 26, at the ninth hour on Holy Thursday, fire is struck from flint at the door of the basilica, and from the fire a candle stuck on a reed is lit. A lamp is also lit at the fire and kept until Holy Saturday, when it will be used to light the candle that has just been blessed. This seems to be a strictly Gallican custom. The blessed and lit candle is solemnly carried into the basilica and used to light seven lamps standing before the altar; then the whole church is illumined. At this point the ministers enter for the celebration of Mass. The various lamps are solemnly extinguished again during Matins and Lauds.

From this time on, the usages found in the various *Ordines* intermingle, and the problem becomes complicated. At Mainz in the tenth century, for example, the procession into the church may be done in two ways: in silence or to the accompaniment of the hymn *Inventor rutili luminis, dux bone* ("O good Leader, Creator of the gleaming light").[111] In the thirteenth century a three-branched candlestick is in use,[112] but this was eliminated in the reform of 1951. The use of a three-branched candlestick may have been taken over from Jerusalem, where the bishop lit three candles, and after him the clergy and finally the entire congregation did the same.[113] But, while the 1951 reform suppressed the three-branched candlestick (the point of which was not very clear), it introduced the practice of lighting the candles of all the faithful; this custom had not hitherto existed in the Roman liturgy, though it did at Jerusalem.

How was the candle blessed? Originally, it seems that the ceremony consisted simply in tracing a sign of the Cross on the candle. The minister who was to do the blessing stood at the center of the sanctuary in front of the altar, asked that the others pray for him, and drew the sign of the Cross on the candle. Then he received from the subdeacon the light hidden away on Good Friday and lit the candle. Thereupon he said, "The Lord be with you," and a prayer, and continued with the "Lift up your hearts" etc.[114] Several *Exsultet* formulas have come down to us, among them the poem with which we are familiar. In 384, St. Jerome wrote a long letter to Praesidius in which he rather spitefully attacked our *Exsultet* for frivolity.[115]

The readings

The readings are an essential part of the Paschal Vigil, but the various Rites differ in the number, choice, and length of the readings. The Coptic Rite, for example, has a very large number of readings, as does the Byzantine Rite. The Roman Rite has known different systems over the centuries. The history has not yet been fully clarified, and we cannot go into it here. Suffice it to say that the Gregorian Sacramentary has four readings,[116] and the Gelasian ten,[117] while at Rome there were six lessons, later on twelve. During the period when the popes were Easterners, that is, in the seventh and eighth centuries, there were twelve lessons, sung in both Latin and Greek.[118]

The blessing of the baptismal water

The blessing of the baptismal water seems to have been in use by about the second century. Two important texts of the blessing have come down to us. One was composed by Bishop Serapion of Thmuis (ca. 350). The celebrant asks that the waters be filled with the Spirit; just as the Word went down into the water of the Jordan and sanctified it, so may he now descend into the water of the font and render it spiritual.[119] The other text is by St. Optatus of Milevi (writing ca. 370) and takes the form of a brief acclamation of praise addressed to the water.[120]

Later on, around 400, the *Constitutiones Apostolorum* describes the blessing of the water by the priest. The latter praises and blesses the Lord because he has sent his Son for the world's salvation. Now we have the baptism of regeneration as a symbolic embodiment of the saving Cross. May God therefore sanctify the water and make it the medium of his grace and power so that everyone who is baptized in accordance with Christ's command may be crucified with Christ and may die and rise with him to adoptive sonship, thus dying to sin and being made alive for holiness.[121]

The Verona Sacramentary (5th–6th cent.) has a short formula for the blessing of baptismal water:

> We turn to you in prayer, Lord, eternal Creator of all things and all-powerful God, whose Spirit swept over the waters of creation and whose eyes looked from heaven upon the Jordan as John bestowed his baptism of repentance on those who confessed their sins. We pray your holy Majesty to be secretly at work in this water and to thoroughly cleanse the interior man in those who will be baptized in it. May they be reborn from their deadly sins and live again according to the new man who is created in Christ Jesus, with whom you live and reign in the unity of the Holy Spirit throughout the ages.[122]

St. Ambrose speaks of the blessing in his *De sacramentis*. He is addressing the newly baptized and explaining to them the sacrament they have received: "Attend now to this next point. The priest comes and stands by the font; he says a prayer, calling upon the name of the Father and the presence of the Son and the Holy Spirit. He uses heavenly words, for he uses the words of Christ, who told us to baptize 'in the name of the Father and of the Son and of the Holy Spirit.'"[123]

Litanies

Since it took time to get from the church, where the liturgy of the word had been celebrated, to the baptistery, where the water was to be blessed, a litany was sung. At Rome a litany served as a processional song. That is why we find a litany at various points in the celebration of the Easter Vigil. In *Ordo* 17 a litany is sung before the blessing of the candle as the clergy and subdeacons enter; another is sung after the blessing of the candle while the priests and deacons, with their lighted candles, are taking their places for the readings.[124] According to another *Ordo*, a litany is also sung during the procession to the font.[125] Finally, a litany is sung that serves as an entrance song for the Mass and ends with the *Gloria in excelsis*.[126] In some places a litany is also sung while the bishop is conferring the sacrament of confirmation after baptism.[127]

The litanies were usually repeated, sometimes as often as seven times. In time the antiphon *Sicut cervus* ("As a hart longs for flowing streams . . .": Ps. 42:2) was introduced for the procession to the font. Then it became customary to divide up a single litany, part being sung before the blessing of the font and the baptisms, part afterwards, with the *Kyrie* of the litany serving as the *Kyrie* of the Mass.

Until Vatican Council II and the most recent reform of Holy Week, the Vigil Mass had preserved some special features in an effort to imitate what was done in early times. For example, there was no *Agnus Dei*, a prayer that had been introduced during the fraction by Pope Sergius I (687–701). There was also no kiss of peace, because at cockcrow, when Easter day began to dawn, a kiss of peace was exchanged, with the greeting, "Peace be with you."[128] The experts in the recent reform judged that the preservation of these peculiarities had no value for the life of the faithful.

14. THE LIGHT OF CHRIST

The new fire

When the Church introduced the blessing of the new fire, she was simply giving a sacral dimension to a straightforward material necessity. A new source of light was needed for the nighttime Office, since the lamps had been extinguished at the end of the Lucernarium, or evening Office. What this blessing of the new fire shows, as do the blessing of the paschal candle and the consecration of the baptismal water, is the effects of redemption. The world is already taking on a new appearance, as subhuman creatures take their place in the global unity and cease to be man's enemies. These creatures are servants once again and thus instruments of grace.

The catechumen has long since been awaiting the moment of his enlightenment. Now he sees the act of creation being mimed before his eyes. The Lord is asleep in his tomb, but he is also now making his own and acting out the words the prophet Osee had written: "Death, you shall die in me; hell, you shall be destroyed by me" (13:14).[129] The third antiphon at Vespers on Holy Saturday reminds all that they are to expect Christ's victory over death, for he had said, "Destroy this temple, and in three days I will raise it up" (John 2:19).

In short, the now sleeping Lord will soon be the victorious Master of the world. In the canticle for Vespers on Holy Saturday, the Church bids the faithful sing a passage from the Letter to the Philippians that presents both the fact of the resurrection and the title the Lord has to it:

> [he] emptied himself. . . . And being found in human form he humbled himself and became obedient unto death, even death on a cross. Therefore God has highly exalted him and bestowed on him the name which is above every name, that at the name of Jesus every knee should bow, in heaven and on earth and

under the earth, and every tongue confess that Jesus Christ is Lord, to the glory of God the Father (Phil. 2:7-11).

Christ the Lord is thus given dominion over the whole universe; the Letter to the Philippians expresses it as sovereignty over everything in the heavens, on earth, and under the earth.

In the Letter to the Colossians, Paul again asserts the unqualified lordship of Christ as conqueror of death:

> He is the image of the invisible God, the first-born of all creation; for in him all things were created, in heaven and on earth, visible and invisible, whether thrones or dominions or principalities or authorities — all things were created through him and for him. He is before all things, and in him all things hold together (Col. 1:15-17).

The Letter to the Ephesians contains a similar assertion:

> [God's might was] . . . accomplished in Christ when he raised him from the dead and made him sit at his right hand in the heavenly places, far above all rule and authority and power and dominion, and above every name that is named, not only in this age but also in that which is to come (Eph. 1:20-21).

We should note carefully Paul's insistence on Christ's triumph and present dominion over the entirety of creation. The paschal mystery means the renewal of creation as a whole; that is the normal and logical consequence of man's redemption. Man was set in the midst of the world and called upon to bestow names upon creatures; they in turn were meant to be his servants. Once man himself acquires a new existence as servant of God, the creatures around him are likewise renewed and begin once again to serve, for they were created for man's sake so that he might be steward of them and make them contribute to the glory of God.

Fire is one such creature that is now man's servant, the

fire "which was struck from the flint and is destined for our use."[130] The fire becomes at the same time God's servant, and we can therefore ask him: "Make this new fire holy, and inflame us with new hope. Purify our minds by this Easter celebration and bring us one day to the feast of eternal light."[131] It thus symbolizes a new beginning in our lives.

The new fire is silently sprinkled with holy water. Then a blessed coal is placed in the censer, incense is heaped on it, and the fire is incensed three times. By means of this simple rite the Church acknowledges the dignity of the created world that the Lord has redeemed.

The new light

The candle, too, is a creature renewed and has the sacral function of symbolizing to the world the glory of the risen Christ. That is why the sign of the Cross is first traced on the candle, for the Cross is what gives all things their meaning. The Roman Canon of the Mass (Eucharistic Prayer I) gives apt expression to this universal significance of Christ's redemptive death when it says: "Through Christ our Lord you give us all these gifts. You fill them with life and goodness, you bless them and make them holy."

As the celebrant traces the sign of the Cross and inscribes the Greek letters alpha and omega along with the numerals of the current year, he says: "Christ yesterday and today, the beginning and the end, Alpha and Omega; all time belongs to him, and all the ages; to him be glory and power through every age for ever. Amen." He thus expresses in a few words and actions the entire doctrine of St. Paul on Christ as Lord of the universe. Nothing escapes the influence of Christ's redemptive act; the whole of creation — man, things, and time — now belong to him.

It might be thought that from a pastoral viewpoint the restoration of these rites — some of them ancient, others merely local — was not a very happy idea. Does it not create a kind of dead space in the course of the celebration, inasmuch as the faithful take hardly any part in these ceremonies? People are standing in the dark; they can hardly see what is going on; the words of the celebrant lack unction and are like scattered fragments of a discourse. And yet we have just seen the wealth of teaching this short ceremony contains.

In the recent reform a good deal of freedom was allowed with regard to these ceremonies, since they may be omitted or kept only in part. It was thought proper to retain the practice of inserting the five grains of incense in the candle, although the whole ceremony had its origin in a misreading of the Latin text. The Latin word *incensum*, which in context meant "lighted" and referred to the candle, was mistaken for another word that is spelled the same way but has a different meaning, namely, "incense." It was this misinterpretation that gave rise to the five grains of incense that are inserted in the candle and symbolize the five wounds of Christ: "By his holy and glorious wounds may Christ our Lord guard us and keep us. Amen." The words admittedly do aptly express the mysterious power of Christ's glorious death, but the symbolism is a bit forced. It could disappear without great loss from a liturgy that is already rich enough and ought not to become excessively freighted with symbolism. Our concern, after all, should be that the faithful might concentrate on the central aspects of the paschal mystery.

The celebrant ends the preparation of the paschal candle by lighting it from the new fire, while saying, "May the light of Christ, rising in glory, dispel the darkness of our hearts and minds."

The procession

The ministers now walk in procession behind the lighted candle, which represents Christ, who is the column of fire and light that guides us through the darkness and shows us the way to the promised land. The procession begins when the deacon has chanted for a first time, "Christ our light,"

and the congregation answers, "Thanks be to God." The
deacon then moves forward and, when he has advanced a
bit, chants once again but in a higher tone, "Christ our
light." All again answer "Thanks be to God," and then light
their candles from the Easter candle. The procession advances to the altar, where the deacon sings a third time,
"Christ our light."

We must attend this ceremony with the simplicity and
openness of a child if we are to enter fully into the mind of
the Church at this moment of joy. The world knows only
too well the darkness that fills the earth with unhappiness
and anxiety. Yet at this moment men can tell themselves
that their wretchedness has elicited God's pity and that he
wants to shed his light everywhere.

The prophets of long ago promised that the light would
come: "The people who walked in darkness have seen a
great light" (Is. 9:1; cf. 42:7; 49:9). But the light that will
shine upon the new Jerusalem (Is. 60:1-2) will be the living
God himself, for he shall enlighten his people (Is. 60:19),
and his Servant will be a light for the nations (Is. 42:6;
49:6). St. Paul ends his speech to King Agrippa by saying
that Moses and the prophets had predicted "that the Christ
must suffer, and that, by being the first to rise from the
dead, he would proclaim light both to the people and to the
Gentiles" (Acts 26:23).

Jesus tells his hearers what his own miracles mean; in
particular, before healing the man born blind, he says: "As
long as I am in the world, I am the light of the world" (John
9:5). In the Prologue to the Fourth Gospel, John has already
presented Christ to us as "the true light that enlightens
every man" (John 1:9).

"It was night," observed St. John (13:30) when Judas left
the room after the Last Supper. It was night, too, when
Christ at the moment of his arrest said, "But this is your
hour, and the power of darkness" (Luke 22:53). Now, during the Easter Vigil, it is again night, but on this night the
Church contemplates Christ as the light that dispels all

darkness. "God is light," says St. John, and "in him there is no darkness" (1 John 1:5).

The catechumen who takes part in this celebration of the light has already known from experience that by his natural birth he belonged to the realm of darkness. Now he knows as well that God has "called" him "out of darkness into his marvelous light" (1 Peter 2:9). In a few minutes' time, at his baptism, he will experience what St. Paul wrote to the Ephesians: "Christ shall give you light" (Eph. 5:14). He will cease to be "darkness" and will become "light in the Lord" (Eph. 5:8). As a member of the Church, he will be rescued from the power of darkness and brought into the kingdom of God's Son, where he will share the lot of the saints in the light (Col. 1:12-13).

The light also shines on all the faithful present, and they too must choose once again either to accept or to reject it. No celebration, however pastoral, however moving and meaningful, can force men to choose aright, and even in the presence of the risen Christ men will continue to be divided into "children of this world" and "children of light" (Luke 16:8, JB). In order to become a child of the light one must believe, in concrete, practical ways, in him who is the Light; only through conflict does the believer make his way to the heavenly Jerusalem, the city that has no need of sun or moon, because God's glory is its source of light and the Lamb its lamp (Apoc. 21:23).

The *Exsultet*

The deacon now comes to the celebrant and asks his blessing before singing the Easter Proclamation. Then he incenses the book containing the *Exsultet*, and the Easter candle as well. Finally he begins the Easter Proclamation, or the "Praise of the Candle" (*Laus Cerei*), to give it its ancient name.

The word *Exsultet* that begins the song (or, more properly, its prologue) has given the whole piece its name.

Another name for it is "Easter Proclamation" (*Praeconium Paschale*).

In the prologue, the deacon bids all — heaven, earth, the Church, the Christian assembly — to share the joy that comes from Christ's victory over darkness. The prologue, and indeed the body of the song as well, often took the form of an improvised song about the resurrection.

After the prologue the deacon intones the great hymn of thanksgiving for the history of salvation. The Proclamation sums up this history: the redemptive act that ransomed sinful Adam; the great prefigurations of redemption (the Passover lamb, the Red Sea, the pillar of fire). This is the night when men receive salvation and when Christ wins his victory. The deacon then waxes even more lyrical as he praises this night in which God had shown us his tender love by giving his own Son to ransom a slave. He sings of the fault that was a happy fault, the sin that was a necessary sin, because it won for us so glorious a Redeemer.

Next, the deacon speaks of the candle itself, which the entire Church offers to God. May it burn and never be extinguished; may Christ, the Morning Star that never sets, find it always lit.

This very beautiful poem (St. Ambrose of Milan may have written it [132]) often stirs the congregation deeply at its beginning, for they are still under the influence of the preceding darkness that had been lit only by the flickering light of the candles. Today, however, it will hardly win adherents through its doctrine. The many images, the tightly packed themes, and a lyricism that does not reflect our modern sensibility make this bravura piece rather difficult for the congregation. After the rapid start in the "Christ our light" ceremony, the people may find nothing for them to grasp and become somewhat bored, even though the celebration of the paschal mystery is only beginning.

Regretfully, then (since the *Exsultet* is indeed a masterpiece), we must say that some future reform should shorten the Easter Proclamation and recast it in language more accessible to contemporary man. In this regard, pastors with authority must act courageously to sacrifice a poem that is a theological and artistic success, and to replace it with a composition that may turn out to be even more beautiful if it is a vernacular song with genuine pastoral value. Nothing can be truly beautiful if it is not functional — a principle as valid for liturgy as for architecture. We must live, not in the past or the future, but in the present, and we must study the solid doctrine given us in the *Exsultet* in order that we may present it in a more suitable manner.

The today of the Scriptures

In its *Constitution on the Sacred Liturgy* (no. 7), Vatican Council II lists the various ways in which Christ is present among his people. He is present not only in the Eucharist (the highest form of his presence) and the other sacraments, but also in his word and in the prayer of the Church. The liturgy of the word during the Easter Vigil is an especially notable example of this teaching, for the Vigil is constructed as a dialogue (something we would like to find more frequently in the Church).

At this point when the Church is about to baptize the catechumens, she is undoubtedly motivated by a desire to offer them a final instruction.[133] It would be a mistake, however, to concentrate exclusively on the didactic aspect of the Vigil readings. What we should be primarily attentive to is the presence of Christ, who is teaching us himself.[134] That is the point of reading the Scripture lessons near, and by the light of, the paschal candle. The Old Testament is read, but in the light of Christ, and indeed in the light of a Christ who is present today. This bridging of the centuries is especially striking in connection with the third reading, which narrates the first Passover on which the Hebrews were rescued from Egypt and brought safely through the Red Sea.[135]

In this reading the Lord addresses us and tells us what he did for his Chosen People on the first Passover: how he led them out of Egypt and across the Red Sea and how he destroyed Pharaoh's army. The Lord, the Father, speaks to us, and he speaks through his Son, the true paschal Lamb that has been sacrificed. We, for our part, listen to this Lord who speaks to us here and now. We are in the same position as the Hebrews in the Book of Exodus (ch. 19), who have crossed the Red Sea and whom the Lord now gathered so that he might speak to them.

On that occasion God spoke from the mountain top, and the people listened. The atmosphere for their listening was created by songs and prayers; on hearing, they acclaimed God's words and then offered him a sacrifice as a covenant sign. We are that people, and Christ actualizes the narrative for us in our day; he tells us what he did for us and what he is still doing for us. We listen. Then, filled with his words, we stand and sing to the Lord the joy his word has brought us. We sing back to him, in lyrical form, what he has just said to us, as we engage in a dialogue with him that conveys our wonder and thanksgiving: "I will sing to the Lord, for he has triumphed gloriously; the horse and his rider he has thrown into the sea" (Exod. 15:1).[136]

With his "Let us pray," the celebrant then invites us to pray over this amazing dialogue between the Lord and ourselves. Each person present reflects in silence on what has been said and on the dialogue in which he has taken part. Then the celebrant actualizes, in the form of a prayer, the message that has been proclaimed: "Father, even today we see the wonders of the miracles you worked long ago. You once saved a single nation from slavery, and now you offer that salvation to all through baptism. May the peoples of the world become true sons of Abraham and prove worthy of the heritage of Israel. We ask this through Christ our Lord." (A new, optional prayer effects the same actualization.)

In the light of the paschal candle, and because of Jesus our Messiah, what happened once upon a time in the past is happening again. As the catechumens listen to the reading and the prayer, they can better understand that they are indeed part of the history of salvation. The miracle of the Red Sea will shortly be repeated for them.

We cannot really enter into this liturgy unless we walk the path of typology, for we must not see in the story of the Red Sea simply an illustration of what takes place in baptism. Baptism is not modeled after the crossing of the Red Sea; but neither is the account of the crossing simply an illustrated explanation of the baptismal rite. Instead, baptism is a continuation of the account of the crossing. That is, the passage through the sea takes place this night, and from the historical point of view, the crossing this night is more real than the crossing of long ago; it will be ever more real as we approach closer and closer to the promised land.

Unless we thus understand the Scriptures that are proclaimed in the liturgy, they will be for us nothing but a reminder of the past; they will stir a sense of wonder, but we will not grasp the fact that the events narrated are taking place here and now. The other readings and prayers of the Vigil are part of the same process of actualization that is going on in the light of the paschal candle.

The first reading confronts us with the two creations (Genesis 1:1–2:2). When the Vigil began, we found ourselves in the presence of Christ, the Lord of the universe. Now this Lord of all things himself tells about the creation of the world — a world that he intended as good but which was ruined by sin. The first human beings found themselves in a splendid world of life where everything was good. Now, in the light of the risen Christ, the world is being created once again.

Jesus is the one Lord, "from whom are all things and through whom we exist" (1 Cor. 8:6); he is "the first-born of all creation" (Col. 1:15) and "all things were created through him and for him" (Col. 1:16); he upholds "the universe by his word of power" (Heb. 1:3). The world he created has been ruined, but Christ's task is to restore it completely; point by point, the new creation wrought by Christ corresponds to the first creation. All things in heaven and on earth are to be brought into unity under Christ (Eph. 1:10), for God's plan is to make him the one Head of all.

In the midst of this world that is being renewed stands

man. Unlike Adam, he is "his [God's] workmanship, created in Christ Jesus for good works, which God prepared beforehand, that we should walk in them" (Eph. 2:10). Man has become a new creation, a new being (Gal. 6:15; 2 Cor. 5:17), being stripped of the old self with its past deeds and clad in the new self, the new man "which is being renewed in knowledge after the image of its creator" (Col. 3:10).

The catechumen knows that he is on the way to this marvelous transformation, but he knows, too, that the transformation will not be immediately complete. "We know that the whole creation has been groaning in travail together until now; and not only the creation, but we ourselves, who have the first fruits of the Spirit, groan inwardly as we wait for adoption as sons, the redemption of our bodies" (Rom. 8:22-23). At the same time, however, we know that the completion will someday come and that John's vision in the Apocalypse is true: the old heavens and earth will pass away, and he who sits on the throne will declare, "Behold, I make all things new" (Apoc. 21:5).

The prayer after this first reading shows that the new creation is going on here and now: "Let us pray. Almighty and eternal God, you created all things in wonderful beauty and order. Help us now to perceive how still more wonderful is the new creation by which in the fullness of time you redeemed your people through the sacrifice of our passover, Jesus Christ, who lives and reigns for ever and ever."

The only Son, offered in sacrifice

The second reading is about the sacrifice of Isaac (Gen. 22:1-18), and the choice of it is especially appropriate on this night when the Church is recollecting herself in order to celebrate Easter.

Everyone knows the story. What must be realized is that the sacrifice is an essential "type" in both the Scriptures and the liturgy. In order to appreciate the point of the type, it is not enough to emphasize the faith of Abraham and to draw from it moral conclusions about the need to accept unreservedly all sufferings that God may send us. These reflections are valid enough, but the biblico-liturgical meaning of the text goes beyond them. The Letter to the Hebrews shows us the twofold meaning of the event: "He [Abraham] considered that God was able to raise men even from the dead; hence he did receive him [Isaac] back and this was a symbol" (11:19). The sacrifice of Isaac, an only son, reminds us of the sacrifice of the Father's only Son, while the rescue of Isaac turns our thoughts to the resurrection of Christ.

The story contains a sentence that is important for interpreting the action of Jesus and indeed all the sacrifices the Church offers along with her Christ: "Take your son Isaac, your only son Isaac, whom you love, and go to the land of Moriah, and offer him there as a burnt offering upon one of the mountains of which I shall tell you" (Gen. 22:2). The point being made in the text is clear: Isaac is a loved possession, "your son," and all the more loved because he is "your only Son." The sacrifice being asked is all the more agonizing because Isaac is the only son and because he had been born of a barren mother in order to carry out a mission of great importance in the formation of God's people: Isaac was the son of the promise. Moreover, it was the Lord himself who told Abraham of the son Sara would bear him: "Through Isaac shall your descendants be named" (Gen. 21:12).

When we insisted that the story should not be simply a subject for moralizing, we were not denying that it does invite the catechumens now awaiting baptism to an unconditioned faith in the Lord. On that kind of faith will depend the vital renewal through the sacrament that they are about to receive and that will bring them the sacramental gift of faith. The faith they already have is what has brought them to baptism, yet it is baptism that will instill in them a faith that is the work of the Spirit.

The object they embrace in such faith is the death of Christ as efficacious for redemption and as obedience to God's will, in contrast to the disobedience of Adam. A further object of their faith is the resurrection, which signifies a passage through death to life. All that will be the effect of the covenant. That is why Abraham has always been spoken of as our father in faith.

The reading on the sacrifice of Isaac is, then, essentially paschal in character. On the one hand, it shows an act of unconditional obedience to God's will, even to the extent of offering up an only son and having God accept the offering. On the other hand, the sacrifice leading to death leads also to ultimate life and to the restoration of a people through fulfillment of the promise.

The responsorial psalm (Ps. 16) is well chosen, since from the very first days of the Church it was interpreted as a prophecy of the resurrection (cf. Acts 2:25-29): "The Lord is my chosen portion and my cup; thou holdest my lot. . . . My body also dwells secure. For thou dost not give me up to Sheol, or let thy godly one see the Pit" (vv. 5, 9-10).

The congregation meditates briefly on the mystery, and the prayer pulls the various threads together: "God and Father of all who believe in you, you promised Abraham that he would become the father of all nations, and through the death and resurrection of Christ you fulfill that promise: everywhere throughout the world you increase your chosen people. . . ."

The Church: City and Bride

The fourth reading speaks to the faithful and the candidates for baptism of the building of the Church that has come forth from the side of Christ and is now his Bride. There is great depth and richness in the "theology" of the Church that is thus proclaimed during the Paschal Vigil and presented in close connection with the mystery of death and resurrection. This Church is the "sacrament" of the encounter with God, and a "sacrament" that, by Christ's will, contains within itself all the signs of salvation.

The passage from Isaiah (54:5-14) hymns the merciful love and fidelity of God, while also giving an enthusiastic description of the City which divine love has built and continues to build without ceasing. Here is how the prophet expresses God's tender love: "For a brief moment I forsook you, but with great compassion I will gather you. . . . With everlasting love I will have compassion on you" (vv. 7-8). The Lord then recalls the Deluge in the days of Noah and his own promise never again to let the waters flood the earth. He has sworn not to be angry at his people, and nothing can change his love for them.

God then promises to build the City: "I will make your pinnacles of agate, your gates of carbuncles, and all your walls of precious stones. All your sons shall be taught by the Lord. . . . In righteousness you shall be established" (vv. 12-14). Isaiah here anticipates the Apocalypse of St. John in describing the earthly Jerusalem in a celestial fashion. We also find in the passage the theme of the Church as a Bride that St. Paul will enunciate in Ephesians (5:25-28) and the Second Vatican Council will repeat in its *Dogmatic Constitution on the Church* (no. 7).

The responsorial psalm (Ps. 30) emphasizes the mercy of God in raising us up and bringing us back to life when we were doomed to death. He has thus "turned . . . my mourning into dancing" (v. 11). The prayer then shows the present relevance of, or actualizes, this vision of the building of the Church: "Almighty and eternal God, glorify your Church the fulfillment of your promise."

The mystery of water and the mystery of the word

Life is the theme of the fifth reading (Is. 55:1-11), and it is approached from two angles. First, life is seen in terms of the food that nourishes it, as God freely offers to all a life-giving water: "Every one who thirsts, come to the waters" (v. 1). Second, the Lord offers a life that has its source in an everlasting covenant. On this night, then, the newly baptized Christian will be given a divine nourishment for his new life, and he will also become a sharer in an everlasting covenant.

If this is to happen, the believer must be receptive to God's word. This receptivity usually takes the form of faith pure and simple, since God's thoughts are not our thoughts. But the faith is justified, since God's word is powerful and accomplishes what he wants: "So shall my word be that goes forth from my mouth; it shall not return to me empty, but it shall accomplish that which I purpose, and prosper in the thing for which I sent it" (v. 11).

A strict exegesis would doubtless not justify seeing in this passage any allusion to the sacraments. Christian tradition, however, and the insertion of the reading into this particular liturgical celebration require the presence of such a meaning. Water and word are efficacious sacraments and transform the sinner into a new creature. The prophet urges us to "seek the Lord while he may be found, call upon him while he is near; let the wicked forsake his way, and the unrighteous man his thoughts" (vv. 6-7). God's word converts men, and the water he provides nourishes anyone who decides to obey the word. In short, we enter upon a vital relationship to God, and we become aware that our life depends on the water he offers us and on the efficacious word he addresses to us.

The responsory is likewise taken from the Book of Isaiah (12:2-6). It sings of our joy and exultation at what the Lord offers us: "Behold, God is my salvation; I will trust, and will not be afraid; for the Lord God is my strength and my song, and he has become my salvation" (v. 2).

The prayer reminds us that God proclaimed through the prophets the great deeds he will accomplish this night. It then goes on to say: "Help us to be your faithful people, for it is by your inspiration alone that we can grow in goodness."

Wisdom, the source of life; the efficacious word

Men who are transformed by God are also given a guide and a law so that they can move onward and advance toward the goal. The sixth reading (Bar. 3:9-15, 32–4:4) praises the wisdom given those who have received new life through water and the Spirit.

The important thing for us, in the liturgical context, is the Christian and Christological interpretation of Baruch's poem. If we look only at Baruch's words in their immediate historical context, it is evident that wisdom, though personified, is not really a person. In this same wisdom, however, the Church sees Jesus Christ. On this point there is a solid interpretative tradition.

The sapiential books of the Bible provide a vision of Wisdom that is rich but also quite complex. Wisdom is described as living with God (Wis. 8:3), but also as "a breath of the power of God, and a pure emanation of the glory of the Almighty" (Wis. 7:25). St. John completely identifies this Wisdom with Christ, frequently applying to him what the sapiential books say of Wisdom. Here are some examples.

Wisdom is at God's side from the beginning of the world (Prov. 8:22-23; Sir. 24:9; Wis. 6:22); John presents the Word of God in the same way in his Prologue (1:1) and in the priestly prayer of Christ after the Last Supper (17:5). Wisdom is an outpouring of God's glory (Wis. 7:25); the Word, for St. John, is a manifestation of the Father's glory (1:14; 8:50; 11:4; 17:5, 22, 24). Wisdom is a reflection of the eternal light (Wis. 7:26); Jesus comes forth from God, who is Light (1 John 1:5). Wisdom illumines men's paths (Wis. 9:11); the Word is the Light of the world and of men (John 1:4-5; 3:19; 8:12; 9:5; 12:46). Wisdom comes from heaven and seeks to remain among men (Prov. 8:31; Sir. 24:8; Bar. 3:29, 37; Wis. 9:10, 16, 17); Jesus, the Son of Man, has come down from heaven (John 1:14; 3:13, 31; 6:38; 16:28). Wisdom has for her mission to make heavenly realities known to men (Wis. 9:16-18); Christ reveals to men what he has himself received from his Father (John 3:11-12, 32; 7:16; 8:26, 40; 15:45; 17:18).

Further parallels might be given, but they would perhaps be a bit forced. Can anyone doubt that there is a conscious reference back to the Old Testament texts? Even the

Synoptics set up similar deliberate parallels and references. For example, Christ's invitation, "Come to me, all who labor . . ." (Matthew 11:28-30) is an evident echo of the Book of Sirach (24:19; 51:23) and of the Book of Proverbs (9:3). St. Paul, too, sees Christ as being "the wisdom of God" (1 Cor. 1:24).

All Christians must seek out this Wisdom and follow her teaching, for "she is the book of the commandments of God. . . . All who hold her fast will live" (Bar. 4:1). We must all retrace our steps and advance toward her in her splendor; such is the privilege given to the baptized. The responsory psalm (Psalm 19) bids us sing: "The law of the Lord is perfect, reviving the soul; the testimony of the Lord is sure, making wise the simple" (v. 7).

The prayer asks God for the wisdom that should guide the faithful in all that they do: "Father. . . . Listen to our prayers and always watch over those you cleanse in baptism."

A new heart and a new spirit

The seventh and last of the Old Testament readings for the Vigil is from the Book of Ezekiel (36:16-17a, 18-28). It is quite familiar to Christians, yet it never fails to rouse their enthusiasm when they listen to it with faith and with a sense of gratitude for their experience of its truth.

The essential theme of the reading is, on the one hand, the dispersal of a people because of their sins (a dispersal reflected in the divisions within us that our infidelities cause) and, on the other, the benevolence of God who, for his name's sake and in order to glorify his name that has been profaned, wishes to unite us into a single people, just as he sought to gather again the dispersed Israelites. He no longer seeks to unite a single nation, but to gather mankind from all nations and lands. He transforms men by pouring out purifying water upon them and giving them a new heart and a new spirit. The Lord puts his own Spirit in them and makes them capable of following his law, observing his commandments, and being faithful to him. They will dwell in the land which he will give them; they will be his people, and he will be their God.

The text needs no further commentary. So clearly does it apply to those who will be baptized during the Vigil and to all Christians whom the same baptism has formed into a single body, that further explanations would be an unnecessary distraction.

We ought, however, advert once again to the way in which the liturgy uses the text. In itself the passage does not foretell Christian baptism, and yet no one will feel that the Church is misusing or betraying the text in making it a part of her catechesis for baptism. She rightly uses the words to sing of God's initiative in taking pity on men and in saving them by purifying them. It is the Lord who purifies, just as it was the Lord who created. Moreover, we receive the Spirit as a gift when God thus sanctifies us (Rom. 5:5).

The paschal movement of the passage from Ezekiel is reflected in St. Paul's words to the Romans: "While we were yet helpless, at the right time Christ died for the ungodly. . . . Since, therefore, we are now justified by his blood, much more shall we be saved by him from the wrath of God" (Rom. 5:6, 9). We have become new men. Ezekiel's theme is taken up by St. Paul (Eph. 4:24); in the Fourth Gospel, Jesus develops it in his conversation with Nicodemus: "Unless one is born of water and the Spirit, he cannot enter the kingdom of God" (John 3:5).

Two psalms are offered as responses to this splendid reading. Both speak of encountering God — the God who gives life (Ps. 42) and the God who purifies and renews (Ps. 51). Psalm 42 reminds us of how the catechumens will shortly approach the altar after being baptized. Psalm 51 asks God to create a clean heart for us and to restore to us the joy of being saved.

Three prayers are supplied after this seventh and last reading. The third, which is used if there are to be baptisms, best expresses the yearning of every believer. "Almighty and eternal God, be present in this sacrament of your love. Send your Spirit of adoption on those to be born again in baptism. And may the work of our humble ministry be brought to perfection by your mighty power."

Alive for God

With the singing of the *Gloria* we pass from the anticipations of the paschal mystery in the Old Testament to its reality in the New.

St. Paul's Letter to the Romans (6:3-11) puts briefly the theology of our baptism. He speaks of our liberation through the sacrament: We are there immersed in death with Christ and laid in the tomb with him, but there too we rise with him to a new life. The old self is nailed to the Cross with Christ so that our state of sin might be rendered powerless and we might no longer be enslaved to sin. Now we are dead to sin and alive for God.

Paul shows the conclusions that must be drawn from the fact of our baptism into Christ. Since the baptized person has died with Christ, he is no longer under the domination of sin. The consequences of the first Adam's disobedience are overcome, since the obedience of the second Adam has reconciled us to God and made us members of his people, which is the Church. Our union with Christ is real now and is becoming ever more full and complete, but it will reach its perfect and definitive form only at the end of time. We are therefore saved now, but in principle and according to the degree of our union with God; this means we are saved according to the concrete ways in which we apply the means of salvation that are offered to us.

Christian life, then, is a life of freedom and belongs to those who have now been rescued from enslavement to sin. But the freedom will be lasting only if it is always exercised in ways that respect the new situation given us by our baptism as adopted children of the Father.

The responsorial psalm (Ps. 118) sings of the wondrous deeds the Lord has done for us: "The right hand of the

Lord does valiantly, the right hand of the Lord is exalted. . . . I shall not die, but I shall live, and recount the deeds of the Lord" (vv. 15-17).

The risen Lord

The Gospel readings for the Vigil follow a three-year cycle; each deals with the same event, the resurrection of Jesus. To understand them properly, however, we should set them side by side and compare them, taking St. Mark's text as our starting point, since Mark seems to be the first witness to the women visiting the tomb.[137] By studying some inconsistencies in the account, the exegetes endeavor to go a step further and get back to Mark's sources; we shall not follow them in this venture, since it would be irrelevant to our purpose here.[138]

It is easy enough to show the similarities between the various narratives in the Synoptics and John. More important, however, is the fact that each of the evangelists approaches the event differently, depending on his own personality and on the task of evangelization that is his. St. Matthew gives a doctrinal synthesis on the resurrection, with the intervention of the angels serving as an introduction to the appearances of the risen Christ to the women (Matthew 28:9-10) and to the Eleven (Matthew 28:16-20). He is also concerned with apologetics, since "to this day" the Jews have been claiming that the Christians simply stole Christ's body (Matthew 28:15).

St. Luke is more interested in the empty tomb; the women discover that it is empty, even before the angels intervene (Luke 24:2-3). Subsequently, some disciples, Peter among them, come to the tomb to check on the women's story (Luke 24:12, 24).

St. John is less interested in details, but he nonetheless, like Matthew, does not exclude apologetic concerns. He makes the point that the discovery of the empty tomb by Mary Magdalene (20:1) makes less probable a transfer of the body (20:2, 6-7, 13, 15). In the main, however, John is true to the central theme of his Gospel as a whole, namely, faith, and studies the varied reactions of the disciples in terms of faith. Peter and John, for example, are described as coming to a belief in the resurrection (20:3-10); Mary Magdalene is seen passing from grief at the absence of the body to a joy at the Savior's new presence (20:11-18).

St. Mark's account is the basis for the other narratives. In his Gospel the empty tomb manifests God's power, and the visit of the women is the occasion for asserting that Christ has comquered death after his mission had apparently ended in failure.

With these facts as basis and background, the various apparitions of the risen Christ, whom the Apostles at first recognize only with hesitation (since if it is indeed the Lord and if he is present in the body, then his body is also a body transformed!), acquire a central place in the teaching of the early Church. This is clear from the sermons in the Acts of the Apostles and the First Letter to the Corinthians (15:3-8). The fact that Peter and the disciples went and verified the women's story lends special authority to the teaching on the resurrection.[139]

The important thing in the liturgical proclamation of the resurrection during the Easter Vigil is not the historical fact of the empty tomb. The empty tomb, after all, is not the object of our faith, any more than the precise manner of Christ's resurrection is. The important thing is that we should conform our lives to that of the risen Christ, in order that, having died with him, we may also rise with him.

That is the real goal of the faith of those who are preparing for baptism and will shortly receive the sacramental faith that saves. Such, too, is the real goal of the faith of all Christians; the problem of how the Lord rose from the dead is unimportant.

Three sacramental stages

When the baptism of adults is celebrated during the Easter Vigil and by the community that prepared the catechumens for the sacrament, the unity that once marked the three sacraments of Christian initiation (baptism, confirmation, Eucharist) is restored. After the homily and a short litany, the water is blessed, the catechumens receive baptism and confirmation, and the community begins the celebration of the Eucharist, the first in which the newly baptized will share.

We want to dwell briefly here on the connections between the three stages of the one total sacrament of initiation. In showing the connections, our starting point must be the history of salvation and the action of the Holy Spirit, who directs the development of that history.

At the first creation, the Spirit of God swept over the waters as God was creating the world in unity (Gen. 1:2). It was God's intention that close relations of mutual service should bind subhuman creatures to each other and to man, and men to each other and to their divine Lord. Man's catastrophic rebellion against God destroyed this unity, and the Old Testament shows us God constantly endeavoring to re-establish it by offering men repeated covenants.

Throughout this Old Testament history it is easy to see the Holy Spirit at work in those whose role it was to guide the people of God and reunite them. Thus, it was the Spirit who raised up the Judges for the salvation of Israel (Judg. 3:10-11; 14:6; 1 Sam. 10:1-6; 11:2-11; Exod. 35:31; etc.). The Spirit is bestowed upon the prophets so that they may bear witness; important here is the connection between the Spirit and the word (Is. 8:11; Jer. 1:9-15; 20:7; Ezek. 3:12-14, 24; 8:3; 11:5; Amos 3:8; 7:14; Is. 61:1-8). Through a consecration the Spirit is also given for priestly service. The Spirit makes the Servant a prophet, a king, and a priest who offers God a pleasing sacrifice that he accepts as expiation for the sins of men (Is. 53). Joined to the priestly service here is the mission of the prophet and the witness.

Yet all these missions were unsuccessful. At the end of the ages, therefore, the Lord sends his own Son. Here again we find the Spirit at work in bringing about the birth of the eternal Word as a man. The birth of the Word made flesh from the Virgin's womb is due to the action of the Spirit, and once again God's intervention — in this case, his coming in person — is aimed at the restoration of unity. From the moment of his conception, moreover, the Word incarnate is Messiah, Prophet, Priest, and King.

We can link our baptism directly to the incarnation. By the power of the Spirit, the Word came among men and took a human nature to himself. By the power of the same Spirit, who acts now through the instrumentality of the baptismal water, we become new creatures and adopted children; we are "divinized." Baptism gives us a specifically "Christ-ian" existence, which is that of an adopted son or daughter of the Father.

In the life even of Jesus himself, the Spirit intervened in a special way at his baptism in the Jordan and at his transfiguration. By his baptism Jesus was officially assigned to carry out his roles as Messiah, Prophet, Priest, and King. These functions already belonged to him ever since his birth as a man, but now he was publicly, officially deputed to carry them out so as to create a new people. In this context, the words of the Father point to the mission of this Son who was so pleasing to him. If the Father is pleased with the Son, it is because the Son does his will. Tradition has therefore justifiably enriched the word "Son" with the further meaning of "Servant," that is, the one who proclaims God and offers sacrifice by offering his own life for the redemption of his people.

At his baptism, then, Jesus is consecrated for the sacrifice he will offer his Father as a Priest chosen from among men. The baptism also signals the beginning of Jesus' preaching, and the transfiguration is the point at which he begins to predict his own death and resurrection. To the intervention of the Spirit in the life of the incarnate Word in order officially to bestow upon him his mission we can connect the intervention in our lives of the Spirit of Pentecost. Confirmation, which gives us Christian "perfection" and thus complements the "Christ-ian" existence given us at baptism, is the sacrament officially assigning us our Christian mission. It deputes us to be witnesses and to offer sacrifice.

Christ carried out his own priestly mission first and foremost through the paschal mystery of his death, resurrection, and ascension, and his sending of the Spirit. We too fulfill our priestly task when we offer sacrifice in union with the ordained priest who has been consecrated by the Spirit so that he may make the sacrifice of Christ present for us.

These various considerations drawn from the history of salvation and the action of the Spirit make clear the close union that exists between the three sacraments of initiation. The first two of these sacraments give us a mode of existence which theologians call a "character" and which is definitive. Through baptism we are destined for a Christian life under the sway of the Spirit, and we become adopted sons and daughters of God. Confirmation puts an official seal upon our existence and role as Christians. The third sacrament of initiation, the Eucharist, has for its purpose to revive and renew in us the character we received in baptism and confirmation. In celebrating the Eucharist we give witness and proclaim to the world the death and resurrection of Christ until he comes again.

Wellspring of life

Once the liturgy of the word is completed, the liturgy of baptism begins. The cantors start the ceremony by singing the litany that will lead up to the blessing of the baptismal water. The water is blessed in the baptistry if the place is so situated that the faithful may easily take part in the ceremony; otherwise the water to be blessed is placed in a vessel in the sanctuary.

The prayer now used for the blessing of the baptismal water is no longer the one found in the old liturgical books for the Easter Vigil. Yet, even though it is much shortened, it has preserved the important passages that link the blessing with the history of salvation. We still find in it the "types" of baptism, that is, the past events that are not simply illustrations but find a genuine fulfillment in the Church. The prayer mentions in turn the Spirit who breathed over the waters at the beginning, the waters of the Deluge (signifying death to sin and the rebirth of the just man), the crossing of the Red Sea, the waters of the Jordan, and the water that flowed from the wound in Christ's side. Then Christ's command to go and baptize all nations is recalled, and the blessing proper ends with a prayer: "By the power of the Holy Spirit give to the water of this font the grace of your Son. You created man in your own likeness: cleanse him from sin in a new birth of innocence by water and the Spirit."

In his *De sacramentis*, St. Ambrose comments on the various scriptural "types" of baptism. With regard to the Deluge, he says:

> We began to explain yesterday that the Deluge is a prefiguration of baptism. What is the Flood, after all, but the means by which the just man dies to sin and is preserved in order to propagate justice? The Lord saw that the sins of men were multiplying; he therefore rescued only the just man and his posterity when he bade the waters rise above even the mountaintops. Thus all fleshly corruption was itself destroyed in the Flood, and only the stock and example of the just man remained. Is not the Flood, then, the same as baptism, in which all sins are washed away and only the spirit and grace of the just man revive?[140]

Tertullian writes in his treatise on baptism:

> After the waters of the Deluge had cleansed away the ancient stain, that is, after what I might call the baptism of the world, the dove was sent forth from the ark and returned with an olive branch as a sign that heaven's wrath had ceased. This olive branch was a sign of peace extended even to the pagans. By a similar ordinance, but one that is spiritually effective, the Dove which is the Holy Spirit is sent upon the earth, that is, upon our flesh as it emerges from the bath

with its old sins wiped away. The Dove comes bringing the peace of God, a messenger from heaven, where the Church, prefigured by the ark, has her dwelling.[141]

An inscription in the Lateran baptistery from the time of Sixtus III gives poetic expression to the maternal aspect of the font:

Here a race divine is born for heaven,
begotten by the fruitful Spirit in this font. . . .
Naught separates those reborn and made one
by the one font, the one Spirit, the one faith.
Mother Church gives birth in these waters
to the virginal fruit she conceived by the Spirit. . . .[142]

St. Justin, in his *First Apology*, had already seen in the baptismal font an image of the Church's maternal womb.[143] St. Leo the Great takes up the theme in one of his sermons: "For every man who is reborn, the water of baptism is like the Virgin's womb, since the same Holy Spirit who filled the Virgin fills the font."[144]

These various types of baptism and the font (Deluge, womb, etc.) became part of the early Church's teaching on baptism. St. Ambrose comments on most of them in his catechetical writings. He speaks as follows, for example, of the bitter waters of Marah:

Moses had entered the desert, and the thirsting people had reached the spring of Marah and wanted to drink. But no sooner did they draw the water than they tasted its bitterness and could not drink it. Then Moses threw a piece of wood into the spring, and the bitter waters turned sweet.

What does this tell us but that every creature subject to corruption is a bitter water to mankind? It may be sweet for a moment, it may be pleasurable for a moment, but it is bitter, since it cannot take away sin. Drink it and you will go on thirsting. . . . But when it receives the Cross of Christ, the heavenly sacrament, it becomes sweet and pleasant — rightly "sweet" because it takes guilt from us.[145]

Born again of water and the Spirit

The decisive moment is now at hand for which the Church has long been preparing the catechumens by means of frequent exorcisms. The priest asks them whether they believe; then he proceeds to baptize them.

At an earlier time, these two actions, now separate, formed a single whole. The candidates put off their garments and went down into the pool of water that was the baptismal font. As they stood there, the priest asked them: "Do you believe in God, the Father almighty, Creator of heaven and earth?" The candidate, moved by the grace of the Holy Spirit, answered, "I believe." The priest then submerged the candidate's head under the water of the pool or else collected a little water from the pipes feeding the pool and poured it over the candidate's head as he stood in the pool. The priest then questioned the person again: "Do you believe in Jesus Christ, his only Son, our Lord, who was born and suffered?" The answer came again: "I believe," and the priest performed the second immersion or infusion. Finally, "Do you believe in the Holy Spirit, the holy Catholic Church, the communion of saints, the forgiveness of sins, the resurrection of the dead, and everlasting life?" The third profession of faith was followed by the third immersion or infusion. Such was the early form baptism took; it consisted of the triple question-and-answer and the triple immersion.

That type of baptism imaged forth in a more perfect way the reality of which St. Paul speaks: "We were buried . . . with him by baptism into death, so that as Christ was raised from the dead by the glory of the Father, we too might walk in newness of life" (Rom. 6:4). The baptized person also showed outwardly his active receptivity toward the baptismal grace given to him by answering "I believe." Later on, however, toward the seventh century, when it was primarily infants who were being baptized and who could not answer for themselves, the questions came to be directed to the sponsors. For the act of baptism itself, the question-and-answer sequence was replaced by a simple assertion on the part of the minister: "I baptize you in the name of the Father and of the Son and of the Holy Spirit."

The priest now goes on to anoint the newly baptized person with holy chrism, signifying that the person now shares in the Messiah's role of Prophet, Priest, and King. The person is then given a white garment, which he is urged to wear unstained until the day of judgment. The garment is a sign of the resurrection; the candidate has gone down into death with Christ, then risen to life again with him, thereby becoming a new creature. Finally, the newly baptized is given a lighted candle and bidden to walk as a child of light and to keep the candle lit until the Lord comes for the everlasting marriage feast; at that moment the faithful Christian will go out with the saints and the elect to meet him.

St. Ambrose reminds the newly baptized Christian of the questions he was asked and the answer he gave:

> They asked you, "Do you believe in God, the Father almighty?" You answered, "I believe," and you were immersed, that is, buried. Again they asked you, "Do you believe in our Lord Jesus Christ and in his Cross?" You said, "I believe," and were immersed again. You were thus buried with Christ; but anyone buried with Christ also rises with Christ. A third time they asked, "Do you believe in the Holy Spirit?" You said, "I believe," and you were immersed a third time so that the triple profession of faith might free you from the many sins of the past.[146]

The Saint explains another aspect of the immersion and the emergence from the font:

> Listen carefully, for in order to break the bonds of Satan even in this world, a way was found for a man to die while still alive and to rise again. What do we

mean by "still alive"? We mean that he is living a
bodily life when he comes to the font and is immersed in it. Water comes from the earth, does it not?
In baptism, therefore, a man satisfies the sentence
passed by God, but without being swallowed up in
bodily death. By being immersed, you suffer the sentence, "Dust you are, and to dust you will return."
Once that sentence has been executed, there is room
for the heavenly remedy and blessing. Water comes
from the earth, but the nature of our bodily life did
not permit us to be covered with earth and to rise
again from the earth. Therefore we are cleansed not
by earth but by water, and the font is a kind of
tomb.[147]

The Fathers generally like to think of the baptismal font as
both a tomb and a life-giving mother.

St. Ambrose focuses his attention above all on the rite of
immersion. He has already described it; now, in his commentary on it, he takes as his point of departure the well-
known sentence of St. Paul in his Letter to the Romans
(6:3):

The Apostle therefore cries out, as we have just heard
in the reading, that whoever is baptized is baptized
into the death of Jesus. What does he mean by "into
the death of Jesus"? His point is that just as Christ
died, so you must taste death, and that just as Christ
died to sin and lives for God, so you have died,
through the act of baptism, to the attraction that sin
used to have for you, and you have risen through the
grace of Christ. The "death," then, is indeed a death,
but it is a symbolic death, not a bodily death. When
you were immersed, you received the likeness of his
death and burial and the sacrament of his Cross, for
Christ hung on the Cross and his body was fixed to it
with the nails. You were thus crucified with him and
are now attached to Christ, attached by the nails of
our Lord Jesus Christ lest the devil be able to detach

you from him. Let these nails of Christ keep you his, though human weakness draws you away.[148]

In his *De mysteriis*, St. Ambrose points out the meaning of the white garment that is given to the newly baptized Christian:

> You then received white garments as a sign that you have put off the wrappings of sin and put on the pure veils of innocence. . . . For Christ's garments became as white as snow when, in the Gospel, he showed the glory of his resurrection. . . . After donning these white garments through the bath of rebirth, the Church says in the Canticle, "I am very dark, but comely, O daughters of Jerusalem." She is very dark through the weakness of the human condition, comely through grace; very dark because made up of sinners, comely through the sacrament of faith.[149]

The Saint continues his commentary on the Canticle of Canticles: The Lord sees his Church as beautiful because she has been redeemed by his blood; he engages in dialogue with her, with the text of the Canticle supplying his words to her.

Many other Fathers of the Church likewise commented on the baptismal rites. It is impossible for us to give further examples here, but what St. Ambrose says gives us a good idea of what the Fathers in general taught.

In the ancient baptismal rite, the baptized were clad in or received an alb (after the postbaptismal anointing) and then advanced toward the bishop. The latter laid his hands on them, anointed their heads, and gave them the kiss of peace. Carrying their candles, the newly baptized then moved on to the altar, where for the first time they would share in the celebration of the Eucharist. The Eucharist was for them, as for the rest of the faithful, the high point of the Easter Vigil. They would now eat the Body and drink the Blood of the dead and risen Christ and thus receive the pledge of everlasting life.

As the procession moved toward the altar, the newly baptized sang Psalm 23(22), "The Lord is my shepherd." Patristic commentaries on this psalm are numerous and often quite interesting; we must however read the psalm in its entirety if we are to understand the patristic interpretation of it.

> The Lord is my shepherd, I shall not want;
>> he makes me lie down in green pastures.
>
> He leads me beside still waters;
>> he restores my soul.
>
> He leads me in paths of righteousness
>> for his name's sake.
>
> Even though I walk through the valley of the shadow of death,
>> I fear no evil;
>
> for thou art with me;
>> thy rod and thy staff,
>> they comfort me.
>
> Thou preparest a table before me
>> in the presence of my enemies;
>
> thou anointest my head with oil,
>> my cup overflows.
>
> Surely goodness and mercy shall follow me
>> all the days of my life;
>
> and I shall dwell in the house of the Lord
>> for ever.

Let us turn once again to St. Ambrose for commentary:

> Learn again what sacrament you received. Listen to what holy David says, for he too foresaw this mystery and rejoiced at it. He said that he lacked nothing. Why? Because he who receives Christ's Body will not hunger for ever. How often have you not heard the twenty-second psalm, but not understood it? See how it applies to the heavenly sacraments![150]

Elsewhere the Saint tells us just at what point Psalm 23 was sung: "He has sloughed off the ancient error and renewed his youth like the eagle; now he hastens to this heavenly banquet. He comes in and sees the sacred altar made ready, and he cries out: 'Thou preparest a table before me!'"[151]

The Fathers interpret the "table" of Psalm 23 as referring to the Eucharist that the newly baptized Christians are about to receive for the first time. But the preceding verses too have their Christian significance. For example, they see the words "He leads me beside still waters" as indicating baptism. St. Cyril of Alexandria writes: "This grassy place [= the 'green pastures'] is the paradise whence we fell; Christ brings us back to it and settles us therein through the waters that give rest, that is, through baptism."[152]

The anointing with oil was understood as referring to confirmation. St. Cyril of Jerusalem thus interprets it in the fourth of his *Mystagogical Catecheses*: "He has anointed your forehead with oil, in the form of the seal you have received from God; this was that the seal might be impressed upon you and you might be consecrated to God."[153] The psalm also mentions an overflowing cup; the same commentator compares it to the cup of the Eucharist: "'Your cup intoxicates me like the best wine.' Here is mention of the cup which Jesus took in his hands and over which he gave thanks and said, "This is my blood which is shed for many for the forgiveness of sins.'"[154]

The new rite of initiation provides that adults be baptized and right away confirmed and that any children then be baptized. After this, the rest of the faithful renew their baptismal promises.

The celebration of the Eucharist then begins. Here is how the preface sings of the mystery:

> Father, all-powerful and ever-living God,
> we do well always and everywhere to give you thanks
> through Jesus Christ our Lord.
>
> We praise you with greater joy than ever
> on this Easter night
> when Christ became our paschal sacrifice.

He is the true Lamb who took away the sins of the
    world.
By dying he destroyed our death;
by rising he restored our life.

And so, with all the choirs of angels in heaven
we proclaim your glory
and join in their unending hymn of praise. . . .

The whole service ends with a prayer that all may be
united in love: "Lord, you have nourished us with your
Easter sacraments. Fill us with your Spirit, and make us
one in peace and love."

The "perfect Christian"

The catechumen has now completed his initiation; he is a
"complete," "finished," "perfect" Christian. Now that we
have seen the stages in this initiation, we want to go back to
the second and third stages so that we may gain an understanding of what this Christian layman's life in the
Church means.

Here we run into a problem: What is the meaning of
confirmation? The question is a complicated one and has
been the subject of much discussion. This, however, is not
the place for reviewing the controversies; we are not interested here in scholarship but only in helping the Christian to understand better what he is and to comprehend
what the former catechumen has now become.

In the discussion of and preaching on confirmation, it is
usually said that the sacrament makes the baptized person a
witness; he is now a witness to, and a soldier of, Christ.
This approach seems rather narrow. We may also ask
whether the interpretation of confirmation as the sacrament
of witnessing is not due to a particular situation. I am referring to the fact that in most Western countries confirmation
is the last of the sacraments of initiation to be given, being
administered often quite a few years after the Eucharist has

been received for the first time. In these circumstances, emphasis has been placed on the idea that the sacrament gives the strength and courage for bearing witness, and that it "completes" the formation of a Christian.

We may ask whether such a theology of confirmation is not the result of circumstances, instead of being the source of the liturgical practice found in many parts of the Church. This is not to deny that the theology has a certain validity. The Church certainly has the right to preach a theology of the sacraments that has a real basis in the sacraments. She may also emphasize at a given moment one aspect of a complete theology rather than another. Moreover, in her liturgical practice she can act in a way that corresponds to the theology being preached.

The Church of today could, for example, determine that the central focus in the theology of confirmation should be on witnessing, and could therefore prescribe that the sacrament is to be conferred when the recipient reaches adulthood and after admission to the Eucharist. Christ himself gave no precise instructions on this matter, and the Church, his Body, has the right to take the initiative and issue such instructions.

As a matter of fact, however, the present practice of the Church is not such that we can deduce a specific theology from it. Usage differs widely. In the Eastern Church the three sacraments of baptism, confirmation, and Eucharist are always given together, even to an infant. Elsewhere confirmation is given immediately after baptism or conjointly with first Communion or several years after first Communion. What conclusion can we draw from such a varied practice — conclusions not about pastoral practice but about what a Christian is?

If we are to understand the action of the Spirit in this sacrament, it would be better to begin, not with the effects the Spirit produces in men, but with his role in the history of salvation, that is, in God's plan for the world. To start with the effects of the Spirit's action in man is to get ourselves into difficulty right from the beginning. For if the

Spirit has already acted in baptism, how are we to conceive of him acting in confirmation? Conversely, if he does act in confirmation, how are we to conceive of him having already acted in baptism? If we concentrate on effects, we will be led to think that there is really only one sacrament involved in baptism and confirmation, and that confirmation is simply an aspect of baptism. But then we would be denying the formal teaching of the Church, which distinguishes them as two sacraments. (The fact that baptism, confirmation, and Eucharist are three distinct sacraments does not prevent us from legitimately considering Christian initiation to be a single whole with three stages.)

It will be profitable, then, to approach the problem, not by inquiring into the effects of the Spirit's action in man, but by distinguishing his various activities in God's plan for the world. Such an approach brings us back to what we said earlier about the unity of the three sacraments of initiation.[155]

We see, to begin with, that the Spirit is at work in the creation of the world; according to the opening verses of Genesis he seems to act as the mighty "Breath" that he is by his very being. Once the world has been created, the Spirit's habitual role is to bring into existence, raise up, and transform, and above all to unify. Unity is the goal that controls the whole work of creation: the union of man with God, union within man, the union of men with one another, the union of men with subhuman creatures, and the union of subhuman creatures with one another in the service of man and for the glory of God.

Sin rends, separates, dislocates. Once sin has come on the scene, God's plan becomes that of bringing man back to union and of restoring unity to the world. Can we discern how the Lord God goes about implementing his plan for rebuilding? In the Old Testament we see the Spirit of God acting to raise up men for needed tasks; we cannot say that the Old Testament presents the Spirit as a distinct Person in God, but we certainly can see the Spirit of God acting in the prophets, for example. In order to reach man at the latter's own level, that of an incarnated spirit, God sent envoys, representatives, so that in touching and hearing them and in seeing the signs they offered, men could come in contact with God himself. (Recall how important the theology of "mission" is in the Old Testament.)

God's preliminary work needed implementation, and therefore, because he always loved the world, he sent his only Son. Now, in touching Jesus, men could truly be in contact with the Father. But as God's plan enters this new stage, there is also a major action of the Spirit, for it is by the power of the Spirit that Jesus is conceived in the Virgin's womb. It is through the action of the Spirit that the Word becomes a man in the fullest and most concrete sense. From his conception, Jesus is Messiah, Prophet, Priest, and King, and is thus qualified for the role he must play in the plan of salvation.

Before he begins to exercise that role, Christ is officially declared before men to be Messiah, Prophet, Priest, and King; this happens at his baptism and involves the intervention of the Spirit. A voice from heaven describes Jesus as the one on whom the Father's favor rests; the dove descending is the symbol of the Spirit. Later on, at the transfiguration, in an account that has a function similar to that of the baptism, we see the Spirit manifesting himself once again, and we hear the voice declaring, "This is my beloved Son, with whom I am well pleased; listen to him."

If we ask where the essential fulfillment of Christ's mission as Messiah, Prophet, Priest, and King is to be found, we must say that it is to be found in the paschal mystery. He fulfills his role most perfectly and completely in this mystery, which includes his priestly action on Calvary, his resurrection and ascension, and his sending of the Spirit, who will unify the Church.

We can now see which were the major actions of the Spirit in the carrying out of the plan of salvation in Christ. He acted at the moment when the world was created in unity, in the conception of Christ, in Christ's official deputation to his role as Savior, and in the restoration of unity at Pentecost.

Against this background we may now inquire into the activities of the Spirit within the Christian. The Fathers of the Church, like St. Paul, explicitly state that the Christian has become so like Christ in his death and resurrection that if we look at Christ, we can understand what takes place likewise in the Christian. It is legitimate, in other words, to parallel what happened in the case of Christ and what happens now in the Christian. If such and such were the activities of the Spirit in the plan of salvation and especially in the person of Jesus, then his activities in the Christian will be similar.

Consequently, just as the Word became a human being through the action of the Spirit, so the Christian becomes a Christian through the Spirit's action in the font. The early Church thought of the font as being both tomb and mother: in the font we are immersed in death with Christ so that we may rise with him; from it we receive a new life in a second birth through water and the Spirit. When the Christian is thus reborn, he receives powers and qualifications that are essential for being what he should be. The postbaptismal anointing makes it quite clear that he is now prophet, priest, and king.

At a second stage, we can draw a parallel between what took place for Christ at the Jordan and in his transfiguration and what takes place for the Christian at his confirmation, which is the Spirit's second action in him. Like Christ, the Christian is now officially deputed to his role as prophet, priest, and king.

What do these roles mean for the Christian? When does he carry them out most intensely? For an answer we must keep looking at the parallel between Christ and the Christian. Christ most perfectly carried out his role as Messiah, Prophet, Priest, and King in the paschal mystery (Passion, resurrection, ascension, sending of the Spirit). When, then, does the Christian actively exercise the role the Spirit gave him in confirmation? He does it first and foremost in the celebration of the Eucharist, which makes present the paschal mystery and especially the death on the Cross.

In confirmation, then, the Spirit officially deputes the Christian to the sharing with Christ of his paschal mystery; the Christian does this, above all, by celebrating the mystery through an active participation in the Eucharist. Here we have theological justification for the practice of always administering confirmation before the Christian is admitted to the celebration of the Eucharist, since it is to participation in the Eucharist that his confirmation officially deputes him.

There is no text from Christian antiquity that proves a necessity of administering confirmation before the person can participate in the Eucharist. We think, however, that a passage from St. Hippolytus's *Apostolic Tradition* speaks of a prescription that is not simply juridical: after describing baptism and confirmation, he writes: "Then let them join the whole people in prayer; they are not to pray together with the faithful until they have received all that." [156] In the context, Hippolytus seems to be referring to the prayer of the faithful at the beginning of the Eucharistic liturgy. This would mean that in Hippolytus's eyes confirmation makes the Christian "perfect" or "complete," that is, enables him to take part in the celebration of the Eucharist, the greatest prayer the Church has.

It is in this Eucharist that the Christian is now called upon to give his witness. And indeed by celebrating the Eucharist with the Church, the Christian gives the most powerful of all testimonies, since it is not only a human testimony but one with sacramental efficacy. For, "as often as you eat this bread and drink the cup, you proclaim the Lord's death until he comes" (1 Cor. 11:26). In thus bearing witness through active participation in the Eucharist, the Christian performs a priestly act.

No confusion is really possible between this priesthood and that of the ordained priest. The priesthood of the believer is a genuine priesthood, not simply a "priesthood" by some extension of the term. The priesthood of the ordained priest, however, is ministerial; through his action the reality of the paschal mystery is made present in the real presence of the Eucharist. The priesthood of the believer, on the other hand, consists in his power and right to take a fully active part in the sacrifice of Christ that the action of the ministerial priest has rendered present.

To be a "perfect" or "complete" Christian, then, means primarily to fulfill the priestly role and, by so doing, to bear witness. For the fulfillment of that role, the Christian is made part of the Church that the Spirit of Pentecost has gathered into unity; the same Spirit structures the Body of Christ and gives it its apostolic mission.

This, then, is the height now reached by the catechumen whom the Church began preparing for baptism at the beginning of Lent. He is now part of the Church and has the mission of living the paschal mystery and spreading its influence around him.

Climax of the Vigil: The Eucharist, Pasch of the Church

We must be on guard lest, after giving so much attention to the blessing of the fire, the singing of the *Exsultet*, the blessing of the water, the celebration of baptism and confirmation, we end up celebrating the Eucharist as though it were an ordinary, everyday Eucharist. As a matter of fact, however, the Eucharist is the climax of the Vigil service. It is to it that baptism and confirmation are leading, and this Eucharist is, moreover, the most solemn of the year, more solemn even than that of Holy Thursday evening.

The Eucharist is in a true sense the Pasch, or Passover, of the Church.[157] It is constantly effecting the Church's passage to definitive life, constantly actualizing the paschal mystery and purifying men. The forgiveness of sins in baptism depends on the Eucharist; the early Church felt that we must be purified before participating in the Eucharist, but at the same time it thought of the Eucharist as cleansing from sin those who were truly repentant. The Church is thus constantly being built in solid foundations by the repetition of the Paschal Supper; it is constantly being brought into the presence of the one sacrifice of the Cross and constantly offering it, with the Son, to the Father.

The Eucharist is also very closely connected with the Lord's resurrection. For if Christ is not risen, the Eucharist is emptied of content and meaning. The Eucharist presupposes the resurrection and gives men a share in it: the same Jesus said "I am the resurrection and the life" (John 11:25) and "I am the bread of life" (John 6:48). Without the resurrection, the Eucharist would be a simple fraternal meal; it would not communicate divine life and be creative.

There is a further side of the Eucharist that we should bear in mind: the Eucharistic Christ, because he is the risen Christ, truly rules the world. He has overcome our death by his resurrection and is now slowly transforming the world through the Eucharist, which is rendering the world incorruptible.[158]

Especially, then, on this night of Christ's resurrection, the celebration of the Eucharist is the climax of the Church's activity and thus the key to the whole celebration of the Paschal Vigil.

STRUCTURE AND THEMES OF
EASTER SUNDAY AND
THE EASTER SEASON

The distribution of readings

The following tables will list the readings from Scripture for the Easter season, both at Mass and in the Liturgy of the Hours.

Beginning in the second week of Easter, the principle of continuous reading is applied at Mass, both for the first reading (continuous reading of Acts) and for the Gospel (continuous reading of St. John). As a result, we may not look for close parallels between the two readings at each Mass; the two collections of readings, however, do provide an important doctrinal synthesis.

In the Office of Readings, the First Letter of St. Peter is read during the octave. The next four weeks are given over to a semi-continuous reading of the Apocalypse, and the final two weeks to a reading of the Letters of St. John.

In the following table, the number given before each reading will be used later on to refer to it.

READINGS FOR THE EASTER SEASON
Sundays and Feasts

Sundays		Acts of the Apostles		The Apostle		The Gospel
I. Christ is risen	1	We ate and drank with him after he had risen Acts 10:34a, 37-43	2	Look for the things that are above, where Christ is risen Col. 3:1-4	3	*Morning:* Jesus risen from the dead John 20:1-9 *Evening:* They knew him in the breaking of bread Luke 24:13-35
			or			or
			2 bis	Be a new leaven 1 Cor. 5:6b-8	4	Gospel of the Easter Vigil
II. The community of believers grew; doubting Thomas	5	A. The community of believers Acts 2:42-47	8	A. Rebirth through the risen Jesus 1 Peter 1:3-9	11	A. Jesus appears on Sunday evening John 20:19-31
	6	B. One heart and one Acts 4:32-35	9	B. The Sons of God overcome the world 1 John 5:1-6	12	B. [same]
	7	C. Growth of the community Acts 5:12-16	10	C. Christ who was dead lives forever Apoc. 1:9-11a, 12-13, 17-19	13	C. [same]

III. The risen Christ appears to his followers

14 A. Sermon of Peter on the risen Christ
Acts 2:14, 22-28

15 B. Sermon of Peter: Christ died and rose
Acts 3:13-15, 17-19

16 C. Sermon of Peter: the apostles are witnesses
Acts 5:27b-32, 40b-41

17 A. Redeemed by the blood of the Lamb
1 Peter 1:17-21

18 B. Christ, the victim
1 John 2:1-5a

19 C. The Lamb receives power and riches
Apoc. 5:11-14

20 A. They knew him in the breaking of bread
Luke 24:13-35

21 B. Christ appears and eats with the disciples
Luke 24:35-48

22 C. Peter, fisherman and shepherd
John 21:1-19

IV. The Good Shepherd

23 A. Sermon of Peter: Jesus is Lord and Christ
Acts 2:14a, 36-41

24 B. Sermon of Peter: No salvation but in Christ
Acts 4:8-12

25 C. Sermon of Paul and Barnabas: Salvation to the ends of the earth.
Acts 13:14, 43-52

26 A. We are healed and have come back to our Shepherd
1 Peter 2:20b-25

27 B. We have become children of God
1 John 3:1-2

28 C. The Lamb leads to the living waters
Apoc. 7:9, 14b-17

29 A. Christ the Sheepgate
John 10:1-10

30 B. The true shepherd his life for his flock
John 10:11-18

31 C. Christ gives eternal life to his flock
John 10:27-30

Ascension	50 A. Account of the Ascension — Acts 1:1-11	51 A. Christ seated at the Father's right hand — Eph. 1:17-23	52 A. All power is given to Christ — Matthew 28:16-20
	B. [same]	B. [same]	53 B. Christ exalted to the Father's side — Mark 16:15-20
	C. [same]	C. [same]	54 C. Christ was taken up to heaven — Luke 24:46-53
VII. Witnesses to the Son glory of Christ; the prayer of Jesus	55 A. Prayer of the community — Acts 1:12-14	58 A. Insulted for the name of Christ — 1 Peter 4:13-16	61 A. Father, glorify your Son of Christ — John 17:1-11a
	56 B. Choice of Matthias as a witness to the resurrection — Acts 1:15-17, 20a, 20c-26	59 B. We have seen, and we await the sending of the Son as savior — 1 John 4:11-16	62 B. May they be consecrated by the truth — John 17:11b-19
	57 C. Stephen's vision and martyrdom — Acts 7:55-8:1a	60 C. I am the Alpha and the Omega — Apoc. 22:12-14, 16-17, 20	63 C. May they be one in us — John 17:20-26

Pentecost				
Vigil	64	Babel and the scattering of mankind Gen. 11:1-9	68	The Spirit prays for you Rom. 8:22-27
	65	The Lord on Sinai Exod. 19:3-8a, 16-20b	69	The Spirit is given, a flood of living water John 7:37-39
	66	The dry bones Ezek. 37:1-14		
	67	I will pour out my spirit on my servants and handmaids Joel 2:28-32		
Sunday	70	They were filled with the Spirit Acts 2:1-11	72	I send you; receive the Spirit John 20:19-23
	71	Baptized in the one Spirit into a single body 1 Cor. 12:3b-7, 12-13		

READINGS DURING THE OCTAVE OF EASTER

	Witnesses to the resurrection		Faith and conversion through proclamation of the resurrection
Monday	73	Witnesses to the resurrection Acts 2:14, 22-32	74	The risen Christ meets the women who are to tell his brothers of his resurrection Matthew 28:8-15
Tuesday	75	Be converted, believe and be baptized Acts 2:36-41	76	Appearance to Magdalene: "I have seen the Lord." John 20:11-18
Wednesday	77	Peter cures a paralytic Acts 3:1-10	78	The disciples at Emmaus Luke 24:13-35
Thursday	79	Sermon of Peter: Jesus died but rose again Acts 3:11-26	80	The prophecies have been fulfilled: Christ rose on the third day Luke 24:35-48
Friday	81	Salvation is to be found only in Jesus Acts 4:1-12	82	Appearance at the Sea of Tiberias: Jesus gives the disciples bread and fish John 21:1-14
Saturday	83	We cannot be silent about what we have seen Acts 4:13-21	84	Go and proclaim the good news to all mankind Mark 16:9-15

READINGS FOR WEEKDAYS DURING THE EASTER SEASON

		Continuous reading of Acts			Continuous reading of John
Second Week					
Monday	85	Prayer for the Spirit and courage to preach	4:23-31	86	Rebirth from water and Spirit for the kingdom	3:1-8
Tuesday	87	The faithful were of one heart and one mind	4:32-37	88	Christ comes from God, reveals the Father, and returns	3:7-15
Wednesday	89	The apostles escape from prison and preach in the Temple	5:17-26	90	God sent his Son to save the world	3:16-21
Thursday	91	We testify to the resurrection	5:27-33	92	The Father has put everything in the Son's hands	3:31-36
Friday	93	The apostles are beaten for the name of Jesus	5:34-42	94	Multiplication of bread; Jesus eats with his disciples	6:1-15
Saturday	95	Appointment of seven men who are filled with the Spirit	6:1-7	96	Jesus walks on the water	6:16-21
Third Week					
Monday	97	Stephen speaks with wisdom and the power of the Spirit	6:8-15	98	Seek the food that does not perish	6:22-29
Tuesday	99	Martyrdom of Stephen	7:51-59	100	My Father gives you the true bread from heaven	6:30-35
Wednesday	101	The good news is preached everywhere	8:1-8	102	Whoever sees the Son will live for ever	6:35-40
Thursday	103	Philip baptizes an Ethiopian	8:26-40	104	I am the living bread come down from heaven	6:44-51
Friday	105	Paul, God's instrument for the Gentiles	9:1-20	106	My flesh is real food and my blood real drink	6:52-59
Saturday	107	The Church progresses and is consoled by the Spirit	9:31-42	108	To whom shall we go? You have the words of eternal life	6:60-69

Fourth Week						
Monday	109	11:1-18	Even the pagans are converted	110	10:1-10	I am the gate for the sheep
Tuesday	111	11:19-26	The good news is preached to the Greeks	112	10:22-30	The Father and I are one
Wednesday	113	12:24-13:5a	The Spirit chooses Saul and Barnabas	114	12:44-50	I have come into the world to be its light
Thursday	115	13:13-25	Jesus of the race of David has been raised up	116	13:16-20	Receive the one I send, and you receive me
Friday	117	13:26-33	Sermon of Paul: God has raised up Jesus	118	14:1-6	I am the Way, the Truth, and the Life
Saturday	119	13:44-52	We now turn to the Gentiles	120	14:7-14	He who sees me sees the Father
Fifth Week						
Monday	121	14:5-18	Sermon of Paul and Barnabas: Turn from idols to the living God	122	14:21-26	The Spirit will teach you everything
Tuesday	123	14:19-28	Address of Paul and Barnabas to the community, telling what God had done for them	124	14:27-31a	I give you my peace
Wednesday	125	15:1-6	The problem of whether to circumcise the Gentiles	126	15:1-8	If you remain in me and I in you, you will bear much fruit
Thursday	127	15:7-21	Counsels of Peter and James: Do not burden the converted pagans	128	15:9-11	Love me and you will have joy
Friday	129	15:22-23	No unnecessary burdens	130	15:12-17	Love one another
Saturday	131	16:1-10	The Spirit sends forth Paul and Luke	132	15:18-21	I have chosen you; you no longer belong to the world

SUNDAY READINGS IN THE LITURGY OF THE HOURS

First Sunday	157	The Israelites pass dryshod through the Red Sea Exod. 14:15–15:1a	Fifth Sunday	161	The wedding day of the Lamb Apoc. 18:21–19:10
Second Sunday	158	A new life Col. 3:1-17	Sixth Sunday	162	The word of life; God is Light 1 John 1:1-10
Third Sunday	159	The Lamb breaks the seals of the book Apoc. 6:1-17	Ascension	163	He ascended on high with a host of captives Eph. 4:1-24
Fourth Sunday	160	The sign of the woman Apoc. 12:1-17	Seventh Sunday	164	The commandment of faith and love 1 John 3:18-24
			Pentecost	165	Those led by the Spirit are the children of God Rom. 8:5-27

WEEKDAY READINGS IN THE LITURGY OF THE HOURS

First Week

Day	Page	Reading	Theme
Monday	166	1 Peter 1:1-21	Thanksgiving
Tuesday	167	1 Peter 1:22-2:10	The way of God's children
Wednesday	168	1 Peter 2:11-25	Christians are aliens in the world
Thursday	169	1 Peter 3:1-17	The imitation of Christ
Friday	170	1 Peter 3:18-4:11	Waiting for the Lord's coming
Saturday	171	1 Peter 4:12-5:14	Exhortation to the faithful and the elders

Second Week

Day	Page	Reading	Theme
Monday	172	Apoc. 1:1-20	Vision of the Son of Man
Tuesday	173	Apoc. 2:1-11	To the churches of Ephesus and Smyrna
Wednesday	174	Apoc. 2:12-29	To the churches of Pergamum and Thyatira
Thursday	175	Apoc. 3:1-22	To the churches of Sardis, Philadelphia, and Laodicea
Friday	176	Apoc. 4:1-11	Vision of God
Saturday	177	Apoc. 5:1-14	Vision of the Lamb

Third Week

Day	Page	Reading	Theme
Monday	178	Apoc. 7:1-17	A great throng with the seal of God
Tuesday	179	Apoc. 8:1-13	Seven angels chastise the world
Wednesday	180	Apoc. 9:1-12	The plague of locusts
Thursday	181	Apoc. 9:13-21	The plague of war
Friday	182	Apoc. 10:1-11	The seer is confirmed in his role
Saturday	183	Apoc. 11:1-19	The two witnesses

*If the Ascension is celebrated on this day and on Sunday, today's reading is shifted to Friday, Friday's to Saturday, and Saturday's to the Seventh Sunday.

EASTER SUNDAY

15. THIS DAY THAT THE LORD HAS MADE

"This is the day the Lord has made"

The day has dawned at last, the day of days; indeed, the feast we celebrate we call simply "the Day of the Lord." At this moment we experience a reality that is both past and present: "The Pasch is indeed 'the Passover of the Lord.' Has the Spirit ever made any truth more clear than this: that Easter is not a figure or a story or a distant image, but the real Passover of the Lord?"[159]

As the celebrant enters the church to celebrate the Mass of Easter Day, he reminds all both of baptism and the blood of the covenant by sprinkling those present with holy water. Meanwhile all sing: "I saw water flowing from the right side of the temple, alleluia. It brought God's life and his salvation, and the people sang in joyful praise: alleluia, alleluia."

The great news is proclaimed once again in the entrance song, but this time it is Christ himself who proclaims it through the mouths of his faithful: "I have risen: I am with you once more; you placed your hand on me to keep me safe. How great is the depth of your wisdom! Alleluia." The hand the Father placed on the Son he now places on the Church and on each of us.

"We ate and drank with him"

The first reading in today's Mass is from Peter's sermon in the house of Cornelius the centurion. These two men were deeply moved when they met for the first time. Cor-

159

nelius had had a vision in which he was told to send for Peter. Peter came, learned of what had happened, and responded with the catechesis that forms today's reading [1].

The passage raises historical and literary problems that we shall not go into. In any event, it is generally accepted that the account is historical as far as its substance goes. It can readily be admitted that, under the inspiration of the Holy Spirit, Luke has made contributions of his own in respect to both the literary form and the exposition of the problems caused by the law-gospel conflict in the life of the young Church.[160]

It is chiefly because of verses 40-43 that the Church today bids us read this discourse that Cornelius's conversion elicits from the deeply moved Apostle. Cornelius's vision and conversion mark a major turning point for Peter and the entire Church, for the Spirit seems to be clearly pointing out the direction the Church should take. The Spirit has now revealed that "in every nation any one who fears him and does what is right is acceptable to him" (Acts 10:35). Yet the revelation that the Church's mission is universal turns Peter's world upside down. Others had already learned this truth, either from personal experience, as Paul did in his own sudden conversion, or from the experience of converting others, as Philip did in baptizing the Ethiopian official. Peter, on the other hand, while never denying it (after all, he stated the truth on Pentecost! [Acts 2:14]), had not come to a personal realization that the Spirit was demanding the mission to the pagans. The chief of the apostles will not forget his experience, as he makes clear in his explanation to the church at Jerusalem (Acts 11:1-8) and in his words to the Council of Jerusalem (Acts 15:7-9).

The few verses read today sum up both the Church's mission and the essential object of saving faith: God raised Jesus up on the third day and had him appear to the witness-chosen beforehand by God. One requirement for being an apostle was to have been a witness of the resurrection. That is why Peter adds, "us . . . who ate and drank with him after he rose from the dead" (Acts 10:41). The mission of the apostles and of the entire Church is to bear witness to this resurrection and to proclaim it as the object of a faith that saves because it brings the forgiveness of sins (v. 43).

The three essential points of this message are meaningful for each of us and should stimulate our reflection: the universalism of the Church; the witness to the resurrection of Christ; our faith in the risen Christ. The preaching of the Church, and the witness each of us must give, can be summed up, at every point in time until Christ comes again, in the paschal message that Christ is risen from the dead and is now living.

The responsorial psalm (Ps. 118) proclaims our new condition, now that the mystery of the resurrection has been fulfilled in us: "The right hand of the Lord is exalted, the right hand of the Lord does valiantly! I shall not die, but I shall live, and recount the deeds of the Lord" (Ps. 118:16-17).

If you have been raised with Christ . . .

The second reading rouses us from a contemplation that might possibly be that of the mere spectator and thus leave us personally uncommitted. For the baptized Christian, the resurrection of Christ is not merely a historical event; it affects him personally, and its reality and the demands it makes on him are felt each day of his life: "If you have been raised with Christ . . ." (Col. 3:1) [2].

St. Paul tells us that these demands are laid upon us by our baptism. In his Letter to the Romans, and with the ritual of baptism as his point of reference, the Apostle teaches that we have been buried with Christ in death; consequently, we must also live a new life with him (Rom. 6:4-5). The way Paul speaks might make us think that our risen life is entirely in the future. The Letter to the Colossians, however, makes it clear that we live here and now with the risen Jesus and that our lives must be the lives of men who are risen with Christ.

The concrete conclusion that follows from this premise is

perfectly clear and forms the basis of Christian morality: "Set your minds on things that are above, not on things that are on earth" (Col. 3:2). The Christian must live according to what he really is; this means that his life is lived under the sign of hope. Only in faith does he understand that his personal renewal is something already real. While on earth, he passes through a time of testing, and only as in a mirror, indistinctly, does he come in contact with the mysteries of salvation (1 Cor. 13:12; 2 Cor. 5:6-7). Nonetheless, he does possess the pledge that is the Spirit (2 Cor. 1:22; 5:5; Rom. 2:23; Eph. 1:13-14). We must strengthen within us the new life we received in baptism. That life is truly ours, but we must live it in paradoxical condition: We must be in the world without belonging to it (Col. 2:20; 1 Cor. 7:31); we must suffer even though we are already risen (2 Cor. 4:10-11). In this way we Christians make up what is lacking in the sufferings of Christ, even as we live by his resurrection and wait to "appear with him in glory" (Col. 3:4).

Here is a doctrine that is both optimistic and demanding. The opening prayer of the Mass translates it into fervent prayer: "God our Father, by raising Christ your Son you conquered the power of death and opened for us the way to eternal life. Let our celebration today raise us up and renew our lives by the Spirit that is within us."

A new dough

The Easter Sunday liturgy provides an alternative second reading, taken from the First Letter to the Corinthians (5:6-8). This reading makes the point that the feast of Easter is not a celebration limited to externals, but that, on the contrary, there is only one way of properly celebrating it: to put away all corruption and wickedness. These are the "old yeast" and we must get rid of them so that we may celebrate with the unleavened bread of sincerity and truth. We ourselves must be like Passover bread that is unleavened. We must be a new dough.

St. Paul likes to relate Christ's Pasch and ours to the

Pasch of the Church as she first celebrated it in the context of the Jewish Passover. The first ritual step taken for the latter celebration was to rid the house of any old yeast. Paul also, and more importantly, compares the sacrifice of Christ to the sacrifice of the Passover lamb. As the Passover sacrifice commemorated the liberation and Exodus from Egypt, so the blood of Christ the Lamb sealed the new and eternal covenant.

The Easter Sequence sums up in poetic style the meaning of the feast. In this poem the Church sings: "We know that Christ has indeed risen from the dead. Do you, conqueror and king, have mercy on us." "They did not know . . . that he must rise from the dead."

The Gospel passage proposed for reading at a morning Mass on Easter Sunday [161] might well stir our enthusiasm by its literary character and by the apologetic emphasis it contains. By "apologetic emphasis" I mean the importance John attributes to the witness of Mary and of the two disciples, namely, Peter, the chief of the apostles, and John, who, though not the chief, runs ahead of Peter to the tomb [3].

The account is undoubtedly important for its details, especially since John, while agreeing with the Synoptics on a number of points, also has his own way of describing the events. Nonetheless, it seems to me, especially since the Church has already greatly emphasized the event itself of the resurrection during the Easter Vigil service, that we should pay special attention to the final sentence of the passage: "For as yet they did not know the scripture, that he must rise from the dead" (John 20:9).

Here was a blindness that the disciple whom Jesus loved made no attempt to hide. That should encourage us to renew our own faith. Here were men who had lived with Jesus and had listened time after time to his teaching and his references to his death and resurrection. Yet they did not even now understand him or the Scriptures with all those prophecies of the resurrection that we heard read during the Vigil. As a matter of fact, the two disciples in today's

Gospel believe only when they see: Peter, who enters the tomb, sees and believes; John, who arrives first, looks in without entering (that privilege is for Peter) and likewise sees and believes.

The account, which poses numerous problems for the exegete, contains three important points: the empty tomb, the haste of the disciples, and their faith.

The discovery takes place "on the first day of the week." Here we have the reason for the celebration of Sunday. The Jews celebrated Saturday, because that was the day on which the Lord rested after his six days' work of creation. But the Lord rose "early in the morning" on the first day of the new week, and that is the day Christians would henceforth celebrate. It would be for them, however, not only the first day of the week but also the eighth day, a day that in a sense falls outside the system of the week. For it is not only the day on which God began the work of the first creation but also the day of the new creation and the resurrection from the dead.

Christians did not think of this day in terms of apologetics, that is, as a proof that the mission of Jesus had been successful. They thought of it as first and foremost the day when the whole of creation is renewed.

The rock has been taken from the door of the tomb. Mary Magdalene, seeing this, runs to tell the disciples. John makes it a point to tell us who the two disciples are that hasten to check on Mary's report: they are Peter, the leader of the new Church, and "the other disciple, the one whom Jesus loved." The latter, so eager in his love for Christ, reaches the tomb first, but he holds back and lets Peter enter the tomb, for Peter's testimony will carry greater weight with the community as a whole. The other disciple does however see immediately that the tomb is empty, even if everything in it is neatly disposed (as Peter could attest). That other disciple then entered the tomb, and "saw and believed." We are reminded of the story of Thomas, which will be read on the second Sunday of Easter: "Have you believed because you have seen me? Blessed are those who have not seen and yet believe" (John 20:29).

The Church and every Christian now have at their disposal two testimonies: that of the ancient Scriptures, as read now in and by the Church, under the guidance of the Spirit of Pentecost; and that of the two disciples and Mary Magdalene.

"He was known to them in the breaking of the bread"

At an afternoon Mass on Easter Sunday, the familiar Gospel of the disciples at Emmaus is read [4]. In it we find exemplified the same kind of failure to understand the Scriptures. Here Jesus himself makes this point as he walks along with the two disciples on the evening of Resurrection Sunday: "'O foolish men, and slow of heart to believe all that the prophets have spoken! Was it not necessary that the Christ should suffer these things and enter into his glory?' And beginning with Moses and all the prophets, he interpreted to them in all the scriptures the things concerning himself" (Luke 24:25-27). Christ gives the kind of catechesis that the Fathers of the Church will later adopt; they will search out the types or prefigurations, and then study the fulfillment of them: type, prefigurement, preparation — antitype, realization, fulfillment.

We have on several occasions emphasized the fact that the Church's traditional liturgical reading of the Scriptures, while not neglecting exegesis, brings to light special values in the Gospel passages she proclaims. Thus, a strict application of the principles of exegesis will not allow us to assert that the meal Jesus took with the disciples at Emmaus was a Eucharistic meal; and yet it is impossible not to see in the words Luke uses a reference to the Eucharist: "He took the bread and blessed, and broke it, and gave it to them" (Luke 24:30). Surely Luke had the Eucharist in mind both here and in Acts 2:42. He may not say in so many words that the

meal at Emmaus is a repetition of the Supper, but he surely
is thinking about it; nor can the Church think otherwise.

In other words, the simple fact that the disciples recognized Jesus in the breaking of bread does not prove that the
meal was a Eucharistic celebration, since it could have
been simply the case that the Lord's manner of performing
the actions made him immediately recognizable. Yet neither Luke nor the Church as she proclaims this text can help
but recall the Last Supper. Moreover, while the disciples
recognized Jesus in the breaking of bread, what inflames
their hearts is above all the Lord's explanations of the
Scriptures: "Did not our hearts burn within us while he
talked to us on the road, while he open to us the scriptures?" (Luke 24:32). It was doubtless that experience that
made them urge Jesus: "Stay with us, for it is toward evening and the day is now far spent" (Luke 24:29). And yet, in
telling their story to the apostles they refer only to the
breaking of bread and do not mention the explanation of the
Scriptures. "Then they told what had happened on the
road, and how he was known to them in the breaking of the
bread" (v. 35).

From that time forward it is in the breaking of bread that
the Church has manifested her faith in the resurrection of
Jesus. The Eucharist is the distinctive sign by which a
Catholic professes his faith in the paschal mystery; he
celebrates that mystery in the joyous Eucharist, which is
inseparable from Easter.

Living the paschal mystery

The Church does not limit her celebration of her Lord's
resurrection to Easter Sunday but continues it until the day
when the Lord sends his Spirit. The reason for this unbroken celebration is that Pentecost marks the full impact
of salvation on the world, and the outpouring of God's life
upon men.[162]

This does not mean, however, that the Christian need not
himself face death. On the contrary, the vision of glory

never comes save after the passage through death. The "rediscovery" of the paschal mystery undoubtedly has made us aware that the term "redemption" tended to be too juridical, to the point at times of making Christians forget that the resurrection too was a mystery of salvation and not simply a kind of appendix or a proof that Christ's mission had been successful. It is also true, however, that the paschal mystery directs our attention back to the beginning of God's creation and to the catastrophe that had left its mark on the world. The paschal mystery includes the incarnation and all the deeds of Christ. Consequently, though it ends in glory, it also requires the passage through death. In fact, we must even maintain that life springs from death.

These remarks enable us to pinpoint the true nature of Christian asceticism. Of the Christian, as of Christ himself, it must be said not simply that his glory comes after death, but that his self-renunciation and his death are already part of his paschal victory.

The paschal mystery and the Fathers

Our purpose here is not to provide an anthology of patristic texts on the paschal mystery; that would require more pages than we have at our disposal. We wish only to bring to the reader's attention some thoughts of the great writers whose voices still echo in the Church.

An author whose poetic freshness and profound yet simple theology still have power to move us deeply is Melito of Sardis.[163] His poem *On the Pasch* displays, as early as 160–70 (the most probable period of composition), a procedure that will be typical of the later patristic catecheses, namely, the use of typology. The poet gives a typological interpretation of Exodus 12:3-28, namely, just as Israel was protected by the blood of the lamb, so the new people of God will be preserved by the blood of the sacrifice on the Cross. The person, nature, and work of Christ are presented in the framework of the economy of salvation, that is, of the developing plan God has for mankind's redemption. The

Passion of Christ is foretold by types. Finally he wins the victory in his resurrection.

Here is how the poem begins:

> The Scripture account of the Hebrew Exodus has been read, and the words of the mystery have been explained: how the lamb is sacrificed and the people saved. Therefore, beloved, observe and understand! The paschal mystery is new and old, eternal and temporal, corruptible and incorruptible, mortal and immortal. It is old according to the Law, new according to the Logos; temporal in its prefiguration, eternal in the grace it bestows; corruptible in the immolation of the sheep, incorruptible in the life of the Lord; mortal through burial in the earth, immortal through the resurrection from the dead. The Law is old, but the Logos new; the figure is temporal, grace eternal; the sheep is corruptible, the Lord incorruptible; he is sacrificed as a lamb, raised up as God. For, "like a sheep he was led forth to be slaughtered," but he was not a sheep; he was led forth like a silent lamb, but he was not a lamb. The figure is gone and outstripped, the truth has been found [fulfilled]. For instead of a lamb it is God who has come; instead of a sheep, a man, and in the man the Christ who contains all things. Thus the sacrifice of the sheep and the Passover rite and the letter of the Law have given way to Christ Jesus.[164]

Further on, Melito explains that what is prefigured in the Old Testament is fulfilled in the New: "The people [Israel], therefore, were like the outline of a plan, and the Law was like the letter of a parable; the Gospel, however, is the explanation and fulfillment of the Law, and the Church is the place where it is carried out."[165]

However, it is when Melito defines the Pasch on the basis of a false etymology that he best expresses the meaning of the mystery and opens the door for an interpretation that will always remain valid, even when its erroneous etymological basis is removed. Melito writes: "What, then, is the 'Pasch'? The name is derived from what happened, for the verb *paschein* [to suffer; also, to celebrate the Passion = Pasch = passage] is derived from *pathein* [to have suffered]."[166]

Here is a valid theology despite its being based on a false etymology. The Pasch *is* a passage through suffering to victory; *paschein*, "to suffer," is indeed connected, in its content, with *pascha*, "passage." As a result, the word *passio* will connote triumph through suffering, rather than simply suffering itself. This is true of the *Passio*, or Gospel of Christ's Passion, that is proclaimed on Good Friday: it is first and foremost an account of Christ's victory through suffering. So too, the *passio* of a martyr, despite its legendary details, means chiefly an account of how the martyr triumphed through his sufferings.

This, at any rate, is how we must understand the "Pasch" of the Lord as well as our own and the Church's "pasch." It was worth our while to recall the false etymology that served as a point of departure, for it helps us understand the way in which the Fathers approached the paschal mystery.[167]

Some patristic texts: St. John Chrysostom and St. Ambrose

In one of his Easter catecheses, St. John Chrysostom reminds his hearers of the power still present in the blood that Christ shed for us:

> Do you wish to know the power of this blood? Go back to what prefigured it, to the ancient accounts of what happened in Egypt. God was about to inflict the tenth plague on the Egyptians, slaying their first-born because they were holding his first-born people captive. But how could he avoid harming the Jews along with the Egyptians, since all alike dwelt in the same place? See now the power of the prefiguration so that you may understand the power of the reality that

fulfilled it. The blow inflicted by God was about to descend from heaven, and the destroying angel was about to make the round of the homes.

What did Moses do? He told the Jews: "Sacrifice an unblemished lamb and smear your doorposts with the blood."

What do you respond to Moses? "Can the blood of a mindless beast save men who are endowed with reason?" "Yes," he says, "not because it is blood but because it is a figure of the Savior's blood. Just as an emperor's statue, though it lacks all sense, safeguards men endowed with reason and sense when they seek refuge at it, not because it is a piece of bronze but because it is an image of the emperor, so this lifeless and unfeeling blood saved living men, not because it was blood, but because it prefigured the blood of the Lord."

Here is another way to appreciate the power of this blood. Observe where it began to flow and what its source was. It flowed down from the Cross and the from the Lord's side. While the dead Jesus still hung on the Cross (the Gospel tells us), a soldier approached and opened his side with a spear, and water and blood flowed out. The water symbolized baptism, and the blood the mysteries. . . .

Blood and water flowed from his side. Beloved, do not pass this mystery by unheeding, for I have yet another mystical interpretation to offer you. I said that the water and blood were the symbols respectively of baptism and the mysteries. Now it is from these two sacraments that the Church is reborn, in the bath of rebirth and renewal in the Holy Spirit, through baptism and the mysteries. The symbols of baptism and the mysteries, however, came from Christ's side. Therefore it is from his side that he formed the Church, just as he formed Eve from the side of Adam. . . .

Have you seen how Christ made his Bride one with

himself? Have you observed the food with which he nourishes her? Well, it is the same food that has formed and nourished us. . . .[168]

Note the procedure, which is a favorite with the Fathers. It consists in going back to the types and figures in the Old Testament and making these the basis for instructing Christians on the sacraments and situating the sacraments in the history of salvation. Such a catechesis highlights the connection between the sacraments of Christian initiation and the Pasch.

In his explanation of the Creed, St. Ambrose approaches the resurrection from a special point of view, seeing in it a sign of Christ's divinity, which the incarnation had in no way diminished:

> "On the third day he arose from the dead." There you are told of his resurrection. "He ascended into heaven, and sits at the right hand of the Father." You see that the flesh could in no way detract from the divinity, but that on the contrary the incarnation brought Christ a great triumph. Why, after rising from the dead, does he take his seat at the Father's right hand? Because he has thus brought back to the Father the fruit of his "good pleasure." There are two facts of which you are sure: he rose from the dead, and he sits at the Father's right hand. The conclusion is that the flesh could not diminish the glory of the divinity.[169]

In emphasizing this unwonted aspect of the resurrection and ascension, the Doctor of the Church should not be regarded as developing an apologetic argument. His aim is rather to call our attention not only to the glorification of Christ but to ours as well, for once sins have been forgiven, the flesh is not of itself an obstacle to the glorious transfiguration.

St. Leo the Great

St. Leo is what we might call the classical catechist of the great mysteries of the Lord, such as the incarnation, passion, and resurrection. In discussing each of the mysteries, he likes to emphasize three points: the actualization of the mystery that the Church celebrates in her liturgy as a present and not a purely past reality; the integration of the mystery being celebrated into the overall history of salvation; the consideration of the mystery as being not simply an event but an example as well. Christ's actions have a present reality and, as such, are fully efficacious, but at the same time they are an example for us.

St. Leo begins a sermon on the Passion by saying:

Beloved, the Lord's glorious Passion, concerning which we promised we would speak today, is most to be admired for the mystery of humility it embodies. It redeemed us all, and it instructs us, so that after having paid our ransom it also helps us to holiness. . . .

Beyond a doubt, beloved, the Son of God so closely united human nature to himself that Christ is one and the same not only in that individual who is the first-born of all creatures but in all his saints as well. As the Head cannot be separated from the members, neither can the members be separated from the Head. For although it is true not of this life but of eternal life that God is all in all, yet even now he inhabits, and cannot be separated from, his temple which is the Church, as he promised when he said: "Lo, I am with you always, to the close of the age." The Apostle concurs when he writes: "He is the head of the body, the Church; he is the beginning, the first-born from the dead, that in everything he might be pre-eminent. For in him all the fullness of God was pleased to dwell, and through him to reconcile to himself all things."[170]

From the very beginning of this sermon, St. Leo makes it clear what a mystery of Christ is for us: a fact, and indeed a sanctifying fact, but an example as well. Taking as his starting point the incarnation and the bonds uniting Christ and his Church, the Saint draws concrete conclusions for us. He continues: "Thus our Savior, the Son of God, gave all who believe in him an efficacious sign and an example; through rebirth they lay hold of the former, through imitation they follow the latter."[171]

We have already seen how the Fathers like to refer back to scriptural types. St. Leo does not neglect this method:

> Everything that was formerly done in obedience to the law — the circumcision of the flesh, the varied sacrifices, the observance of the Sabbath — was a testimony to Christ and a prophecy of his grace. He is the end of the law, not in the sense that he empties the law of further meaning, but in the sense that he fulfills it. Though he is the author of the old as well as the new, he changed the mysteries hidden in the figurative promises by bringing to pass what was promised; he put an end to prophecy, because he who was prophesied had now come.[172]

St. Leo goes on then to present salvation as a present reality in the liturgy, so much so that we are in contact with the mystery we celebrate. The passage is extremely important for a theology of the liturgy.

> All that the Son of God did and taught for the reconciliation of the world is not simply known to us through the historical record of the past; we also experience it through the power of his present works. . . . It is not only the courageous, glorious martyrs who share in his suffering; all the faithful who are reborn also share it, and do so in the very act of their rebirth. For when men renounce Satan and believe in God, when they pass from corruption to a new life, when they lay aside the image of the earthly man and take on the form of the heavenly man, they go through a kind of death and resurrection. He who is received by

> Christ and receives Christ is not the same after his
> baptism as before; the body of the reborn Christian
> becomes the flesh of the crucified Christ.[173]

Commenting on St. Paul's words in his First Letter to the
Corinthians: "Christ has been raised from the dead, the first
fruits of those who have fallen asleep" (15:20), St. Leo
writes: "He who was the first human being to rise from the
dead was part of the totality that followed; moreover, we
piously believe that what first took place in the Head will
take place in the members as well, since 'as in Adam all
die, so also in Christ shall all be made alive.'"[174]
In the Saint's two sermons on the resurrection, we find
passages that speak to some of our contemporary preoccu-
pations. He speaks, for example, of the state of Christ's
risen body:

> He would also show them the wounds in his side, the
> holes left by the nails, and all the marks of his recent
> Passion — all this in order to show that the divine and
> human natures remain distinct in him, and in order
> that we might be sure the Word is not identical with
> the flesh he assumed, but might confess that the Son
> of God is both Word and flesh.
>
> Paul, the Apostle of the Gentiles, does not disagree
> with this belief, beloved, when he says: "Although
> we used to know Christ according to the flesh, now
> we no longer know him thus." For the resurrection of
> the Lord signals, not the end of the flesh, but a trans-
> formation of it, nor does the increased power mean
> that the substance is consumed. The nature remains;
> only its state changes. The body that could once be
> crucified is now impassible; the body that could once
> be slain is now immortal; the body that could once be
> wounded is now incorruptible. Rightly, then, does
> Paul say we no longer know Christ's flesh in the state
> in which it used to be known, for now everything
> weak and passible has been eliminated, so that while

remaining what it was in its essence, it is no longer
what it was as far as its glorified state is concerned.[175]

The second sermon on the resurrection is especially rich;
it follows a method with which we are by now familiar:
"The Cross of Christ by which mankind was saved is both a
sacred sign and an example: a sacred sign through which
the power of God works, and an example to stimulate men's
devotion. Once men have been freed from the yoke of slavery, they are given this further blessing, that they can then
imitate the work of redemption."[176]

To the feast we call the Pasch the Hebrews gave the
name *Phase*, or "passage," as the evangelist shows when he
writes: "It was before the festival of the Passover, and Jesus
knew that the hour had come for him to pass from this
world to the Father" (John 13:1 JB). But in which of his two
natures did he make this passage? In ours, of course, since
the Father was in the Son and the Son in the Father beyond
any possibility of separation. Nonetheless, since the Word
and his human nature are but a single person, the nature he
assumed is not separated from him who assumed it. Consequently, the honor given to him who is exalted means an
increase of glory for him who does the exalting. St. Paul
says as much: "Therefore God has highly exalted him and
bestowed on him the name which is above every name"
(Phil. 2:9).

Paul is here referring to the exaltation of Jesus in the
human nature that had been assumed by the Word; just as
the divinity is inseparable from Jesus in his sufferings, so it
is coeternal with him in his divine glory.

The Lord wanted his faithful followers to share in the
passage to glory that would shortly be his. He prepared
them for it when, with his Passion imminent, he prayed to
his Father not only for his apostles and disciples but for the
entire Church: "I do not pray for these only, but also for
those who believe in me through their word, that they may
all be one; even as thou, Father, art in me, and I in thee,
that they also may be [one] in us" (John 17:20-21). "There-

fore, too, as the Apostle says, 'we await a Savior, the Lord Jesus Christ, who will change our lowly body to be like his glorious body,' he who lives and reigns with the Father and the Holy Spirit for ever and ever. Amen."[177]

This quite simple theology of the paschal mystery emphasizes our close and very concrete participation in the mystery that we are already living out in our lives. It was the great merit of the Fathers that they gave such vibrant expression to it. No one has ever been able to improve on it without complicating it and without making abstract and conceptual something meant to be lived out in concrete experience.

SECOND SUNDAY OF EASTER

16. BELIEVING WITHOUT SEEING

The faith of Thomas

On the second Sunday of Easter the same Gospel pericope is read in all three years of the cycle. The passage relates the appearance of Christ to his disciples and the faith of Thomas, who had been absent on the occasion of Christ's first appearance to them. Thomas had withheld his assent and was waiting to verify in a personal, concrete way the Lord's resurrection. We all know of the deeply moving encounter between Christ and his doubting disciple, and of the gentle but firm way in which the Lord brought Thomas to faith, even while proclaiming a demanding ideal of unconditional faith: "Blessed are those who have not seen and yet believe" (John 20:29).

It is important that the liturgy, before embarking on a presentation of the Church's paschal life, should emphasize the nature of Christian faith. This passage from John's Gospel [11] was perfect for the purpose.

As the reader may know, chapter 20 of St. John's Gospel is regarded as the last of his writings. It is one of the best constructed chapters in the whole Gospel, and its content is extremely important for the life of the Church as a whole and for the life of each member. Why so? Because, although the apostles were in a position to have concrete experience of the risen Christ, that kind of experience must in the future be replaced by a purely spiritual faith. In the future, to be converted would mean to believe in the word, the kerygma or authoritative proclamation of the Church, without there being any possibility of controlling through external evidence the truth the Church proclaims.

This new situation means a new difficulty for the Christian of later times as compared with the apostles; at the same time, however, it marks a certain superiority of the later Christian over the first disciples. For when Thomas wanted to control belief by facts and when the Lord was forced to tell him, "Blessed are those who have not seen and yet believe," he was uttering a reproach that also applied to the other disciples, including John, of whom we are told that "he saw and believed" (John 20:8). Neither Peter nor John believed what Mary Magdalene told them; instead they ran to the tomb to see for themselves. Mary herself, no less than Thomas, had a quasi-material experience of the resurrection (John 20:17; 20:25, 27).

The starting point, then, was a faith that went beyond any physical control of evidence for the resurrection, but was nonetheless still dependent on an experience of the visible and tangible. The goal was a much broader and deeper kind of faith that must characterize the Church as a whole and each individual member. For the Church, in days to come, would have to proclaim the resurrection and, with the help of the Spirit, rouse faith in the risen Jesus. Let us look now at the profound meaning this Gospel pericope has in its liturgical proclamation. (In so doing, we shall leave aside the critical exegetical problems with regard to verses 30-31, which, according to some, mark the end of the Fourth Gospel, and the problem of the possible revision of verse 21 by a contemporary of John, possibly one of his disciples.)

The appearance of Christ occurs at a new gathering of his disciples. John dates the event precisely: "eight days later" (v. 26). On that day "his disciples were again in the house"; the word "again" would seem to indicate that the disciples did not gather daily. Christ appears in their midst with a body that is his own yet transformed, for he comes through "doors [that] were shut." This glorified body still bears the marks of the Passion, so much so that Thomas is forced to cry out, "My Lord and my God!" Here is a clear assertion about the person of Jesus, and the first to be put in such concrete words in the New Testament writings. We must bear in mind that faith is the theme of John's Gospel. The miracles of Jesus and the concomitant intensification of Jewish disbelief form the very framework of this Gospel. Here, on Thomas's lips, we have the climactic affirmation that will henceforth be used by the Church and the individual Christian when in the presence of Christ the Lord: "My Lord and my God!"

Let us turn now to verse 29. It contains two statements that need to be carefully distinguished. The first applies to Thomas and, as we noted earlier, to the other disciples as well: they believed because they had seen. The second statement, however, is addressed to the entire Church: "Blessed are those who have not seen and yet believe." The first part of this verse, then, is addressed to the apostles, the second part to the Church and to us. And yet the first part of verse 29 is important for us too. Our faith, after all, is not faith in a doctrine but faith in a historical person, in the Jesus who died and rose. The reality of the historical person and his glorification is assured us by the apostles, whose essential role was to be witnesses to others.

The end of the pericope (vv. 30-31) make clear the purpose of John in writing his Gospel. He has carefully chosen the "signs" or miracles of Jesus that he found the most suitable for rousing faith. His Gospel is in the service of the Church's faith and mission, which is to bring men to faith in Jesus. The recently founded Christian community will perdure and grow only if its faith is strong and persevering. In the Fourth Gospel, faith is either stimulated by the "sign" or miracle, or it is the direct result of the "sign."

The same law holds in the sacramental life of the Church. If a person is to enter into that life, he must already have the gift of faith to some degree. And yet, at the same time, faith is a gift received in and through the sacrament itself. If we are to be transformed and to live in Christ, we need faith, which is the condition for the sacramental life and the access to the "signs." Yet it is these very "signs" that bestow faith on us and assure its growth and strength.

The life of the first community

The faith we have been discussing is a faith that does not depend on seeing; it does, however, depend on the full experience of the sacramental signs and, even more basically, of the ecclesial community, which is itself a sign of the death and resurrection of Christ. That is the kind of faith that characterizes the first Christian community, as it must characterize every community that claims Christ for its Lord.

The first reading in each year of the three-year cycle presents this first Christian community to us. Cycle A shows us the group in its life of faith [5]. The activity of this united community for which Christ prayed in chapter 17 of the Fourth Gospel has four components that are especially singled out: fidelity in listening to the instruction of the apostles; a life of brotherly communion; the breaking of bread; and common prayer. These four characteristic activities are briefly stated in the first reading.

The first community was the fruit produced by the Spirit of the risen Christ; it was also constantly being sustained and built up by the hearing of the words of the apostles, who had been witnesses to the resurrection. Note how the passage begins by emphasizing the patience and continuity that characterize each of the four activities: the first Christians "devoted themselves to" (literally: they persisted or persevered in) the four activities that their life as a group comprised.

The faithful listened, then, to the teachings and instructions of the apostles. From now on, it was through the apostles that the Lord would speak; they are the men the Lord has "sent," and it is their task to present the faith to others, since they have been witnesses of all that occurred from the beginning to the day when the Spirit was sent (Acts 1:8, 21; Luke 24:48). The teaching and instruction the apostles gave has come to us in those marvelous documents whose truth is guaranteed by their divine inspiration: the four Gospels and the letters of the apostles, the latter being, as it were, a more concrete commentary on the Gospels, with emphasis on particular points of which the faithful needed to be reminded. Other readings from the Acts of the Apostles will give us an idea of how the apostles went about their task of instructing men; especially to be noted are the sermons of Peter and Paul.

This picture of the first Christians perseveringly listening to the instruction of the apostles will always be relevant to the Church. Heresy and schism result precisely from a failure to listen perseveringly and from a refusal to accept the teaching of the Lord's envoys. Surely this example of the first community is especially necessary today.

The faithful also lived in close communion with one another. Fraternal communion, however, does not mean having a shared mystical vision of reality or repeating platitudes that never flow over into action. On the contrary, the *koinonia* — a word which people today are constantly using in and out of season, but which Luke uses only in this passage — quite clearly means, in its context here, the sharing of all possessions, as is made clear in Acts 2:44-45, "And all who believed were together and had all things in common; and they sold their possessions and goods and distributed them to all, as any had need."

The *koinonia*, or communion, is thus very realistic and affects men at the material level. And yet, if the communion were limited to this, it would not suffice to make the community "Christian," for we can find the sharing of possessions practiced apart from any reference to Christianity. "Communion" here looks beyond material sharing to an attitude inspired by a living faith and manifested in prayer and especially in the celebration of the Eucharist in the homes of the community.

The faithful devoted themselves, we are told, "to the breaking of bread." The words and their specific meaning are much discussed. We may admit, however, with a good number of exegetes, that the words refer to the Eucharist and not simply to the ritual that marked the beginning of an ordinary meal. At the same time, we should not focus on this verse with the intention of giving a historical or theological proof that a Eucharistic celebration was indeed meant. It is better to say simply that Christian tradition has seen in the words a reference to the Eucharist. As for its being celebrated in homes, that is something that is frequently mentioned (1 Cor. 16:19; Rom. 16:5; Col. 4:15; Philemon 2).

The faithful also devoted themselves to prayer in the temple. This explains why the patterns of Christian prayer will be those of Jewish prayer before it. What we now call the "liturgy of the word" at Mass took over the scheme of the Jewish liturgy and especially of prayer in the synagogue. When St. Justin Martyr describes the Christian celebration on Sundays, his account of the liturgy of the word might well be an account of the Jewish synagogal liturgy.[178]

The final point made in today's first reading is that the community grew because the Lord drew into it those whom he was calling to salvation.

Such was the character of the first Christian community. The first reading in Cycles B and C will fill out the picture a bit more.

Psalm 118, chosen as responsorial psalm for this reading,

sings of the stone that was rejected by the builders but nonetheless became the cornerstone.

One heart and one soul

The first reading in Cycle B once again characterizes the community, but this time by means of a trait that was among the most eye-catching of all: the unity that allows St. Luke to speak of the community as possessing "one heart and soul" [6]. The sharing of possessions, however, is also mentioned once again, while a new characteristic makes its appearance: the witness given by the apostles.

If, then, the early community as a whole, because of its unity and its sharing of possessions, played a prominent part in the life of the Church, we should not let that make us forget the role of the apostles. The latter have a place apart in the Acts of the Apostles, and their most characteristic function is to give witness. They continue to be teachers, as we have already seen, and the community listens devotedly to them, but they also carry out this ministry of witnessing on the broader scene to the world at large. They do this in two ways: through preaching (preaching that is frequently bold and courageous, leading to beatings and imprisonment) and, in imitation of Christ, through miracles, as the Book of Acts specifically mentions (2:43; 5:12). The purpose of these miracles is to rouse faith in the presence of the risen Christ. In Acts, Peter is the one who most frequently gives witness by his sermons and miracles (3:1-10; 9:32-35, 36-42). The envoys of Christ are thus able to see in their own persons the fulfillment of Christ's promises (Luke 9:1; 10:9).

A growing community

The first reading in Cycle C emphasizes the growth of the community [7]. What Acts is here reporting is a kind of miracle of faith, and the miracle is due to the Spirit who guides the Church in its mission and expansion. The expansion, in other words, is not the result of propaganda that is intended, as in politics, to augment the number of sympathizers and adherents. The truth is that "the Lord added to their number day by day those who were being saved" (Acts 2:47). The source of the Church's fruitfulness in her mission is Jesus and the Spirit whom he has sent (Acts 2:41, 47; 4:4; 5:14; 6:7; 11:21; 21:20). In today's reading, St. Luke observes that more and more men and women were "added to the Lord" through faith. He is showing how powerful was the gift of the Spirit who led men to faith in the resurrection of Christ and in his various mysteries.

Faith in the risen Christ

The second reading in each of the three cycles focuses on an aspect of the theology of the resurrection.

The risen Jesus and our rebirth

The second reading in Cycle A reminds us that we owe the grace of our rebirth to the resurrection of Jesus [8]. The "blessing" or thanksgiving with which the letter begins (after the greeting) and its reference to rebirth have suggested to exegetes that the letter here incorporates a baptismal liturgy. That is quite possible. At any rate, there can be no doubt that the author is referring to rebirth through baptism. It is another matter, of course, to see in the passage a liturgical composition used in baptism, namely, a hymn composed for the baptismal liturgy of that time.[179]

The structure and style of the first verses are not original but reflect Jewish prayer patterns in which the person praying blesses or praises the Lord, and marvels at what he has done and continues to do for his people. The formula is one that we find even in our oldest Eucharistic prayers.[180] In the passage from the First Letter of Peter, the Jewish prayer form is immediately filled with a Christian content: he who is "blessed" or praised is the Father of our Lord Jesus

Christ who has given us rebirth and a living hope by raising Jesus from the dead. The words "born anew" do not of themselves necessarily refer to baptism; but we must bear in mind the liturgical context of the reading on the second Sunday of Easter, a time when we are still in the atmosphere created by the Easter Vigil, in which rebirth is so closely linked to the death and resurrection of Christ.

The most important point in the reading, however, and the point that should give strength and vitality to the Christian community, is the fact of the resurrection, for that is the basis of the hope shared by all the children of God. Hope here does not mean expectation pure and simple, for we already possess, in a way, the reality for which we hope. The passage makes this reality, that is, the object of our hope, quite clear: it is the inheritance being kept for us in heaven.

Because we are advancing toward the goal, present trials cannot deaden our sense of joy; no crisis, however serious, can lessen the interior joy of the community and of the individual Christian who knows by faith the treasure that is already his. The faith, however, must be of a high order; it must have a quality that is tested by the trials he must yet endure for a while. The joy that springs from faith — the faith that believes without seeing, faith in the person of Christ who died but has risen and is now living in the Church — should transform the Christian and his entire life, for, as the end of the pericope says, "As the outcome of your faith you obtain the salvation of your souls."

If we look back now over the whole liturgy of the word for the second Sunday of Easter in Cycle A, we do not find the kind of thematic unity that forces itself on our attention. Yet, without straining for points of contact, we can say that the liturgy possesses a real unity. Christ appears to Thomas and tells him what he, Christ, understands by faith. This faith, which is of a spiritual kind, being faith in the word of God, gives rise in the Christian community to deep-rooted attitudes of prayer, sharing of material goods, and perseverance in breaking bread together; these attitudes in turn astonish outsiders and bring new members into the community. The community is constantly "blessing" the God who, through faith in the resurrection of His Son, sustains it in the joy of possessing, in sure hope, the inheritance of salvation.

Such is the vitally important and always relevant lesson the Lord himself teaches his disciples who listen to him in the liturgical proclamation that actualizes his word.

Child of God and conqueror of the world

The second reading for this Sunday in Cycle B emphasizes the efficacy of faith; it tells us that the believer is a child of God and overcomes the world [9]. The community that sought to live as having "one heart and soul" [6] needed this encouraging vision at the moment when it had to move out into a hostile world. Earlier in this same letter John had written: "He who loves is born of God" (1 John 4:7). Now he shifts his attention to faith in the person of Christ: "Every one who believes that Jesus is the Christ is a child of God" (1 John 5:1).

This personal faith was all the more necessary at a time when the new community was hardly fully distinct as yet from Judaism; it must inevitably think of Jesus as Messiah and believe him to be the expected Messiah. This is also a frequent topic of preaching in the early Church (Acts 5:42; 9:22; 17:3; 18:28; John 9:22). Faith, then, insofar as it meant adherence to the person of Jesus, could not but be the belief that he was both Messiah and Son of God.

Overcoming the world presupposes such a faith in the Son of God. St. John is certainly concerned to make it clear just what "faith" involves, since there was, and always will be, the danger of self-deception, inasmuch as a person may "believe" and yet in no way alter the way he lives. St. John, therefore, knowing his Church from experience, wants to make plain the realistic conditions that faith requires. Concretely, a person who believes will obey the commandments; that is what enables the faith of Christians to overcome the world and makes faith a conquering power.

Christ had said, in order to hearten his disciples, "Be of good cheer, I have overcome the world" (John 16:33). If we believe in the person of Christ Jesus, we shall share in this victory of his, which is such a favorite theme of John's. In other words, the person (after Christ) who overcomes the world is the one who believes that Jesus is the Son of God and who — we must add with St. John — lives in accordance with this faith of his.

Such a faith would not be possible in a world so opposed to it unless the Spirit himself bore witness. Amid the storm, when the entire world is rejecting Christ, Christians will have the help of the Spirit whom Christ promised them for their witnessing (John 15:26) and will continue to believe unwaveringly in Jesus. It is the Spirit who will make their faith unwavering, because he will make known to us the full revelation that is present in the person of Jesus (John 14:6).

If we look back over the liturgy of the word for the second Sunday of Easter in Cycle B, we find that it embodies a rich conception, namely, that Christ by his resurrection has created a community that is one in heart and mind, a community convinced that it will overcome the world because it believes in the person of Christ, a community enlightened by the Holy Spirit who manifests divine revelation in its fullness.

Christ died but now lives for ever

In continuity with ancient tradition, especially in the Spanish Church, the Church chooses a pericope from the Apocalypse for the second reading in Cycle C [10]. The passage is a thrilling proclamation of the reality of the Lord's resurrection. The Jesus of whom the passage speaks is the Son of Man, the Head of the Church, and the Master of the entire history of salvation.

The letter to the seven churches of Asia is addressed to a

suffering Christian community that is being persecuted but at the same time is persevering with Jesus like the royal nation of priests that it is. The only reason, moreover, why the Church and the Apostle are experiencing this difficult time is their faith in the risen Jesus and their preaching of the word.

It is on a Sunday, the Lord's Day, that John has his first vision (v. 10). This simple fact has a deeper significance, since Sunday is the day when the Church is most deeply aware of the resurrection of Christ. That is also the day on which he writes, and his correspondents are the churches of Asia Minor.

His vision, though written in the style of the time, is easy to interpret. The seven golden lampstands are evidently the seven churches to which John is to write. The central figure, however, is the Son of Man; this is important, because the vision is meant to tell the seven churches the precise object of their faith.

The expression "Son of Man" occurs first in the Book of Daniel (ch. 7). It becomes complex and acquires various meanings in the course of time, but the important thing for us is that Jesus himself uses the expression with the reference to himself (Matthew 17:9 and Mark 9:9-13; Matthew 17:22, Mark 9:30-32, and Luke 9:44-45; Matthew 20:18, Mark 10:32-34, and Luke 18:31-33; Mark 8:31, Matthew 16:13-20, and Luke 9:18-21). The title comes from Jewish apocalyptic, but Jesus enriches it by applying it to the one who came as "Servant" to save men by sacrificing his own life, and to be glorified. In addition, the title has an eschatological aspect as it is used by Christ: The Son of Man will come at the end of time in order to judge. According to the Synoptics, Jesus presents himself to the Sanhedrin as Son of Man (Matthew 26:57-66; 27:2; Mark 14:53-64; 15:1; Luke 22:66-69). John has his own way of putting it: "The Father . . . has given him authority to execute judgment, because he is the Son of man" (John 5:27). The title became important to the faith of the early Christians, and St. Stephen will say when he is about to die: "Behold, I see the heavens opened, and the Son of man standing at the right hand of God" (Acts 7:56).

The Apocalypse enters into even greater detail on the person of the Son of Man. The latter himself tells John who he is: "I am the first and the last" — that is, God — "and the living one" — an expression that conjures up the paschal mystery in which the dead Christ rises to everlasting life and henceforth holds "the keys of Death and Hades."

John's vision in the Apocalypse thus shows us the Son of Man as possessed of the new status that is his by reason of the resurrection. In Christian eyes, the Son of Man is first and foremost the risen Christ who sits at the Father's right hand and will come to judge the living and the dead.

The three readings in Cycle C thus show us the risen Christ as the object of the community's faith and the focus of its life; he draws men to the Church so that he may bestow salvation upon them.

The opening prayer for this second Sunday emphasizes the role of faith and asks God's help in living that faith: "God of mercy, you wash away our sins in water, you give us new birth in the Spirit, and redeem us in the blood of Christ. As we celebrate Christ's resurrection increase our awareness of these blessings, and renew your gift of life within us." [181]

The entrance antiphon exhorts the Christian community to be eager for God's word, which will make it grow toward salvation: "Like newborn children you should thirst for milk, on which your spirit can grow to strength."

THIRD SUNDAY OF EASTER

17. THE RISEN CHRIST APPEARS TO HIS DISCIPLES

[A] "He was known to them in the breaking of the bread"

We have already read and commented on the story of the two disciples at Emmaus, since it was read at the afternoon Mass on Easter Sunday.

The first reading is from St. Peter's sermon on Pentecost [14]. In it Peter proclaims the resurrection of Christ, and does it firmly and even harshly: "This Jesus, delivered up according to the definite plan and foreknowledge of God, you crucified and killed by the hands of lawless men. But God raised him up, having loosed the pangs of death, because it was not possible for him to be held by it" (Acts 2:23-24).

Peter's words are addressed to people who know the facts, and he reminds them that God has sent Jesus to them "with mighty works and wonders and signs . . . as you yourselves know" (v. 22). Despite the signs, they put him to death; others did the evil deed, but the Jews were no less guilty. Now this Jesus has risen from the dead! Peter here quotes Psalm 16, which also serves as the responsorial psalm after the reading: "For thou dost not give me up to Sheol, or let thy godly one see the Pit" (v. 10).

Redeemed by the blood of the Lamb

The second reading continues to develop this life-giving theology of Christ's death and resurrection [17]. The First Letter of Peter reminds us that we have been redeemed by the blood of the Lamb, and the Christian community must bear its true state in mind: "You know that you were ransomed from the futile ways inherited from your fathers . . .

with the precious blood of Christ, like that of a lamb without blemish or spot" (1 Peter 1:18-19).

Peter is here giving a Christian content to Isaiah's Servant songs (Is. 42:1-4; 49:1-6; 50:4-9; 52:13–53:12). We must be on guard, however, against thinking that our redemption was effected solely by the blood of the Lamb, thus separating our liberation from the guilt of sin from the gift of new life that comes through the resurrection. That kind of one-sided theology misses the full content of the paschal mystery; there have been writers accustomed to speak simply of "redemption." There was nothing wrong with the term itself; the mistake was to stop short at the death of Christ and to link our redemption exclusively with this death, the resurrection of Christ being simply a proof of Christ's divinity and of the success of his mission. Many manuals of theology and a large number of spiritual books followed this line. It was even thought at times that the Quartodecimans (who celebrated the Pasch on the 14th of Nisan, date of the Jewish Passover) were celebrating chiefly the death of Christ, while the rest of the Church, which celebrated the Pasch on the Sunday after the 14th of Nisan, was thinking primarily of the resurrection. This interpretation, based on imagination rather than on texts and facts, has now been shown to be false.[182]

We need not force the texts in order to show the liturgical unity of this third Sunday in Cycle A. The Gospel pericope, in the context of the liturgical celebration, acquires a properly Eucharistic reference: the two disciples at Emmaus had come to know him "in the breaking of the bread." The Jesus who broke bread for his disciples at Emmaus is the Nazorean whose death and resurrection Peter proclaims on Pentecost. He is the spotless Lamb who shed his blood and has risen from the dead to liberate us. It is this one Christ who is the object of our faith and of the faith of the Church.

[B] The resurrection on the third day as foretold by the prophets

The Gospel for the third Sunday in Cycle B likewise tells the community about an appearance of the risen Jesus [21]. The new appearance takes place while the two disciples who have returned from Emmaus are still telling their fellows what had happened to them.

The ending of this pericope is very important, for it provides us with insight into the method followed in catechetics by the early Church: the method of starting with Scripture. Here the risen Christ opens the minds of his disciples to the understanding of the Scriptures and shows how the prophets had foretold the sufferings of the Messiah, his resurrection from the dead on the third day, and the fact that "repentance and forgiveness of sins should be preached in his name to all nations, beginning from Jerusalem" (Luke 24:47). The apostles are to be his witnesses.

Here we have a catechesis, but also a mission or program that the risen Christ assigns to his new community. But the catechesis comes after he has first given them a physical demonstration of his resurrection by showing them his wounds and eating a piece of broiled fish that they offer him. Christ wants to make sure that the disciples realize that he is the same Jesus who had lived with them before, that he is now alive again, still in the body, even if a transformed body. He is present with them again as a sign that all the prophecies are now fulfilled.

We must remember, however, that while Jesus thus gives signs showing that he has truly risen, these signs are not enough by themselves. They have to be understood, and this requires faith, since a true recognition of the risen Christ does not stop short at his human nature but penetrates beyond it.

Luke is very much concerned with the theme of the fulfillment of the Scriptures; he is the only one of the evangelists to emphasize it to such an extent. St. John says that the Scriptures could not be understood until Christ had risen from the dead, entered his glory, and sent his Spirit (John 2:22; 12:16; 13:8; 14:26). Luke tells us how the Scriptures in fact came to be understood, but he does not wait for the sending of Jesus' Spirit; instead, he describes the enlightenment as taking place when Christ appears to his disciples after the resurrectiion. Are John and Luke to be reconciled? Yes. The disciples begin to understand the Scriptures from Easter on; at the same time, however, there are moments when their understanding is radically increased, and the coming of the Spirit is a moment that advances this considerably.

The apostles are witnesses to the resurrection and to the fulfillment of the Scriptures. They must now proclaim to the Gentiles what they have seen and what they know. That is the starting point for the expansion of the Church.

Peter and his message

Peter is fully aware of his mission to be a witness and to preach conversion, as his discourse in chapter 3 of the Acts of the Apostle shows [15]. He addresses the people and proclaims the Lord's resurrection, reminding them once again that it was the Jewish people who put the Messiah to death, though he was the Author of life. Peter himself is a witness to the resurrection. He reminds his hearers that in the recent events the Scriptures have been fulfilled. The people must therefore be converted and return to God so that their sins may be forgiven.

Such is the theme of the first reading, and it is closely related to the Gospel of the day, since conversion is precisely what Christ bids his apostles preach as witnesses to the resurrection, which is the central object of faith.

The responsory psalm (Ps. 4) prays the Lord to make himself known: "Lift up the light of thy countenance upon us, O Lord! Thou hast put joy in my heart" (vv. 7-8).

Christ, the Victim for our sins

Faith in Christ brings forgiveness of our sins, but the daily struggle remains. St. John was very conscious of it and speaks of it in the second reading [18]. He seems to have been afraid of any abstract mysticism. The resurrection of Christ is not simply an external fact that should induce wonder; it must lead to conversion, and conversion supposes an effort to observe the commandments and avoid sin. Only if we meet this condition can we be sure that we really "know" Christ, the Victim who was sacrificed for our sins.

The love of God reaches its perfection in the person who faithfully keeps God's word. The believer, then, faces moral demands that he must take very seriously. Yet John is also aware how weak men are, and he assures his readers: "If any one does sin, we have an advocate with the Father, Jesus Christ the righteous" (1 John 2:1).

This statement requires at least a brief explanation. How does John understand Christ's role as "intercessor"? We shall have occasion later on to focus our attention again on the meaning of the term *parakletos*, "Paraclete," which means in general "someone called to another's side," an advocate, a defender whose function is to help and encourage. In our present passage Jesus himself acts as Defender before the Father. He is a Mediator, and the language here refers us to the priestly activity of Christ as presented to us in the Letter to the Hebrews (7:25; 9:24).

It is as Victim for our sins that Christ stands as our Advocate before the Father. But he cannot exercise this role in our favor unless we know him. The Christian must therefore "experience God," as we like to say nowadays. This experience, however, is not some abstractly mystical experience but takes the form of observing the commandments. It is easy to determine whether or not we "know" Christ. Simply ask: Do I observe his commandments? For knowing Christ, like knowing God, is not, in John's view, a narrowly intellectual, conceptual activity;

knowledge in this instance means a concrete, interpersonal relationship with Christ, and the moral quality of our life provides a criterion for determining how real the relationship is.

"Whoever keeps his word, in him truly love for God is perfected" (1 John 2:5). We might think that "love of God" here means our love for him, that is, the love in which we take a certain initiative by giving ourselves to him because we obey his commandments and thus truly "know" him. But the text is susceptible of another interpretation: In the person who observes the commandments and thus knows Christ, divine love is able to enter in without hindrance; it can fill him completely and free him by making him fully an adoptive child of God.

[C] Peter, fisherman and shepherd

The Gospel for the third Sunday in Cycle C tells us of the appearance of the risen Christ to his apostles as they were fishing in the Sea of Tiberias [22]. There is a miraculous catch; Christ gives his disciples bread and fish to eat; Peter avows his love and is appointed shepherd of the Church. The passage has a grandeur about it, and it is so important for the life of the Church of every age that it calls for some words of commentary.

To begin with, the writer of the passage seems to have freighted it with symbolism, and we must find the key that will unlock for us the meaning of the words and the events. Critical exegetical scholarship regards chapter 21 as a later addition to the Gospel, whether by John himself or by one of his collaborators. The Gospel could nicely have ended with chapter 20, although every known manuscript of the Gospel contains chapter 21; evidently this chapter was always known as part of the Fourth Gospel. On the other hand, the exegetes also think that chapter 21 was written long after Peter suffered martyrdom (about thirty years later). These various points must be kept in mind as we listen to the Gospel being read.

This particular passage seems to have been chosen for this Sunday's liturgy in order to call attention to Peter as the witness who converts others and as the shepherd of the Church. The first reading [16] likewise presents Peter as the witness who is willing to be a martyr: he preaches the death and resurrection of Christ, and is beaten for his preaching.

In the Gospel pericope, Peter says that he is going fishing; Thomas, Nathanael, the sons of Zebedee, and two other disciples decide to go with him. We may legitimately discern a deliberate message being conveyed through the simple statement of fact: Peter is a fisherman and will be a fisher of men; but he is accompanied by other apostles and disciples who share his role. However, apart from the command and power of Christ, the fishing is fruitless; St. John emphasizes the point, telling us that "that night they caught nothing" (John 21:3). Then, at dawn, Christ stands there on the shore, and when he gives the order to cast the net, it is soon so filled with fish that it is in danger of breaking.

It is at this moment that John, the disciple whom Jesus loved, recognizes the risen Christ. We should note, here as elsewhere, the difficulty that the disciples had in immediately recognizing the risen Christ, and the concern of John to emphasize that the Christ was real.

The catch is clearly miraculous, and it is the stimulus that causes the disciples to recognize Jesus at last, even though all along he has been only about a hundred yards away. There are one hundred and fifty-three fish in the net, but despite this the net has not broken, as John points out. The number, which is clearly arbitrary, must have had a symbolic meaning that escapes us. Just what the meaning was is not important (since no hint of it is given), but it shows that the author had a specific intention in writing the story and that we must in general be attentive to the symbols he uses.

The apostles and other disciples now eat with Jesus, but it is Jesus who gives them the bread and fish — purely an inescapable reminder of the multiplication of the loaves and fishes (John 6:1-21). There is no multiplication in the present case, but there seems to be the same Eucharistic significance: Jesus gives the bread that is the bread of life, and he gives the fish that is himself. (We may recall that the Greek word for "fish," *ichthus*, was also an acronym used by the early Christians and stood for "Jesus Christ, Son of God, Savior" [*Iesous Christos theou uios soter*].) In addition, just as the story of the multiplication of the loaves and fishes had an eschatological reference, that is, reminded the hearers of the banquet of the kingdom at the end of time (this is why the passage is read during Advent), so this meal of Christ with his disciples has the same eschatological reference. We need not press the symbolism too far and try to find in the details of the account a whole set of eschatological symbols. The fact that the risen Christ, victorious over death, is eating with his disciples, and the presence of the fish, which symbolizes the saved, are sufficiently eloquent; no further details are needed.

Now we come to the main point of the account, at least from the viewpoint of the Church as it celebrates this liturgy of the word, namely, Peter's protestation of love and his investiture as shepherd of the flock. Here, perhaps, we should recall that at the beginning of the story Peter had stripped as he worked in the boat. Should not this fact be noted? John points it out and remarks that Peter threw on some clothes before jumping into the water and going ashore. His nakedness reminds us, does it not, of his human condition, nudity being the sign both of sin and of wretchedness generally?

We may ask why Christ, in his desire to know Peter's love from his own mouth, should ask the question three times. Perhaps the triple repetition simply reflects Christ's concern. May we also see in it Christ's intention of eliciting a triple profession of love that will counterbalance Peter's triple denial? But the repetition seems due rather to the solemnity of the moment and to a form of investiture often used in order to emphasize importance; it is the kind of thing people used to do in sealing unwritten contracts.

In any case, the important thing for us is the investiture of Peter as leader of the flock. It is because of his great role as shepherd that his Lord requires of him a special love beyond that which others have. Peter will have to bear witness to the point of martyrdom and will have to strengthen his brethren in the faith. The account implies that the task entrusted to Peter is entrusted to his successors as well. They too will have to have a love for the Lord greater than that of other men.

The Lord then tells Peter that his role of witness will lead him to a violent death for the glory of God.

Peter, the witness

The first reading [16] shows Peter exercising the function he had received of being a witness to the resurrection. He answers the high priest's accusation of disobedience by saying that the apostles must obey God rather than men. He then goes on to tell the Jews that though they had put Jesus to death, God raised him up and made him the Savior who brings Israel repentance and the forgiveness of sins. He then asserts, as he had on previous occasions: "We are witnesses to these things." The apostles are whipped but nonetheless they depart "rejoicing that they were counted worthy to suffer dishonor for the name."

The Lamb slain and glorified

The second reading proclaims John's fervent vision of the risen Christ's glorification as the Lamb triumphant whom the whole world blesses and praises in a majestic doxology [19]. This Christ, slain but now victorious, is the one who has appeared to the apostles and given them the commission to preach his paschal mystery; he is the one who appeared to Peter and made him shepherd of all who will enter the community.

FOURTH SUNDAY OF EASTER

18. THE GOOD SHEPHERD

The theme of the Good Shepherd appears in the Gospel throughout the three-year cycle, since the three pericopes are taken from chapter 10 of St. John. At first sight, it seemed better to give here, under the fourth Sunday, a complete picture of Christ the Good Shepherd as it is presented in the three passages. But a further factor had to be taken into account, namely, that in each year of the complete cycle the other readings provide a specifying framework for the Gospel pericope. We prefer, therefore, to limit ourselves in each instance to the complex of readings as offered in the liturgy for each year of the cycle.

[A] Christ, the Door of the sheep

"I am the door of the sheep": this statement, which comes after a careful explanatory preparation, is the central theme of the Gospel for the fourth Sunday in Cycle A [29]. How is the statement to be understood? A door opens and closes — and such is the activity Jesus exercises. He speaks of "all who came before me" as "thieves and robbers," for he alone is the Door; anyone, therefore, who attempts to enter by any other door can only be a thief and a robber.

When others came, before Jesus, and called to the sheep, the sheep did not heed and follow them, for in their call the sheep did not recognize the voice of the true Shepherd. Jesus thus condemns his enemies and all who seek to teach without having been sent by the Father. All such come forward on their own authority, and whatever they do is for their own profit; they seek their own glory (cf. John 7:18), and their deeds are destructive. But if anyone enters through the only true Door, which is Jesus, he finds salvation and life. Entering through Jesus is thus a necessity for anyone who wants to be saved; if he enters through Jesus, he enters the fold of which Jesus alone is the Shepherd.

The glorified Christ

In his sermon on Pentecost, Peter exhorts his hearers precisely to enter into the fold through the only true Door: Christ, who is risen from the dead and lives forevermore [23]. The theme of Peter's preaching never varies: it is always Christ, whom the Jews crucified and whom God raised up. The Jews must therefore be converted and accept baptism in the name of Jesus if they are to receive the gift of the Spirit. They must pass through the true Door into the fold, where they will find green pastures. That means, however, that they must turn away from the thieves and marauders, "this crooked generation," and listen to the voice of the true shepherd.

The responsorial psalm (Ps. 23) expresses this faith in the true Shepherd; it also sketches out the journey of the baptized person through the sacramental mysteries. It is the classic psalm to be sung at Christian initiation, and the Church has restored it to its rightful place.

We are healed and have come back to the Shepherd

We must therefore be converted, that is, stop wandering hither and yon and return to the Shepherd who is "the Guardian of your souls" [26]. To this we are exhorted in the second reading. Returning to the Shepherd, however, also means imitating him in our everyday lives. If we suffer, we should praise God for it; suffering, after all, is what we have been called to, since Christ first suffered for us and left us an example so that we might follow after him. We must die to our sins and live holy lives. Such a course is really possible for us, since our Shepherd carried our sins in his own body on the wood of the Cross.

The unity of the three readings is clear by reason of the very broad but meaningful link between them. Anyone who wants to hear and understand and who believes that Christ, really present, is addressing his kindly but demanding message to us today cannot continue to live as he did before. The celebration of the liturgy requires that we examine our conscience and be converted to a truly Christian life within Christ's fold.

[B] "The good shepherd lays down his life for the sheep"

On the fourth Sunday in Cycle B, Christ shows himself to us as the Good Shepherd who gives his life for his sheep [30]. In fact, giving his life is the sign by which we recognize him as a genuine shepherd. But among all the shepherds, Christ alone can give his life in a way that is completely effective, for his sacrifice is unique, being the self-giving of the Son to the Father in obedience to the Father's will. Christ is the only shepherd capable of giving his life in such an efficacious manner.

Because of his total dedication, the Good Shepherd knows his sheep and they know him. The "knowledge" here consists in the active, personal relationship described in the first part of the chapter: the Shepherd calls his sheep by name (John 10:3); he takes jealous care of them (10:8, 12); above all, he gives them life by sacrificing his own (10:10). The sheep in turn know their Shepherd, recognize his voice, and follow him (10:4). We must also note, however, the parallel Jesus uses: he knows his sheep and his sheep know him "as the Father knows me and I know the Father" (10:15). This parallel shows the knowledge to be interpersonal, involving the closest possible kind of union, namely, a union of the kind that exists between Father and Son.

In applying the title of Shepherd to himself, Jesus takes over a favorite theme of the Old Testament. A man can enter into a relation with the Lord and know him only if the Lord himself offers it. It is the Lord who chooses and calls men to the office of shepherd (Is. 16:7; Jer. 1:5). The result is a close relation between shepherd and sheep, comparable to the relation between the Lord and the man who reverences him.

St. John then goes on to speak of one of his central concerns: the Church, its formation and its future. Church means unity, and the unity comes from Christ: "There shall be one flock, one shepherd" (John 10:16). The flock is formed by Christ himself, for it is he who calls the disciple (John 19:35; 20:29; 1 John 1:1-4). It is he who gives his life for the unity of the flock. To that end he has power from the Father.

No salvation but in Christ

The words we just quoted — "There shall be one flock, one shepherd" — have caused questioning and remorse among believers down to our own day. For over against those words there is "the scandal of the separation of Churches," and the faithful of today feel it more than ever before. The quest for union between the Churches is the response men of good will make to the words of Christ with their implicit command; these men hope that the Lord's words are a prophecy that describes the situation at the end: one flock at last.

The first reading emphasizes the need for such oneness: "There is salvation in no one else" [24]. The problem is that each Church believes in good faith that it is indeed with and in Christ! A single flock is possible only under a single Shepherd. The challenge, however, is to accept not only Christ, the one Shepherd, but also the human being who represents the one Shepherd. The drama of the incident reported in the first reading is concentrated precisely in that point: Peter is asked by what power or in whose name he has cured a cripple; he answers that he performed the cure, which was a sign, in the name of the risen Jesus, who is the Cornerstone; apart from this Jesus there is no salvation, for the Lord had made his Christ the foundation of his entire work.

The responsorial psalm (Ps. 118) makes the same point about Christ as the foundation: "The stone which the builders rejected has become the head of the corner. This is the Lord's doing; it is marvelous in our eyes" (vv. 22-23).

"We are God's children now"

Christ is the Shepherd of those who know God and have become his children. This relationship — being a child of God — is what God's love for us has given us. It is also what distinguishes us from, and opposes us to, the world: we are now the children of God, but "the world . . . did not know him" [27]. The theme of the second reading is thus a tragic one. We are now the children of God, and that is all that separates us from the world — but what a radical separation!

At the same time, however, we are ignorant of what we shall one day be, or at least that future state is not clear to us. We are certain, however, of one thing: when the Son of God appears, we shall be like him, for we shall see him as he is. Evidently there is an immense distance between what we now are and that future condition of which we are still ignorant and which others cannot see in us.

This First Letter of John really brings out the great problem that Christianity and the individual Christian face. We know what we really are, and we must live lives befitting men and women who are God's adopted children. But the world does not see or understand what we know to be true. In fact, we ourselves, though knowing that we are now God's children, do not know in any clear way what we shall one day be; that will become clear to us only when Christ returns. In the interim, we must live our lives both apart from the world and in the world, since we have already been bidden to live for the things above.

The entrance song, aware of what we already truly are, proclaims to the world: "The earth is full of the goodness of the Lord; by the word of the Lord the heavens were made, alleluia." The opening prayer expresses an awareness both of what we have become and of the difficulty of our present state: "Almighty and ever-living God, give us new strength from the courage of Christ our shepherd, and lead us to join the saints in heaven, where he lives and reigns with you and the Holy Spirit, one God, for ever and ever."

[C] **The Shepherd gives eternal life to his sheep**

The very short Gospel for the fourth Sunday in Cycle C is rich in the revelation it contains [31]. The key statement in it is: "I give them [my sheep] eternal life, and they shall never perish" (v. 28). The other theme has already been heard in Christ's portrayal of the Good Shepherd, namely, the interpersonal knowledge that is based, as far as man is concerned, on docility in hearing the word and on obedience in following after Jesus in everyday life.

The most important point made there, then, is that eternal life is the Good Shepherd's gift. Jesus is Life: he gives his own life for his flock (10:15) and wants them to have life in abundance (10:10). Now we are told that those who accept the relationship of interpersonal "knowledge" will never perish. This is a new way of promising the eternal life with which the Fourth Gospel is so concerned. Jesus continues the image of the shepherd who possesses and defends his sheep, by saying that no one can snatch them from the hand of the Father to whom he entrusts them, because he and the Father are one.

The baptized Christian feels a new strength flow into him from these words of Christ; he is also compelled to reflect on the responsibility that such a gift demands of him. The protection to which Christ refers is, after all, not a purely mechanical thing, an activity in which our receptivity plays no part. No, acceptance is a positive act, for it means heeding and following; it means being disposed for a difficult life of conflict, but one in which we are sure that victory is possible.

Salvation to the ends of the earth

This eternal life is the subject of the apostolic preaching; we hear Paul and Barnabas preaching it in today's first reading [25]. They had preached it first to the Jews, but were attacked for their pains. Now they turn to the pagans. They cannot remain silent, "for so the Lord has commanded us, saying, 'I have set you to be a light for the Gentiles, that you may bring salvation to the uttermost parts of the earth'" (Acts 13:47). The preaching is effective, and Luke tells us why, in a sentence not easy to interpret: "As many as were ordained to eternal life believed" (v. 48).

The Chosen People of God would not believe in his Son, who died and rose for their salvation. Therefore the preachers of the good news turn to the pagans, whom the Lord has already disposed. They turn to the pagans because salvation is meant to be universal, even if the Chosen People rightly had first place in the implementation of God's saving will. God must dispose men's hearts, for the Shepherd can give eternal life only to those who are willing to hear and accept him and follow him into the one fold.

The responsorial psalm (Ps. 100) picks up the theme of the first reading: "Know that the Lord is God! It is he that made us, and we are his; we are his people, and the sheep of his pasture" (v. 3).

The Lamb and Shepherd

The second reading, from John's apocalyptic vision, speaks of the fulfillment of what we heard about in the first reading [28]. The Apostle sees a huge crowd from every nation and race, people and tongue. They are standing before the throne and the Lamb, clad in white and carrying palm branches. One of the elders explains who these people are and whence they come: "These are they who have come out of the great tribulation; they have washed their robes and made them white in the blood of the Lamb. . . . They shall hunger no more, neither thirst any more. . . . For the Lamb in the midst of the throne will be their shepherd, and he will guide them to springs of living water; and God will wipe away every tear from their eyes" (vv. 14-17).

There is no need to dwell on the universality represented by the huge crowd. They give glory to God, and their whole attitude is one of contemplation and liturgical thanksgiving, for they are a people who have won a victory. They wear the white garments that symbolize the purification received in baptism. The idea of purifying garments in blood is doubtless strange, but the point is clear; the theology of purification and renewal has simply twisted the image for its own purposes. The blood is that which renews mankind and prepares them for the glorious resurrection with Christ; the white garments are thus a sign of victory and resurrection.

The crowd is a single unit directed by the staff of the Lamb, who is thus represented here as a Shepherd. The passage draws upon two classic texts from the earlier Scriptures: Psalm 23, in which the Lord is depicted as Israel's Shepherd, and the Book of Isaiah, chapter 49 (second Servant Song), on which verses 16-17 of the passage are based (cf. Is. 49:10).

John's vision is a vision of the victory of the one flock, which at last is united under a single leader: the Shepherd-Lamb who gave his life for his sheep.

FIFTH SUNDAY OF EASTER

19. MINISTRIES IN THE NEW COMMUNITY

The continuous reading of the Acts of the Apostles and of St. John's Gospel has the drawback that it is not always easy to link the various themes contained in the liturgy of the word. Nonetheless, we may note certain emphases that do give the fifth Sunday after Easter a character of its own. One such emphasis is on the organization of the new Christian community now that its Lord had risen and withdrawn his visible presence from his disciples. There was need of assuring that the services provided in the Church would be continuous, since ministries are indispensable not only for external organization but also for transmitting the word and the sacramental signs that the Lord had left to his followers.

While the reading of the Acts of the Apostles shows us the early Church's concern for the establishment of the needed ministries, the Gospel puts the emphasis rather on the deeper spiritual formation of this community that was called to follow Christ, the Way, the Truth, and the Life [38], to remain in Christ so that it might bear fruit [39], and to live in mutual love [40].

[A] Christ, the Way, the Truth, and the Life

The young Church had to be made deeply aware that no one can come to the Father except through Christ; that is a major theme in this Sunday's Gospel [38]. When Philip asks, "Show us the Father," and thereby reveals the apostles' continued failure to understand, Jesus takes the opportunity to emphasize once again his oneness with the Father: "I am in the Father and the Father in me" (v. 10). Faith in this truth is an absolute necessity; the energy for accomplishing great things comes from belief in the person of Christ. All the activity of the Church would be fruitless if she did not believe unconditionally in the true reality of Christ and in his oneness with the Father. The whole point of Christ's earthly works (according to the fourth Gospel) was to give proof of the unity that exists between the Father and himself.

Now Jesus foretells his departure from the earthly scene. At the moment when he is about to leave his disciples behind, he is concerned with the depth and clarity of their faith, since authentic faith is the basic reality that will direct the life of the young Church. Christ is truly the means of man's encounter with God, and the Church must continue this role of Christ, showing men the way to the Father. The Church is of course not identical with Christ, but Christ wills that the Church be, like him, the sign of the Father. In her lowly state (in this she is, once again, like

Christ) and always under the guidance of the Spirit, she too must be the Way, the Truth, and the Life.

In this passage from St. John, we find once again the word "know": "know" the Father, "know" Christ. The pericope clearly, if implicitly, shows the difference between the idea of "knowledge" as the Hebrew understood it and the idea of knowledge found in the Greek philosophers. To the Greek mind, knowing means abstracting, or else it means contemplating from without an object that is definitively what it is, so that we can form a concept of it. In this view of reality, God is outside of and apart from us; we contemplate him in himself as someone we try to reach by gradually elaborating a concept of him. "Truth" is attained when we grasp the essential characteristics of this God whom we contemplate and who remains always external to us.

For the Hebrew mind, knowing means experiencing the object of knowledge and entering into close relations with it. The Greek thinks of contemplating a God who remains changeless and apart from us; the Hebrew seeks to gain concrete experience of his God in his relations with men, to know him through his works. John's Gospel must be read against its cultural background. This means a context that is basically Hebrew but into which certain Greek elements have made their way; in other words, if we want to understand the terminology of the Fourth Gospel, we must not distinguish too simplistically and undiscerningly between Greek "knowing" and Hebrew "knowing." Nonetheless, Christ himself makes it quite clear what he means by "knowing." He means a concrete experience that is gained by seeing the works he himself does. Seeing them, the observer gains a concrete grasp of Christ's person. Once Christ has returned to the Father, our experiential knowledge of the Father will be gained by means of the signs Christ has left.

The Spirit and the laying on of hands

The Church's chief concern, then, is to continue to give the "signs" of Christ in order to make God visible and to enable men to experience him: to "see our God made visible," as the first preface for Christmas puts it. To this end, she must have at her disposal human beings who will devote themselves to the ministry of the word and to the humbler services that sustain even the material life of the faithful. In fact, it is the Spirit who chooses the individuals and gives them a special charism for the accomplishment of their task. Thus, in the first reading for today, seven spiritual men are chosen; the apostles then pray over them and impose hands on them [32]. Luke notes that the number of the disciples "multiplied greatly" and explicitly notes that among the converts were many Jewish priests.

A chosen race, a royal priesthood

Apart from these individuals with their special roles, the whole Church is a sign giving men access to the Father. As the Church grows, each Christian is a living stone in the building; that is, he is called to be such a stone, but if he is in fact to be such, he must have a vital faith in the person of the risen Jesus.

The second reading in today's liturgy, a passage from the First Letter of Peter [35], has at times been used as the foundation for a somewhat subjective theology that does not properly harmonize with the theology of the ordained ministry (itself admittedly not easy to establish on a Scriptural basis). The "priesthood" of which Peter speaks here has either been unduly limited or unduly extended. Some have interpreted the "priesthood" of the faithful as a simple analogy; that is, baptism and confirmation confer a priesthood that is merely analogous. At the other extreme, the text has been turned into a kind of priestly manifesto, a charter for an undifferentiated priesthood of all the faithful without distinction: every baptized person is in the fullest sense a priest; there can be no hierarchy within the Christian priesthood. The second interpretation was put forward by the Reformers at the time of the Council of Trent: "Every Christian a priest!"

The true meaning of the passage from the First Letter of Peter has been explained by the Second Vatican Council in its *Dogmatic Constitution on the Church*. Here is what the Council says:

> Christ the Lord, high priest taken from among men (cf. Heb. 5:1-5), made the new people "a kingdom of priests to God, his Father" (Apoc. 1:6; cf. 5:9-10). The baptized, by regeneration and the anointing of the Holy Spirit, are consecrated to be a spiritual house and a holy priesthood, that through all the works of Christian men they may offer spiritual sacrifices and proclaim the perfection of him who has called them out of darkness into his marvellous light (cf. 1 Peter 2:4-10).

If we were to stop here, we might interpret the Council as saying that the faithful are only analogously priests and make their offering in an exclusively spiritual way. But the text continues a few lines later:

> Though they differ essentially and not only in degree, the common priesthood of the faithful and the ministerial or hierarchical priesthood are none the less ordered one to another; each in its own proper way shares in the one priesthood of Christ.[183]

There is thus in fact only one priesthood, that of Christ; there are two essentially differing kinds of participation in it: the priesthood common to all the baptized and the priesthood of ordained ministers. The *Constitution* does not, however, give us full clarity on the real priesthood of the faithful. It speaks of the spiritual sacrifices the faithful are to offer; but when there is question of the Eucharist, the Council speaks only of the ministerial priesthood. Are we then to understand the "offering of sacrifice" in two different ways: a spiritual and purely interior offering, which is the task of the common priesthood, and a ritual, visible, external offering of the true sacrifice, which is the task of the ministerial or ordained priesthood? From such a distinction it would follow that the only true sacrifice is ritual and external, and thus offered solely by the hierarchical priesthood.

If such a distinction were proper, it would have serious consequences for the participation of the faithful in the liturgy. The center and high point of the whole liturgy is, after all, the Eucharistic sacrifice. If the sacrifice were offered visibly only by the ministerial priest, while the faithful with their common priesthood could offer only in a spiritual way, the priesthood of the faithful would indeed be merely analogous, and reducible to a nominal attribution to the faithful at large of prerogatives that were really proper to the ordained priest alone. But then how could we speak of the liturgy being offered by the Church as a whole, except in an analogous and metaphorical way? In any true and proper sense, the liturgy would really be the action only of the ordained priesthood.

Now, as a matter of fact, nowhere in the Christian tradition do we find such a distinction between a visible, external, ritual sacrifice and a spiritual sacrifice. On the contrary, in the teaching both of the prophets and of Christ we find that there is only one sacrifice: the spiritual sacrifice that consists in doing the Father's will (Jer. 7:22; Amos 5:21-25; Matthew 9:13; 12:7; Mark 12:33-34; John 4:23-24 and especially 2:14-17; Matthew 26:61; Mark 14:58). Thus the death of Christ is a spiritual sacrifice, the only kind that the Father can accept.

Christians too offer a spiritual sacrifice. The celebration of the Eucharist, being sacramental, is external and ritual, but the sacrifice of Christ that is actualized under the sacramental exterior is itself a spiritual, not an external, sacrifice. The spiritual sacrifice of Christ is rendered present, and the faithful are thus enabled to unite themselves fully with it; they unite themselves to the submission of Christ in doing the Father's will. The obedience and self-giving of the faithful — that is, their spiritual sacrifice — becomes in fact the matter for Christ's own sacrificial offering to the Father, inasmuch as he, the Head of the Church, joins their offering to his own; he unites his whole Church with him in offering his spiritual sacrifice of obedience to the Father's will.

While, then, we must not exaggerate what Peter says in his First Letter and turn the faithful into the same kind of priests as the ordained ministers, neither must we set up an opposition between the sacrifice offered by the ordained priest — an external, visible, ritual sacrifice, which alone would truly be sacrifice — and the sacrifice offered by the priestly faithful, which would consist simply in making an interior, spiritual offering.

We should recall here what was said earlier in this volume about the three sacraments of Christian initiation. God's plan of salvation is to restore the world to unity both within itself and with God so that he may thereby be glorified. Such a goal necessarily requires that men should do the Father's will. The Word incarnate can effect the restoration by offering his life as a sign of the complete dedication of his own will to the Father's. It is because he thus responds to the Father that he is the beloved Son the Father's voice proclaims him to be at his baptism and again at his transfiguration.

Through our baptism the Spirit has made us adopted sons of God; in our confirmation we have been officially deputed to share in the work of Christ. Doing his work requires that his sacrifice (the spiritual sacrifice signified by the shedding of his blood and his death) be actualized for us. The ministerial priest renders this service to the baptized and confirmed, having received from the Spirit the power to render the sacrifice of Calvary present. The ordained priest offers the sacrifice along with Christ, Head of the Church, whose priesthood as Head the ordained minister shares. The baptized and confirmed likewise offer the sacrifice thus rendered present, exercising the priesthood that is theirs as members of the Church. Christ makes his own the good will, the effort to live a better life, the sufferings of each of us, and makes them part of the spiritual sacrifice of praise, whose sign is the sacrifice of the Cross as made present in an unbloody manner.

On this fifth Sunday (Cycle A), then, we must learn to think of the Church as not being made up solely of the ministers who are ordained to provide the Church with a structure. We are uged, on the contrary, to look to our own priesthood, which is admittedly of its own kind, yet which also complements that of the ordained priest. Ordained priests and the rest of the baptized, even if their priesthood be essentially different in degree, must alike offer the one true spiritual sacrifice.

[B] Remain in Christ so that you may bear fruit

In the Gospel for the fifth Sunday in Cycle B, St. John uses a symbolism already familiar from the Old Testament [39]; in fact, it had been used in Hellenistic literature as well, the language being taken from agriculture. Yet, from the beginning, we sense that we must not get lost in symbolic details and that John is seeking to express in material terms the spiritual doctrine that Christ wants to teach. The aim is to bring out the unity and fraternal spirit proper to the Church. We must not, therefore, overemphasize the material details; the symbolism is evidently only a docile instrument, so much so that at points it is, as it were, overwhelmed by the higher doctrinal meaning John wishes to communicate.

The symbolism is that of the vineyard, but a grower who does not know what John is trying to express through it, and does not realize how the symbolism has been built up in the course of the centuries, would find it all very confusing.

The Old Testament applies the symbolism of the vine and vineyard to Israel, which is God's vineyard, but an unfaithful one. God's people, Israel, is his vineyard, yet Israel has attributed her fruitfulness to other gods rather than to the true God who is her Spouse (Osee 10:1; 3:1). The theme of the vine or vineyard is used in this context to highlight both the covenant and Israel's fruitfulness. Isaiah will make extensive use of the image. He describes the anger of God, who loves his vineyard yet receives from it nothing but wild grapes; he will therefore lay it waste (Is. 5:1-7). The situation changes, however, and love triumphs. Israel is a vine that the Lord transplanted from Egypt, where it had been held prisoner, and set in the soil of its own land.

Jeremias likewise deplores the sad state of the chosen vine (2:21; 8:13), which in the end will be destroyed (5:10; 12:10). Ezekiel too describes the infidelity of the vine (19:10-14; 17:5-19).

The Gospel pericope reminds the hearers of the need to bear good fruit and of the vinegrower's anxious concern for his vine. But this is not the main point of the passage. The central interest is in being united with the Lord and in glorifying him by bearing the fruit he wants. The main theme, therefore, is the close union between the Lord and his disciples. The Lord is the true Vine, of which the Father takes such care, and the branches grafted onto it must be careful to remain united to him.

Christ is evidently speaking of his Church and voicing his concern for the future of his Body. His desire is that each of us should remain united to him, for we will bear fruit only if we are one with the Church and thus with him. In this context we cannot but recall the splendid passage from the *Didache* that speaks as follows in a Eucharistic prayer over the cup: "We thank you, our Father, for the holy vine of David, your servant, which you revealed to us through Jesus, your Servant."[184] The *Didache*, however, seems to be thinking simply of the Church that is revealed to men by Jesus. St. John, on the other hand, applies the symbol of the vine directly to Christ who unites the members of the Church to himself and to one another.

There is, then, an exchange of love between Christ and each member of the Church, and between each member of the Church and the other members who are united to

Christ. This love and this union are the conditions required if the branches are to bear fruit and thus give glory to God. We remain in God through faith and through mutual love.

The second reading for this Sunday is a passage from St. John's First Letter [36] and serves as a kind of commentary on the Gospel passage. We will bear fruit, we are told, only if we believe in Jesus and if we love one another as he has commanded us. Through fidelity to the commandments, we remain in God and he remains in us; the gift of his Spirit is his sign to us that he indeed remains in us. We must take careful note of how very concrete John's instruction is, for its down-to-earth character will prevent us from indulging in a purely literary kind of theology of God's indwelling in us and our indwelling in God. John forces us to be very concrete and to measure our union with God by our observance of the commandments, especially the commandment of mutual love, practiced in an atmosphere of authentic faith in Christ.

The gradual expansion of the Church

The first reading for the fifth Sunday in Cycle B describes how Barnabas vouched for Paul to the community at Jerusalem [33]. The reading may seem rather remote from the other two readings of this liturgy, and yet a closer look will show that we are still speaking of the progressive building up of the Church in the years after the resurrection of Christ. Paul had seen the risen Christ and qualifies as an apostle and leader. The Church is gradually expanding as the Spirit brings in new members. The vine is becoming larger as new branches are grafted on through faith in the risen Christ, who is the primary object of the preaching of Paul and the other apostles.

[C] "Love one another"

The Eucharistic meal is finished, and Judas has left the Supper room [40]; the Passion of Christ has already begun. Jesus links his own glorification and that of his Father to the death that he foretells in veiled terms. His words are those of a man who has freely offered his life for the sake of doing the Father's will. His death is, however, also a sign of his love for his disciples (cf. 13:1), who must have the same kind of love for one another. "A new commandment I give to you, that you love one another; even as I have loved you, that you also love one another. By this all men will know that you are my disciples, if you have love for one another" (13:34-35).

As we listen to these words, we must not fail to link them with the Supper that Christ has been celebrating. Neither the words nor the Supper belong simply to the past. Christ speaks the words here and now as we listen to them; Christ is here and now celebrating the Supper he instituted the night before he died, thereby actualizing his glorious Passion and making it the source of our union with him and with each other. The sign by which men will recognize us is the sign of brotherly love that is grounded in the Eucharist, that is, in the ongoing actualization of the paschal mystery that restores the world to unity.

A new city

The new commandment and the new being that is the Christian are creating a new world and a new city. That is the theme of the second reading [37], which is closely connected with the Gospel pericope. John's vision is of the new city, the new Jerusalem (the Church), the new earth, whereon God dwells with men. Everything is renewed: "Behold, I make all things new" (Apoc. 21:5).

We must not, of course, confuse the earthly Church with the kingdom in its final state. While the Church of the present time is indeed the place where God dwells with men, it also contains those who are dead; its people still weep and utter cries of sorrow. On the other hand, the Church is moving toward that ultimate Jerusalem, and we are bidden to go with her, trusting that the mysteries of Christ will be successful in what they seek to accomplish.

The new commandment of love gives rise to the new city that is set over against the world, in whose eyes we Christians are such strange beings; the unbeliever cannot understand our attitudes or the choices we make. Our task, therefore, is to help the Church, whose members we are, to become ever more fully and perfectly the Spouse of Christ, a Bride adorned for her Bridegroom. Love exercised in concrete, practical ways is what will enable the Church to be what she should be.

Negative criticism, on the other hand, is destructive and never constructive. It is easy, after all, to find fault with failures and deficiencies, but much less simple to provide the positive help that remedies a defect and gives others the courage to move forward. Such an attitude does not require that our love be a bland, insipid thing or that we cultivate a complacent, childish admiration for everything the Church says and does. We're quite accustomed nowadays to thinking of the Church as sinful on her human side. Perhaps we're even overaccustomed to it, so that our faith has become less lively. We're preoccupied with counting all the wrinkles, and we forget the spiritual beauty of this Bride that is preparing to meet her Spouse. Is our derisive laughter really a source of fruitfulness for the Church?

Men and women show a special kind of bigness and a special kind of balance when they know how to point out the defects of the institution in a sure but tactful way, while preserving at the same time the unqualified respect owed to the Church which God has established and from which we receive the divine life that is in us. Our criticism, no matter how severe it must sometimes be, should never encourage others to abandon the Church or even to be less than enthusiastic about her. Criticism will not have such effects if it truly proceeds from faith and from love of our brothers and sisters.

The Church grows; elders are needed

The first reading for the fifth Sunday in Cycle C is not closely connected with the other two readings, yet it can be linked to them without forcing the texts [34]. The new Jerusalem that is the Church was growing slowly. If it was to grow, the disciples had to persevere in the faith and had to survive many trials on their way to the kingdom. For this they needed help such as the apostles provided. Meanwhile, however, the number of believers who had made the decision to live the commandment of love as members of the new people of God was increasing rapidly; in particular, the pagan nations were accepting the Good News, and the door of faith was being thrown open to them. Paul and Barnabas therefore installed elders in each community.

What a transformation had taken place since the resurrection of Jesus! Men were bent on attaining unity through mutual love and on building together the new Jerusalem into which even pagans were called.

SIXTH SUNDAY OF EASTER

20. THE SPIRIT AND THE CHURCH

[A] Promise of the Spirit

Christ speaks to his disciples; he also speaks to us who celebrate his Eucharist. Addressing thus his entire Church, he announces in his farewell discourse that he will send the Paraclete and that he will himself return at the end of time [47]; that is the message the Church passes on to us today.

In his farewell discourse, Christ tells us his final wish for us: that we should be faithful to his commandments, since this obedience is the proof of our love for him. St. John is careful to pass these words on to the young Church experiencing so many difficulties and enduring so much conflict. Another theme of the discourse is that of mutual immanence: the Father in me and I in the Father, I in you and you in me. It is a favorite theme of St. John's, for it sheds a great deal of light on the deeper meaning of the Church's life and the life of her individual members. Closely connected both with the observance of the commandments and with the mutual love of Christ and others is the theme of the sending of the Spirit. The Spirit will sustain the Church; at the same time we have the impression that the gift of the Spirit is conditioned by that observance of the commandments that is the sign of love.

The Spirit who will be sent will be "another Counselor," the Spirit of truth, and he will be with us always. What will his role be? It will be to make ever more fully known the mysteries of Christ, that is, the meaning of his life and words and actions. But at the same time the Spirit of truth will give Christians the strength to live in a world that does not understand them or see what they see. For, as Jesus points out emphatically, only those who believe and lovingly obey the commandments can receive, see, and know this Spirit. The Spirit is with and in such people, and not in unbelievers.

"Another Counselor" may seem a rather odd expression, but the meaning is easily grasped. Throughout his earthly life Jesus had been at his disciples' side; now the Spirit will take Jesus' place and continue his work, and the disciples will not be left orphans. As far as the world is concerned, Christ will have disappeared, but the disciples will see him and see him as a living person. This last statement refers to Jesus' return at his resurrection, but also to his return at the end of time. Nonetheless, this knowing and seeing of Jesus does not imply merely a vision of his physical presence, but rather a true understanding of what he is. The disciples will know that he is in the Father and that his disciples are in him and he in them.

Observe how solemnly Christ introduces these words

about the mutual presence and immanence of himself and his disciples: "In that day you will know . . ." (v. 20). "That day" is the day of his glorious resurrection. Yet Christ also has in mind here the Church, with which he will continue to be present until the great Day of definitive encounter. Throughout that whole time he will manifest himself, but only to those who love him, that is, those who accept his word and are faithful to it.

The laying on of hands and the gift of the Spirit

The first reading for the sixth Sunday in Cycle A tells how the Apostles Peter and John laid hands on the Samaritan converts so that they might receive the gift of the Spirit [41]. The reading is evidently related to the Gospel pericope, for the Spirit thus communicated is the Spirit of truth who remains with us and guides us.

Some Samaritans have been converted by the preaching of Philip; Peter and John are then sent into Samaria to continue Philip's work. This they do by imposing hands so that the recently baptized may receive the Holy Spirit. The statement can be misinterpreted to mean that baptism had not conferred the Spirit (as though he had not effected the rebirth through baptism by water for the forgiveness of sins) and that the laying on of hands was required if the Spirit were to be bestowed. No, the point is evidently that some special gift of the Spirit is bestowed through the laying on of hands, even though the Acts of the Apostles does not tell us in what this special gift consists. Later on, at Ephesus, Paul will confer baptism on those who had received only the baptism of John, and then he will lay hands on them for the gift of the Spirit (Acts 19:1-7).

In today's reading the gift of the Spirit takes the form of the gift of tongues and the gift of prophecy. In other words, the gift of the Spirit represents a completion that takes outward form in a kind of witnessing. In any event, we can discern here the link between baptism and that gift of the Spirit that will later on be called "confirmation."

The risen Christ is our hope

The second reading, from the First Letter of Peter, refers to the difficult situation of Christians amid a world that does not understand them [44]. The letter aims at encouraging the persecuted Christians to bear witness to their hope. They must be ready to suffer for having done only what is good and right. Peter then points to the example of Christ, who, though an innocent man, died for the guilty and their sins.

The reason why this passage was chosen for today's liturgy seems to be the implied action of that Spirit of whom we hear in the first reading and in the Gospel. He it is who raised Christ from the dead and gave him the victory over the powers of evil. This same Spirit is our hope, since he gives us rebirth and a participation in the life of God and Christ. In the flesh Christ was put to death, thus sharing the common lot of men, but the Spirit has given him a new kind of life. That is the basis for our hope that we too will be transformed and glorified. For men with such a hope, difficulty and persecution hold no terrors, for they are the way by which we attain a share in Christ's victory.

[B] Giving one's life for one's friends

The theme of the sixth Sunday in Cycle B is love. The salient phrases in the Gospel pericope make this clear: abide in Christ's love; love one another; give one's life for one's friends [48]. In fact, the whole process of salvation is shown to be at bottom a matter of love: "As the Father has loved me, so have I loved you. . . . love one another as I have loved you" (vv. 9, 12).

Everything in this passage has to do with love. Love has been given to us: "As the Father has loved me, so have I loved you" (v. 9). We must therefore be faithful to love: "Abide in my love" (v. 9). We know from elsewhere in what this love given to us consists: "In this is love, not that we loved God but that he loved us and sent his Son to be the expiation for our sins" (1 John 4:10; from the second read-

ing). Christ's great desire is that his disciples and we with
them should live on, or abide, in his love. He also tells us
in what this abiding concretely consists: "If you keep my
commandments, you will abide in my love, just as I have
kept my Father's commandments" (John 15:10). (John, we
should note, never indulges in what might be called an
abstract metaphysics of love; he always gives love a concrete, realistic meaning.)

In speaking of our union with him, Jesus uses the same
terms that he uses to describe his own union with the
Father. While our union with him is only analogous to his
union with the Father, the identity of the language indicates how very close our relation to God can become. The
very love that unites the two divine Persons, Father and
Son, is communicated to men. Christ tells us what the quality of this love is: "Greater love has no man than this, that a
man lay down his life for his friends" (v. 13). Jesus then
identifies his own friends: they are his disciples, and the
laying down of his life for them is a clear reference to his
Passion. We must observe, however, that a "friend" cannot
lay down his life for us unless we have been obeying his
commandments, since otherwise there would have been no
friendship.

It is characteristic of friends that they hide nothing from
one another but share everything. That is what Jesus does,
as he tells us here: "I have called you friends, for all that I
have heard from my Father I have made known to you."

The friendship in question here is, concretely, not a
friendship between mere human beings but between God
and sinful man. Inevitably, then, the initiative in the invitation to friendship must come from God (v. 16). Jesus had
already made this point earlier: "No one can come to me
unless the Father who sent me draws him" (John 6:44). At
the same time, however, this friendship to which God invites us is impossible unless we also love one another (v.
17).

Because of God's love for us and our response to his invitation to friendship, we must "go and bear fruit" (v. 16).

How are these words to be understood? According to the translation just given, "going" and "bearing fruit" are distinct ideas, and we must attend to each of them. The first indicates a mission, the second points to the result of the mission and the love. Other translators prefer to turn the two expressions into one: "go to bear fruit." In any case, love is presented as taking concrete form in the observance of the commandments that is indispensable if we are to bear fruit. Note that the controlling image is still that of the vine, whose branches bear fruit as long as they remain connected with the vine.

A further consequence of the love that unites us to the Father and Son in the Spirit is that we can ask anything of the Father in Christ's name, and it will be given to us.

The passage ends with a repetition of the key idea: "This I command you, to love one another" (v. 17).

God loved us and sent his Son

The second reading [45] also deals with John's favorite theme: mutual love. We must love one another, he says, because all love is from God. "Love is of God, and he who loves is born of God and knows God" (v. 7): here we have some of John's characteristic expressions: love, knowledge, adoptive sonship. We also find John telling us that God's love never remains at the abstract level but manifests itself in concrete ways, most especially in the sending of the Son so that he may give us life (v. 9). There we have the real sign of love: God "sent his Son to be the expiation for our sins" (v. 10).

The proposition that "God is love" (v. 8) had to take concrete form, since love does not exist if it does not manifest itself. But God did manifest his love by sending Jesus. The incarnation of the Word is the supreme sign of God's love for us. Was this an isolated gesture of love? No, for the sending of the Son is bound up with the whole history of salvation. In sending him, then, God did not make an isolated, passing gesture, however grand and glorious; rather, the whole history of salvation is there to prepare for and complete the mission of the Son.

It is important to emphasize the free and unmerited character of God's love for us. He loved first and took the initiative; he chose us, not we him. It is understandable, then, that the Greek text of the New Testament should use the word *agapē* to express this divine love and should reject the terms *eros* (love based on desire that seeks fulfillment; love associated with passion) and *philia* (mutual friendship of equals). The term *agapē* brings out the divine good will and initiative.

John's main concern for the young Church is that charity should rule the life of its members, thus reflecting the love of God that caused him to send his Son. If the expansion of the Church is effected through the revelation to men of God's love for them, then the revelation itself is effected chiefly through the sign of the fraternal love that unites Christians with one another. It is our task to communicate to our fellow men the love of God that made him send his Son, just as it is our task to communicate to them the "knowledge" of God. We can carry out our task, however, only as members of a community that will be a sign of God's *agapē* — in other words, a community whose life is marked by the bonds love fashions.

The Spirit is given without partiality

The love thus manifested by the sending of the Son and the giving of the Spirit reaches out to all men; the Father loves all and intends all to be saved [42]. In the first reading, Peter is forced to acknowledge that the Spirit does indeed breathe wherever he wishes (cf. John 3:8). This is an important moment in the history of the Church, for without this acknowledgement the Church would have been the captive of one nation and one race; but instead the Spirit manifests himself even to pagans. As long as a man fears God and acts uprightly, he can become a believer and receive the gift of the Spirit.

The responsorial psalm (Ps. 98) for the sixth Sunday in Cycle B is an enthusiastic response to God's desire for the salvation of all men. "The Lord has revealed to the nations his saving power," says the response, while in verses 2-3 we sing: "The Lord has made known his victory, he has revealed his vindication in the sight of the nations. . . . All the ends of the earth have seen the victory of our God."

[C] The Holy Spirit will teach us everything

In the Gospel passage for the sixth Sunday in Cycle C, Jesus is preparing his disciples for his departure and return to his Father [49]. Chapter 14 of the Fourth Gospel is, of course, a farewell address. Toward the end of it Jesus promises that God will come to those who believe and that he will send the Spirit to teach them everything. We find once again the familiar theme of "remaining" or "dwelling": "We will come to him and make our home with him" (v. 23).

The Father and the Son come to those who believe with a faith that has its origin in the Spirit. This Trinitarian coming is a new revelation for the disciples. The condition for the coming of the Trinity, however, is that the disciple must love and be faithful to Jesus' word.

The departure of Jesus is necessary if the Spirit is to come and carry out his mission of instructing the disciples and making Christ's words alive for them. What Jesus is here doing is to explain the necessity of the mystery of the ascension: If he does not go, the Spirit cannot be sent; and this sending is necessary for the completion of Jesus' work and for bringing the disciples to an understanding of all that Jesus had taught them.

The disciples realize that Jesus is going to leave them, and the news devastates them. Jesus reassures them: He is leaving, but he will return. Yet, even his return will leave the young Church subject to trial and needing to live by faith; men must believe in Jesus without seeing him. The disciples should not be fearful at this thought, for Christ gives them a peace which is that of God himself. They will have the joy of knowing that Christ is glorified and seated at the Father's right hand; the joy of fully grasping the teaching of Jesus; the joy that comes from the indwelling of the Trinity. Such peace and joy are unintelligible to the world, for the joy is a joy amid suffering, the peace a peace amid conflict. Yet they belong to those who believe in the victory of Christ, for this victory is the firm foundation of hope.

The holy city coming down from heaven

The departure of Jesus and the sending of the Spirit prelude the building of a new city, a new kingdom, the Church of the saved. Such is the meaning of the second reading [46]. But the city is not the present Church; neither is it the future Church, as though the vision were talking about the present Church in its perfect state. The vision is of a new creation: the heavenly city. The present Church is, however, a sign of the heavenly city and constantly refers its present life to that future reality.

The new city gleams with the splendor of God. The details of its description are of little interest to us here, though we should note the reference to the twelve tribes of Israel and to the wall built on twelve foundations, which are the twelve apostles. The city has no temple. What is the significance of this statement? Is it a condemnation of all liturgical worship? Is it an echo of prophetic warnings against the dangers of external worship (cf. Jer. 7:4)? Not at all! There is no opposition between liturgy, external worship, and true adoration; there is only complementarity, provided the gesture and the words reflect genuine interior adoration. The point of the statement that the city has no temple is simply that there is no need for a material building, because God himself is the temple of the new city. Neither is there any longer need of sun and moon, since the Lord is the city's light. He is all in all.

We may ask whether such a vision is not discouraging to the Church and does not take the heart out of those who want to work in the present Church. The question implies a misconception. It is, after all, the present Church herself that prepares us for her future elimination and replacement by the new city, just as every celebration of the liturgy takes us a step closer to the elimination of every temple and every liturgy. Why? Because on earth we toil in darkness and see reality only in a mirror and through signs, whereas in the new city we shall see without the mediation of mirrors and shall see God himself face to face.[185]

Choice of leaders for the community

In the first reading we are at a decisive moment for the new Church: it must decide on the attitude it will take toward the people among whom it first came into existence [43]. Radical decisions have to be made, yet a certain flexibility must also be preserved. The scene is the famous Council of Jerusalem, the first example of a Church council. Leaders are chosen from the Jerusalem community, and they set out for Antioch with Paul and Barnabas to announce the decisions reached by the Council.

Two points are noteworthy. The first is that the leading men chosen by the Council and sent out from Jerusalem are the ones with authority; any others claiming the right to lay down the law have no mandate to do so, and no one should pay any attention to them. The second point is that the conciliar decision has been made with the help of the Holy Spirit. It is this second point that establishes a connection between this reading and the Gospel of the day. The Spirit whom Jesus has sent teaches everything and bestows perspicacity of judgment on those who exercise authority in the Church. Circumcision will not be required of Gentile converts. The only prohibitions are not to eat meat sacrificed to idols, or blood, or the meat of strangled animals, and to abstain from illicit sexual unions.

At first sight this reading seems to have little connection with the overall theme of this Sunday in all three cycles. But it does in fact have a connection, for it is dealing with the formation and growth of the Church. It provides us with a typical example of the difficulties that the establishment of the Church entailed, and of how the Spirit of Christ helped the disciples reach a sound decision in a matter that was agitating a local church.

21. THE ASCENSION OF THE LORD

In the liturgy for the feast of the ascension, the first two readings are the same in all three years of the cycle; for the Gospel, however, a different pericope has been chosen in each of the three years. Of the three Gospel passages, however, only those from Mark [53] and Luke [54] narrate the ascension. Luke tells the story again in the Acts of the Apostles, in a passage used for the first reading of the feast [50], while the second reading, from the Letter to the Ephesians, gives a theology of the mystery [51]. The three Gospels locate the ascension (explicitly or implicitly) after a discourse in which Jesus sends his apostles forth into the world to proclaim his resurrection, to teach, and to baptize. The Acts of the Apostles locates the ascension in the same context.

Since the liturgies for the three-year cycle overlap, we shall treat them as one and discuss all the readings together.

"He was lifted up, and a cloud took him out of their sight"

The first reading, from the Acts of the Apostles [50], puts the mystery of the ascension into its historical context. Luke intends that what he writes here should be read in continuity with what he had already written in his first book, that is, the Gospel. Both here and in the Gospel, chapter 24

[54], Jesus leaves his disciples only after giving them explicit instructions. Matthew and Mark, too, relate the final instructions that Jesus gives his disciples before leaving. them and ascending to heaven.

We should note the way in which Luke, in the Acts of the Apostles, speaks of Christ giving these final instructions: he gives them in the Holy Spirit. The evangelist here points out that the Spirit who will be guiding the apostles in their missionary work is already present and active in the final words Christ speaks before his departure. Nor does Luke fail to give a reason why Christ gives his instructions to a limited group. This is the group to whom he has shown himself alive after his Passion, appearing to them during a period of forty days and giving them proofs of the resurrection; this was the group, too, to which he had been speaking about the kingdom of God.

In Luke's account here, Jesus insists that the apostles must stay in Jerusalem and wait for the fulfillment of the Father's promise. Luke is also the one who, both in his Gospel and in the Acts of the Apostles, emphasizes the place that Jerusalem has in the events of the mystery of salvation. It is at Jerusalem that Jesus is presented in the Temple and recognized as the Messiah by Simeon and Anna (2:22-38). It is at Jerusalem that Jesus, still a child, will teach the teachers of the law (2:41-50). The ascent to Jerusalem later on is therefore significant: the public life of Jesus had begun at Jerusalem, and so it must end there.

It is at Jerusalem too that the apostles will receive their baptism in the Holy Spirit, which will give them the strength and courage they need if they are to be witnesses in Jerusalem, throughout Judea and Samaria, and to the ends of the earth. In their last conversation with Jesus just before his ascension, the apostles ask whether the fulfillment of the Father's promise means that Israel is about to be restored. Jesus answers with firmness and restraint. The answer implicitly distinguishes between the imminent coming of the Spirit who will give the strength the apostles need for bearing witness, and the definitive establishment of the kingdom. Before the latter can occur, the gospel must be carried beyond the boundaries of Israel; the kingdom will come at a time the Father has determined.

After reporting Jesus' instructions, Luke narrates the ascension itself. He writes as a historian of events, in a sober way. The "cloud" is the cloud found in various theophanies in both the Old and the New Testaments; but Luke strikes no note of triumph in his description. Jesus simply vanishes into the cloud, and the angels tell the disciples that he will some day return.

Despite what Luke says, we may well find the account perplexing, for Luke provides no theological interpretation. He prepares us for Jesus' departure, and we know that if Christ does not ascend to heaven and take his place at the Father's side, the Spirit cannot come. But if we had only Luke's account, we would be unable to elaborate a theology of the ascension.

Though there is no triumphal ring to Luke's story, the liturgy strikes this note in the responsorial psalm (Ps. 47): "God has gone up with a shout, the Lord with the sound of a trumpet. . . . For God is the king of all the earth; sing praises with a psalm! God reigns over the nations; God sits on his holy throne" (vv. 6, 8-9).

[A] Christ is seated at the right hand of the Father

The second reading gives a more doctrinal vision of the ascension [51], showing us Christ as the sign of God's strength and wisdom. The passage is one of enthusiastic praise for the victorious Christ. He is the Christ of glory, whom God raised from the dead, set at his own right side, and made Master of all things. Above all, God has made him Head of the Church, which is his Body and fullness.

The passage is thus another summary of Paul's theology (see also, for example, Col. 2:10; Eph. 1:15-16; 3:6; 4:4, 12, 16; 5:23, 29). The Church is here called the "fullness" of Christ, his *plērōma*. Paul uses the same term elsewhere in Ephesians when speaking of the perfect man (3:19; 4:13).

Christ does not, of course, require any perfection from outside himself. The Church is his "fullness" because in her the saving action of God is seen in a maximum degree. The Church is the privileged locus of the action of God and Christ.

The victory and glory of Christ, now Master of all things, is a source of hope for us, because what belongs to Christ belongs also to his followers. We can see in the heavenly Christ the inheritance that shall some day be ours.

"All authority in heaven and on earth has been given to me"

The passage from St. Matthew's Gospel [52] gives us Christ's last words before his departure. He speaks of his glory and power: "All authority in heaven and on earth has been given to me." The moment is a solemn one, and when the disciples see Jesus, they fall down in homage; his presence is already so filled with majesty that it forces men to their knees in adoration.

Until now, some had had their doubts. That is why Jesus presents himself to them as "Lord" and possessor of supreme authority; he is Lord of both heaven and earth. He also gives the disciples their mission, which is universal in scope: they are to make disciples of all nations and baptize them in the name of the Father and the Son and the Holy Spirit; they are also to teach men to observe Christ's commandments. In short, they are to transmit a complete program of Christian life, once they have proclaimed the basic message of faith in the Christ who has been raised from the dead and now lives forever. The account ends with a promise of Christ's efficacious presence to his Church: "And lo, I am with you always, to the close of the age."

[B] "After he had spoken to them, the Lord Jesus was taken up into heaven"

In the reading from Mark's Gospel (Cycle B), Christ's final words have to do with faith, baptism, and the signs that will accompany those who believe [53]. He bids his disciples go and proclaim the Good News to all creation. The words reflect the evangelist's experience as viewed in the light of the Spirit. It is hardly probable, after all, that Christ gave so concrete an order. If he had, how could we explain either the hesitations of the apostles in the early years or their insistence that the gospel must be preached even to the Gentiles?

The apostles are to preach the Good News. The result of their *kerygma* (an authoritative proclamation not based on arguments) will be the faith that saves, or, if men reject the proclamation, their condemnation. Faith in turn leads to baptism, or rather it is professed in the reception of baptism. Note that the condemnation is pronounced against those who *refuse* to believe. There is thus a middle ground left open in Christ's statement; we may not simply condemn all who do not believe, but must examine their basic attitudes and motivations.

Those who believe will have power to perform "signs." This is especially true of the apostles, who must use the signs to back up their preaching. In the Fourth Gospel (14:12), Christ again says that "he who believes in me will also do the works that I do; and greater works than these will he do." And we know from the Acts of the Apostles the wonders that the apostles did perform in order to confirm the truth they preached and to arouse or intensify faith.

After relating Christ's final words, Mark mentions the ascension itself. We should note especially his addition of the fact that Jesus now took his seat at God's right side. What Mark is emphasizing here is the glorification of Jesus' humanity.

As Mark tells it, the apostles let no time elapse between Christ's commission to them and their departure for their missionary work: they go forth and preach the Good News everywhere. The evangelist notes that the Lord continued to work with them, thus fulfilling his promise as recorded by Matthew: "Go . . . I am with you always, to the close of the age" (28:20).

[C] "He was carried up into heaven"

Luke's account of the ascension in the Gospel [54] must be compared with his account in Acts; the latter was written at a later date, and in it Luke refers back to his Gospel.

The pericope contains an important statement by Christ: "Thus it is written, that the Christ should suffer and on the third day rise from the dead, and that repentance and forgiveness of sins should be preached in his name to all nations, beginning from Jerusalem" (24:46-47). There are several essential points made here which together form a doctrinal synthesis that can be described as the paschal mystery of death and resurrection. Those who had been witnesses of the events are to go forth to proclaim them and thus bring men to conversion; they are to make their proclamation to all the nations, but they are to start at Jerusalem. Christ will even tell them to stay in Jerusalem until the promised Spirit comes (cf. Acts 1:1-11).

In Luke's Gospel account of Jesus' final words, the Lord teaches his disciples the meaning of the Scriptures, as he had done for the disciples at Emmaus when he told them: "Was it not necessary that the Christ should suffer these things and enter into his glory?" (24:26). Jesus then promises to send the Spirit. Finally, he blesses the disciples and ascends into heaven. Here again, there is no air of triumph about the story; the facts are related very simply. Nonetheless (but expressing the evangelist's own reaction at a later time?), the apostles fall to the ground in worship of Jesus; they understand now that he is glorified, and they return to Jerusalem rejoicing.

"It is to your advantage that I go away"

Has the Christian of today any reason to be really interested in the ascension that took place so many centuries ago? After all, our concern now is to live the life of the Church under the guidance of the Spirit. How can the ascension be anything to us but a past historical event, albeit an important one, in the life of the Savior?

Let us ask St. Leo the Great what he thinks about the ascension. In the first of his two sermons on the mystery, the Saint makes the point that the ascension of Christ means that his human nature is now enthroned at the Father's side. He then turns his thoughts to us, the disciples Christ has left behind:

> The ascension of Christ thus means our own elevation as well; where the glorious Head has gone before, the Body is called to follow in hope. Let us therefore exult, beloved, as is fitting, and let us rejoice in devout thanksgiving. For on this day not only have we been confirmed in our possession of paradise, but we have even entered heaven in the person of Christ; through his ineffable grace we have regained far more than we had lost through the devil's hatred.[186]

In this sermon, then, the Saint sees in Christ's ascension and heavenly glorification the pledge of what we too shall someday be and a vision of what we already are. In St. Leo's view, the feast of the ascension is not simply the celebration of a historical event; it is also a celebration of what we ourselves now are.

In the second sermon, the Saint returns to this same theme, which, as he sees it, is the real object of the feast: "At Easter the Lord's resurrection was the source of our joy; today his ascension into heaven is our reason for rejoicing, for today we recall and duly venerate the day on which our lowly nature was elevated, in Christ, far above the heavenly host."[187]

But St. Leo goes further in responding to our modern questions about the practical meaning of the feast of the ascension. In the same second sermon he writes:

> Forty days after his resurrection, our Lord Jesus Christ was raised up to heaven before his disciples' eyes, thus ending his bodily presence among them. He would remain at the Father's right side until the time divinely appointed for multiplying the children of the Church had passed. Then he would come, in

the very body in which he had ascended, to judge the living and the dead. Thus what formerly had been visible in our Redeemer now took the form of sacred rites; and in order that faith might be purer and stronger, bodily vision was replaced by teaching whose authority the divinely enlightened hearts of the faithful might accept and follow.[188]

St. Leo makes an important point in this passage, namely, that on the visible scene the Redeemer is replaced by sacred rites; it is through these sacramental signs that we now encounter the Christ who has ascended to the Father's side.

St. Leo's theological approach here has inspired most modern study and presentation of the sacramental life. Its starting point is Christ's assurance to his disciples: "It is to your advantage that I go away" (John 16:7). But Christ had previously said: "He who has seen me has seen the Father" (John 14:9). How then can he say: "It is to your advantage that I go away," when his going deprives us of real contact with the Father? Christ's second statement would indeed be meaningless unless his departure led to a contact of all believers both with him and with his Father. That is precisely what has happened: Christ's departure paved the way for the activity of the Spirit in the sacraments, which are the symbolic extensions of Christ's glorified body throughout the world. Unless Christ were both glorified and departed from us, the sacraments would be impossible. Any contact with a Christ still present in bodily form on earth would be limited by the conditions of space and time. Now, however, Christ is present to us in every place and at all times through signs that draw their efficacy from his Spirit.

The incarnation of the eternal Word made it possible for the world to encounter God and thus changed the course of history. The ascension of the glorified Christ and the subsequent sending of the Spirit allow all believers to touch Christ, to see and know God, and to live his life, by providing a mode of contact with the Lord. Each sacrament is a sign of his presence; this is especially true of the Eucharist, which is specifically the sign of the presence of his now glorified body. Reflection on each of the sacraments (including the word that is part of the rite, and against the background of the sign-nature of the Church herself) will enable us to see how truly Christ spoke in saying that his departure was to our advantage. It will also enable us to understand better the deeper significance of the ascension in the history of our salvation.[189]

The prayers for the feast of the ascension

The reformed liturgy provides two prefaces for the feast of the ascension. The second of them, used already in the Roman Missal of 1570, links resurrection and ascension, the purpose of the latter being to make us sharers in the divinity of Christ: "In his risen body he plainly showed himself to his disciples and was taken up to heaven in their sight to claim for us a share in his divine life."

The first preface expands upon the same point: "Christ, the mediator between God and man, judge of the world and lord of all, has passed beyond our sight, not to abandon us but to be our hope. Christ is the beginning, the head of the Church; where he has gone, we hope to follow."

The other prayers of the Mass concentrate chiefly on our passage to heaven as prefigured in the Lord's ascension. "God our Father, make us joyful in the ascension of your Son Jesus Christ. May we follow him into the new creation, for his ascension is our glory and our hope." Or again: "Father, in this eucharist we touch the divine life you give to the world. Help us to follow Christ with love to eternal life where he is Lord for ever and ever."

A preface in the Verona Sacramentary (a preface that resembles the first, and newer, of the current prefaces) sums up the reason for our joy on this feast:

> Rightly do we exult and rejoice on today's feast. The ascension into heaven of the man Jesus Christ, Mediator between God and men, is not an abandon-

ment of us to our lowly state, for he exists now in the glory that he always had with you and in the nature he took from us and made his own. He deigned to become a man, in order that he might make us sharers in his divinity.[190]

SEVENTH SUNDAY OF EASTER

22. JESUS PRAYS FOR HIS DISCIPLES

[A] "Father, glorify thy Son"

The focus of the Gospel reading is on the glory of the Christ [61]. Jesus had earlier spoken of this glory when he said: "The Son of man is to come with his angels in the glory of his Father" (Matthew 16:27); and Mark reports Christ's words to the effect that if anyone is ashamed of Jesus, Jesus will in turn be ashamed of him when he comes in his Father's glory (Mark 8:38; cf. Luke 9:26).

In the Fourth Gospel, Jesus speaks more pointedly of this glory that will be his: "The hour has come for the Son of man to be glorified" (12:23). It is a glory he does not seek for himself, but there is an Other who seeks it for him (8:50). John ends his account of the miracle at Cana by saying: "This . . . manifested his glory; and his disciples believed in him" (2:11). Finally, in the priestly prayer, Jesus asks that those whom the Father has given him may contemplate his glory (17:24). There is thus a connection between glory and faith by which the glory of Jesus is contemplated.

There can be no doubt that Christ's hearers understood this "glory" to be connected to his person. The word "glory" to us is chiefly a synonym for "reputation" or "renown"; the Semite, however, took it rather to mean "a value that elicits respect." That is why the "glory" of Yahweh can be identified with God himself and his omnipotence. His glory is manifested in his interventions, as, for example, the well-known miracle at the Red Sea (Exod. 14:18) or his various appearances to men (e.g., Exod. 16:10). God's "glory" is his self-manifestation; thus Moses asks the Lord to show him his glory (Exod. 33:18). This presence of the Lord in all his splendor is later on somewhat materialized, so to speak; thus the glory of Yahweh is said to fill the temple (1 Kings 8:10).

In the New Testament, "glory" is connected with the person of Jesus and is consequently manifested by various actions of his earthly life, as we noted in connection with the miracle of Cana. Especially, however, do we see Jesus' glory at his baptism and his transfiguration (Luke 9:32, 35; 2 Peter 1:17). Even the Passion will reveal his glory, and Paul will speak of "crucifying the Lord of glory" (1 Cor. 2:8).

John, above all, is the one who directly connects "glory" with the person of Jesus. This glory is manifested by the unity between Father and Son (10:30), by Jesus' works (11:40), and in a very special way by the paschal mystery of his death and resurrection. The glory belonged to him since before the creation of the world (17:24), but his death, resurrection, and ascension make it manifest to all.

Jesus has now been taken up into glory (1 Tim. 3:16), for God has glorified his Servant (acts 3:13). He has raised him up and given him glory (1 Peter 1:21).

We are now in a position to understand better the pericope read in this day's liturgy (Cycle A). The prayer remains, however, a complicated composition. In the part read today, Christ is saying that he has glorified his Father by carrying out the task entrusted to him; now he in return must be glorified by the Father. Any glory given him, however, means the glorification of the Father as well, since there is no separation between the two glories. The glory that the Son gives the Father consists in the accomplishment of his mission; he has made the Father known to men, who have come to realize that he came from the Father and have accepted the word that had been communicated to the Son and that he in turn has communicated to them. They have believed, and they know; consequently, they have eternal life, for eternal life consists in knowing the only true God.

The climactic statement in this reading is that Jesus is glorified in his disciples. He can say this because they make clear the successful accomplishment of his mission: he has united them to himself and transformed them into his likeness; they now belong to the Father, just as they do to the Son. The Son's glory is the Father's glory, and the Father's glory is the Son's glory, and the Son's glory is ours as well.

The Spirit in its glory rests upon us

The second reading connects the glory of Christ with the way in which the Christian should live [58]. God's Spirit, the Spirit in its glory, rests upon us, and therefore nothing, not even persecution or insult, can take our joy away. In fact, condemnation for being a Christian is an occasion for giving glory to God. During our trials and until the time when Christ's glory will be manifested on the last day, we must share that glory and live joyously. The interim is simply a delay and should therefore be a joyful time.

Persevering in prayer

The apostles and other disciples were steadfast in prayer; with them were some women, among them Mary, the Mother of Jesus. They were all gathered on the upper floor of a house; there the little community, Mary included, contemplated the glory of the risen and ascended Christ while they waited for the promised Holy Spirit [55].

[B] Consecrated in truth

In this section of Christ's fervent prayer, there are three principal themes: life in the truth; life in unity; life in the world but not of the world [62].

God's word is truth, and Jesus has communicated it to his disciples; now these disciples must be consecrated in and by the truth. What does "truth" mean for St. John? "It means eternal reality as revealed to men — either the reality itself or the revelation of it."[191] The final words of today's pericope — "consecrated in truth" — thus reveal their full weight of meaning: When Jesus asks the Father to consecrate his disciples in truth, he is asking that they "be sanctified upon the plane of absolute reality."[192]

The disciples are thus meant to attain to the holiness of God himself, since Jesus is putting them into the very sphere of God. They are God's adopted sons, chosen as such by the Father and given to him by the Son. Consecration in truth and participation in the holiness of the Father will in turn bestow upon them the plenitude of joy — that joy which Christ himself experiences now as he looks back at what has been successfully accomplished.

The disciples must, however, remain united and one, just as the Father and the Son are one. We have met with this theme already; it is a favorite of John's and will be developed further in the next part of the chapter (vv. 21-24). The one reality that the body of disciples should become is identically the one reality that is the Father and the Son. If they remain in this unity, the disciples will be able to remain also in the truth, that is, in the eternal absolute reality.

Such an existence does not remove the disciples from the world, but it does set up an opposition between them and the world. The world cannot understand them, and it will end up by hating them because they are such a stumbling block for it. What is said of the disciples here applies to every Christian: he is in the world, for the sake of the world's life, but he is not of the world. This tension is part of every baptized Christian's life. The opposition is one that can neither be glossed over or watered down, under penalty of not remaining in either truth or unity.

We have seen God's love

The second reading consists of reflections by St. John (First Letter) that run parallel to chapter 17 of the Gospel [59]. The themes of unity and of God's indwelling in us are taken up. While no one has ever seen God, the apostles have been witnesses of the Son in his mission as Savior of the world. We do not see God, but we do see his love at work. He is Love, and anyone who abides in love abides in God. "Abide in love" is the same as "remain in the truth" and "be consecrated in truth." If we have faith, we can discern the love of God at work in our midst. We can also recognize it in ourselves, for in us it achieves its perfect operation, consecrating us in truth.

Here is the source of the Christian's dignity and joy, but also of his responsibility to the world. The Christian is a person who by faith sees how the sacramental signs actualize the history of salvation. His way of life has been established by the Spirit for the period that runs from the ascension to the end of time. Our need now is to abide in love so that we may abide in God and God in us. Such is our privileged situation; we know what consequences flow from it. It is the foundation of the Christian outlook and the Christian moral stance. Morality is a word that has often been debased, but we can see how it far transcends juridicism and codes of precepts. Morality points to and helps preserve our union with God and our fellows.

A witness to the resurrection

The loving faith of which we have been speaking rests ultimately on witness given to the resurrection; the community whose life is one of loving fidelity to truth is founded on the testimony of those who saw the risen Christ. The group of apostles, reduced to eleven by the betrayal and death of Judas, felt it necessary to restore its full complement of twelve, and therefore chose Matthias to join their ranks. Along with the others, he was to be a witness to the resurrection and thus a witness to the Father's love that had been revealed in the mission of the Son.

The Church has continued through the centuries to be a community of faith and love, and the successors of the apostles, with the Spirit's aid, have continued to help the people of God, the Church, to abide in truth and love. That is the bishop's chief function. The successors of the apostles are thus the foundation of the community that continues to live in the world without being of the world, but, on the contrary, being hated by the world. That is the Christian ideal; the gift of the Spirit enables Christians to attain the ideal amid conflict and despite their own weakness.

[C] Perfect unity, sign of the Son's mission

In the last part of John 17, Christ's priestly prayer broadens in scope, as he prays not only for those who already belong to the little community but for all who will enter it in the future [63]. His thoughts focus here on unity. The unity he has before him is the unity that marks the life of Father and Son and makes of them a single Being. The members of the little community have received from Jesus a share in the glory that the Father had given to him. They have been given that share so that they too might be one as Father and Son are one.

It follows from this that the life of the community is chiefly devoted to showing forth the love that is manifested by unity. If the members are successful in this, they will be signs amid the world: "By this all men will know that you are my disciples, if you have love for one another" (John 13:35). In this context, Jesus once again emphasizes the opposition between the world and the disciples. The world has not known the Father; it has refused his love, rejected his Envoy. The disciples, on the other hand, have accepted both the love and the Envoy; that is why they can be children of God (1:12).

This final section of the priestly prayer may be said to sum up John's thoughts on the fulfillment of God's plan of salvation; the key words in the synthesis are love, unity, indwelling. The disciples in Jesus, and Jesus in the disciples; the disciples with Jesus in the Father; the disciples united with one another; the world being restored to the unity God intended for it when he first created it. The prayer is a hymn to the glory of God and Christ.

The Son of Man at the Father's right hand

This hymn of glory is addressed to the Son who has risen from the dead and ascended into heaven. It also shows us what the object of Christians' contemplation should be; they are to "behold my glory" (17:24). In the vision given to him as he undergoes martyrdom, Stephen achieves this contemplation [57]. He is hated by the same world that rejected the Son and Savior; now, like Christ, he gives his life, and therefore the vision of Christ in glory, seated at the Father's side, is given to him at the moment of death. He is the first of many believers to sacrifice themselves for the glory of the Father and the Son.

The Alpha and the Omega

The second reading [60] is a contemplation of the Lord who is Alpha and Omega, the first and the last, the beginning and the end; at the same time, it is a proclamation of the Lord's coming. The Christian community is encouraged to await that coming, not in a passive way, but with the cry "Come, Lord Jesus!"

Those who have washed their robes so that they may have access to the tree of life and may be able to enter the city gate, that is, those who have believed, been converted, and been washed of their sins in baptism, are called. They hear the Spirit and the Bride saying, "Come!" Therefore, "Let him who is thirsty come, let him who desires take the water of life without price" (22:17). The image taken from the prophet Isaiah (55:1) and now used during the Advent season had acquired a sacramental meaning for the young Christian community.

The choice of such a reading at this point in the liturgy suggests a twofold attitude that we should cultivate: expectation of the Spirit to whom the Church of today addresses its appeal, "Come, Holy Spirit!" and expectation of Christ's return on the last day. For if the Spirit comes, he does so in order to lead the Church toward its completion on the final day when it encounters the Lord; the Spirit is pledge of his coming and proclaims it to the Church. The Pentecostal event we are now about to celebrate has thus a double weight of meaning: it means strength and light for the pilgrim Church; it leads us to await Christ in company with the Spirit, our Advocate and Guide as we move toward the day of Christ's return.

PENTECOST SUNDAY

23. THE MISSION OF THE HOLY SPIRIT

I. Vigil Mass

We have come to the end of the fifty-day Easter season.
The day that terminates the season is not a feast of the Holy
Spirit but proclaims that God has sent him and that the
Church has received him as a gift. The Gospel for the Vigil
Mass emphasizes this point, since Jesus' allusion to the
Spirit is spoken on "the last day of the feast" [69]. It was on
the last day, too, of the fifty-day period after Easter that the
gift of the Spirit was bestowed upon the apostles and that
they departed to give witness to the life, death, and resurrection of Jesus. Because Pentecost was so closely related
to Easter (the whole fifty-day period after Easter was a
single long feast), the Church adopted the practice of conferring the sacraments of Christian initiation on Pentecost
on those who had not been able to receive them during the
Easter Vigil. In the reformed liturgy, therefore, the "Vigil"
of Pentecost has been given back its true structure as a vigil
celebration.

There are four Old Testament texts [64–67], a single second reading [68], and a Gospel pericope; the readings are
the same in all three years of the cycle.

Babel and the scattering of mankind

The unity in which the world was created was not wel-
comed by Adam or those who came after him. The story of
Babel and the scattering of mankind brings home the breaking of unity by sin [64].

The reading is well chosen, since the Spirit is he who

brings back into unity what had been scattered, just as he had been present and active when the world was created in its original unity. It is quite fitting, therefore, that at the moment when the Church is about to celebrate the sending of the Spirit, she should recall the disunity and dispersion represented by the tower of Babel.

The descendants of Noah did not turn out any better than the human beings the Lord had earlier decided to destroy in a violent way through the Deluge (Gen. 6:5). In this story of the scattering of mankind at Babylon (Babel = Babylon), some scholars see a conflation of two stories, one relating to the city of Babylon, the other to the tower that was to reach the heavens. Possibly, but the exegetes generally do not see the text, in its present form, as requiring a dissection that would produce two stories; as it stands, the story is now one, even if it was shaped out of what had earlier been two stories.

The story of the destruction of Babylon and its tower comprises verses 2-5, 6b-7a, 8-9a. The emphasis here is on dispersion. The city was named Babel *(Babilu)*, because its inhabitants had been ejected from it *(ibbabilu = cast out —* according to one etymology) and scattered throughout the world. Note the details: "They had brick for stone, and bitumen for mortar" (v. 3); the writer is a Palestinian, and in Palestine stone and mortar were used for building. In any case, the people were forced to stop building and were scattered abroad.

The problem of languages was less important, and the populations in question perhaps did not regard it as so great a misfortune. In fact, the Egyptians sometimes thought of the multiplicity of languages as wealth from the gods.

Luke, in Acts, implicitly regards the tower of Babel as being at the source of the most profound division between men. The Spirit comes to repair the damage, and the sign he gives on Pentecost is that each listener hears in his own language the message preached by the apostles (Acts 2:4, 8).

This first reading has been chosen, then, because the

Church wishes to remind us of creation's original unity, of the division caused by sin, and of the restoration of unity by the Holy Spirit.

The Lord speaks to Moses on Sinai

The choice of this next reading [65] is, to some extent, due to its framework or scenario. The Lord comes down in the midst of fire, and the mountain is covered with a cloud of smoke. Fire, smoke, and flames, along with thunder and lightning, are the Old Testament signs of the Lord's presence. The signs point to, while hiding, the majesty and holiness of God; they are signs that both attract and repel, for man wants to see God, yet to see God is to die.

Passages that speak of fire as a sign are numerous in the Old Testament (for example, Exod. 3:2; 13:21; 40:38; Deut. 1:33; 4:11-12, 33; 5:22; 9:15; Neh. 9:12; Is. 4:5; 10:17; 31:9; 66:15, to list but a few). On Mount Horeb, Moses sees a bush that is on fire yet is not consumed (Exod. 3:2); it is a sign of God's presence and is similar to the sign in today's reading. A dialogue ensues here between God and Moses. The Lord had earlier (vv. 3-6) assured Moses that if Israel proved faithful to the covenant, it would become a kingdom of priests and a holy nation. St. Peter, in his First Letter (2:9), would apply these words to the baptized.

It is easy to understand why this text was chosen for the Vigil of Pentecost, and easy to transpose it to the Christian sphere. In fact, it is when the text is read during the Vigil Mass that we perceive its full resonances. The Spirit of Pentecost comes in the sign of tongues of fire; he consecrates a new people and reasserts his covenant with the new kingdom of priests and holy nation that is the newborn Church.

The Spirit and life

The third reading links the Spirit with life [66]. It records Ezekiel's vision of the dry bones that come to life, and the Lord's interpretation of the vision.

The prophet is walking through a desolate place that is strewn with dried-up bones. The Spirit has brought him to this place, and now the Lord asks him how these bones may be brought back to life. The prophet's answer is inspired by faith: "O Lord God, thou knowest" (v. 3). Because of his great faith, the prophet is bidden to pronounce an oracle in words that the Lord himself gives him. He is bidden to command the bones to become alive once more; he does so and describes what happened.

The Lord next orders Ezekiel to invoke the Spirit and to "prophesy" (a word that means not only to predict something but to bring it to pass by predicting it). He prophesied as commanded: "Come from the four winds, O breath, and breathe upon these slain, that they may live" (v. 9). The result: "They lived, and stood upon their feet" (v. 10).

The Lord explains the vision: The dry bones represent the people of Israel, who are now without hope. It is they whom the prophet is really addressing; he is to say to them in the Lord's name, "O my people! I will put my Spirit within you, and you shall live, and I will place you in your own land; then you shall know that I, the Lord, have spoken" (v. 14).

The proclamation concerns Israel's survival and its liberation as a renewed people. In the resurrection that is depicted (supposedly situated, in the vision, in the Valley of Jehoshaphat) the Church has seen the resurrection of the dead. Both Tertullian[195] and Jerome[194] refer to the passage in the context of this doctrine. We can go a step further, however, and see in the story the Holy Spirit, who gives life and creates a new people; the dry bones that are brought to life are the Church, which is brought to life on Pentecost by the Spirit of God.

"I will pour out my spirit"

In his sermon on Pentecost morning, Peter quotes a long passage from the prophet Joel (Acts 2:17-21; Joel 3:1-5). This passage constitutes the fourth of the Old Testament readings during the Vigil [67].

The text is an intricate one; the prophet is speaking of the last day and also reporting some of the catastrophes that will mark it. We are familiar with this approach, since Jesus himself uses it (Matthew 24:6-9; 27:45-54; Mark 13:7; Apoc. 6:11-13). In the Old Testament, Amos (8:9), Isaiah (13:10), and Ezekiel (32:7) all make similar predictions of catastrophes when speaking of the Day of the Lord. The scene, then, in which we are placed is the last day, the day of judgment, when the only ones to be saved will be the just who call upon the name of the Lord; at that point the people of God will enter into its peace.

The passage from Joel also tells, however, of an outpouring of the Spirit on all mankind, a gift of the Spirit to the whole people without exception. Comings of the Spirit are frequent in the Old Testament; let us briefly review some of them. At times the Spirit is given for the salvation of the people; a typical case is the coming of the Lord's Spirit upon the judges for the exercise of their office (Judg. 3:10-11; 14:6; Is. 10:1-16; 11:2-11; Exod. 35:31). At other times the Spirit is given so that men may bear witness in the form of an oracle that brings about what it predicts; we can see here the connection between the Spirit and the efficacious word (Is. 8:11; Jer. 1:9-15; 20:7; Exod. 3:12, 14; Amos 3:8; 7:14; and especially Is. 61:1-8, where the Servant prefigures Jesus, the Servant of the New Testament). Finally, the Spirit is also given in order to consecrate someone for a priestly service (Is. 42:1); in Isaiah 53:11 we are told that the Servant's sufferings will justify many. Jesus will later fill the role of the Servant who gives his life for the ransom of the many.

In the reading from Joel, the Spirit is given to all mankind, and the liturgy sees in this statement a typological prediction of Pentecost. Certain characteristics attach to this coming of the Spirit. It is universal: "I will pour out my spirit on all flesh." It leads to prodigies, such as the gift of tongues (Acts 2:3). The Spirit also (a point placed in special relief in this passage from Joel) proclaims judgment and the end of the world. That is one aspect of the gift of the Spirit whose overall purpose is to rebuild and bring to completion.

The responsorial psalm (Ps. 104) complements the readings, since it is concerned with praising God for the activity of his Spirit. The response situates the activity in a specifically Christian context: "Lord, send out your Spirit, and renew the face of the earth." The whole psalm is thereby turned into a glorification of the life-giving Holy Spirit.

The Spirit prays for us

We turn now to the New Testament, where St. Paul gives us a "theology" of the Holy Spirit [68]. Paul is concerned in this part of the Letter to the Romans with the reality of the Christian's condition while on earth. He speaks very concretely and makes no effort to play down the difficulties the Christian faces. At the same time, Paul is not a pessimist, but, on the contrary, full of hope. The world has been rent asunder and needs to be wholly refashioned; creation in its entirety suffers and groans. So do we. But we have already received the Spirit; how then is our deep interior division to be explained?

St. Paul's answer is that we have indeed received the Spirit, but the deliverance of our bodies is something we still await. We have been saved, but only in hope; what we hope for is itself unseen, and we must await it with perseverance. At the same time, we are creatures who lack a great deal. In fact, of ourselves we are not even capable of crying out to the Father. Here is where the Spirit intervenes in his role of Advocate.

The Christian's condition, then, does differ from that of other men, because he has received the Spirit. Yet he remains weak. Even after the work of redemption has been accomplished, we experience a constant desolating weakness that is inherent in our nature (Rom. 6:19). That will continue to be our situation until the moment when we are glorified with Christ (Rom. 8:11).

Meanwhile, the Spirit intercedes for us. We cannot pray? The Spirit prays in our stead! This prayer of the Spirit in believers is part of the carrying out of God's plan of salvation: "The Spirit intercedes for the saints according to the will of God" (Rom. 8:27). The Spirit's prayer can be summed up in a "Thy will be done!" — a sentiment that the Spirit accepts and proclaims in us and with us. The Spirit, therefore, helps us to pray in order that God's plan may be carried out and in order that we may be able to collaborate in the salvation that is the Lord's gift.

"Out of his heart shall flow rivers of living water"

The Gospel situates us on the solemn day that marks the ending of the Feast of Booths [69]. The Book of Leviticus tells us how this feast was celebrated (23:33-43). We know that the celebration lasted for a week, that it was a time of rest, like a lengthy Sabbath, and that it involved gathering for worship. The people built huts of branches as a reminder of the years their ancestors had spent in the wilderness. There was also a procession in which the marchers carried palms and fruits. At a later period the practice of offering a libation each morning was introduced, while in the evenings the Temple was illuminated.[195]

The illumination of the Temple and the morning libation are important for the understanding of the Gospel text in which Jesus speaks of rivers of living water and of himself as the Light of the world. The mention of water occurs in the short passage read at Mass during the Pentecost Vigil.

When we read this passage, we are reminded, of course, of Jesus' conversation with the Samaritan woman (John 4:11-14). Elsewhere in the Fourth Gospel, Jesus says: "He who comes to me shall not hunger, and he who believes in me shall never thirst" (6:35). Now, in today's pericope, he says: "If any one thirst, let him come to me and drink. He who believes in me, as the scripture has said, 'Out of his heart shall flow rivers of living water'" (7:37-38), words that also remind us of the Book of Isaiah (55:1, 3).

The evangelist here refers to and quotes Scripture, but a search of the Old Testament has not discovered such a text. Perhaps the words are intended as a reference to Ezekiel (47:1-12), who speaks of the water that flows from the temple and, in its passage to the Dead Sea, becomes a stream on whose banks trees grow. Perhaps they refer rather to the rock from which water flowed in the desert (Pss. 78:16; 105:41).[196] Both hypotheses can be defended; in fact, both can be accepted simultaneously, since they are not opposed to each other but can be harmonized. Christ, after all, is regarded in the New Testament as the spiritual Rock (1 Cor. 10:4), and he is also the Temple of the last times (John 2:20-22).

John himself comments briefly on Jesus' words, telling us that the rivers of living water symbolize the Holy Spirit who will be given to those who believe in Jesus. Water as a symbol of the Spirit is, of course, not John's invention; it is already to be found in the Jewish tradition. In the Book of Isaiah, for example, we read: "For I will pour water on the thirsty land, and streams on the dry ground; I will pour my Spirit upon your descendants, and my blessing on your offspring" (44:3).

In John's view, however, the water is not simply a symbol of power or strength, but of a person, namely, the Spirit whom the Father sends: "As yet the Spirit had not been given, because Jesus was not yet glorified." The death, resurrection, and ascension of Jesus will introduce a new stage in the history of salvation, for they will lead to the sending of the Spirit who slakes the thirst of believers.

II. Mass during the Day

"Receive the Holy Spirit. I send you"

The Gospel read during the Mass on Pentecost day tells us of Jesus' appearance to his apostles in Jerusalem on Easter evening [72]. He is suddenly there, even though the doors were locked, as the evangelist notes; he shows his hands and side to his disciples. Should we not connect this action with the greeting Jesus gives his disciples, "Peace be with you"? This is not an ordinary greeting. In John's view, it is connected with the wounds, because peace flows from the Passion and resurrection. (The idea of Christ's display of his wounds as a way of assuring the disciples of his identity is Lukan rather than Johannine.)

Now Christ "sends" his disciples. In doing so, he uses the kind of formula we find frequently in the Fourth Gospel: "As the Father has sent me, even so I send you" (v. 21; see the many other formulas that establish a parallel between the activity of the Father in relation to the Son and the activity of the Son in relation to his disciples: for example, 6:57; 10:15; 15:9; 17:18). For John, however, such formulas express more than a simple parallelism; they do more than affirm the divinity of Christ on the grounds that he acts as the Father acts. They are also a theological statement that believers share in the very life that is common to Father and Son.

The formula here ends rather abruptly: "I send you." He is not sending them to a place but giving them a mission that they must carry out. What is the mission? It is that of forgiving sins, as Christ immediately makes clear. Since, however, Christ draws a parallel between his action in sending the disciples and the Father's action in sending him, he is also telling the disciples that they are to continue the work that Jesus himself has been doing for the reconstruction of the world. They, too, are to do the Father's work. As Jesus reveals the Father and makes him known, so the disciples are to reveal Jesus and make him known.

The passage confronts us with a problem: How is the giving of the Spirit here to be related to Pentecost?

"They were all filled with the Holy Spirit"

St. Luke tells us in today's first reading of how the Spirit came upon the disciples as they were gathered in the upper room [70]. In describing this coming of the Spirit of the Lord, he uses the classical language of the Old Testament. We saw earlier in this chapter how descriptive traits keep recurring throughout the Old Testament: the rush of wind, the fire that divides into tongues and rests on each individual. As a result of this descent of the Spirit, the disciples proclaim the marvelous deeds of God, and each listener hears them in his own language.

Luke thus puts the coming of the Spirit on Pentecost. John, however, speaks of the Spirit being given on Easter evening. Is there a contradiction here between Acts and John? Has John conflated Pentecost and Easter? According to some exegetes, John is not conflating the two events, but neither is he distinguishing them; he is interested rather in giving expression to the paschal mystery as a unitary whole.[197]

We should note that Luke, too, has an anticipation of Pentecost inasmuch as he speaks of the apostles having been chosen by Christ "through the Holy Spirit" (Acts 1:2). It seems more accurate, therefore, to say that these various actions and gifts of the Spirit (including John 20:22) were all a preparation for the definitive coming of the Spirit. When we say that the Church was born on Pentecost, we are undoubtedly simplifying somewhat. After all, the Church was also born from the side of Christ on Calvary, while the various appearances of Christ after his resurrection were so many stages in the formation of the Church. The Church was born on Calvary and born of his resurrection, no less than it was born of the Spirit on Pentecost. The whole first chapter of the Acts of the Apostles is concerned with this gradual formation that was going on even before the Spirit was poured out on Pentecost.

We may say that St. Luke lays greater emphasis on the historical facts, while John is more concerned with the close connection between Calvary, the resurrection, the appearances, and the gift of the Spirit on Pentecost. As for ourselves, it is important to be aware of how the liturgy understands the Gospel text that it links to the account of

Pentecost and to the second reading, in which St. Paul reminds us that we were baptized in one Spirit in order to form one Body.

Baptized in the one Spirit to form a single Body

Here, as on other occasions, the liturgy transcends, without ignoring, exegetical difficulties and presents the Scripture texts in its own way so as to bring them to life for us.

In the second reading St. Paul tells us of his experience of the Spirit in the Church [71]. He describes the experience by referring to the Spirit's various manifestations, but he also insists on the unity of the Spirit who thus manifests himself in a variety of ways. He seems to connect the diversification of the manifestations with the diverse functions that are needed for the Church's life, but despite the diversity, all the activities have their origin in one and the same Spirit.

We receive various gifts that manifest the Spirit, and we receive them for the good of the community as a whole. When, in this First Letter to the Corinthians, Paul explains the diversity of gifts and offices in the Church, he shows how it is the very richness of the Church's unity that leads to a diversity of spiritual gifts. There is, then, a plurality of gifts, but they exist for the sake of the unity and perfection of a Body that is one. That is why Paul can use the image of the human body to describe the diversity that the unity of the Church entails. There is but one Spirit and there is but one Body of Christ. We have all drunk of the same Spirit and we all form a single Body through our baptism.

In the Gospel pericope for today, John shows us Christ in the act of conferring a special charism on the apostles: the charism of the forgiveness of sins and of going forth to preach. In Acts, St. Luke speaks of the coming of the Spirit, a coming that relates to the Church insofar as she addresses herself to the entire world and actually reaches all nations by speaking their various tongues; here the divided world is reunited, and a sign is given that offsets the sign of Babel, now reduced to a simple memory.

From this time forth, the Christian can always be mindful of the outpouring of the Spirit on the apostles. He need only recall his own baptism and he will understand what the Spirit wants of those who are his fellow Christians, according to the gift each one has for the good of the whole Body. He must also learn what special gift he himself has that can be put at the service of all. The gift of Pentecost is not meant to be a stimulus to triumphalism. On the contrary, it is the stimulus for the Church to realize that she must communicate the gifts of the Spirit to each of her members and that she must preserve these gifts and encourage their use for the good of all.

The opening prayer of this Mass expresses succinctly the mystery of Pentecost as a gift to the Church for the sake of the world. The Church, which has the Spirit for her guide, is above all a catholic, or all-embracing, Church: "God our Father, let the Spirit you sent on your Church to begin the teaching of the Gospel continue to work in the world through the hearts of all who believe."

The preface emphasizes the connection between Pentecost and the paschal mystery: "Today you sent the Holy Spirit on those marked out to be your children by sharing the life of your only Son, and so you brought the paschal mystery to its completion." Then, picking up the theme of the second reading, it adds: "The joy of the resurrection renews the whole world."

The prayer after Communion reminds us that the Spirit is permanently at work in the Church, especially through the sacraments: "Father, may the food we receive in the Eucharist help our eternal redemption. Keep within us the vigor of your Spirit and protect the gifts you have given to your Church."

The paschal mystery

Now that we have made our way through the major seasons of the Christian year — Advent, Nativity and Epiphany, Lent, and the Easter season — we are in a position to appreciate better the unity of the paschal mystery.

We can see that everything in the Church's life has this mystery for its center, leads into it, and depends upon it. The celebration of the incarnation would simply be the recalling of a historical event if we did not know that the incarnation is the necessary starting point for Christ's carrying out of the Father's will that he offer a sacrifice on mankind's behalf for the sake of the covenant. We are also better able to grasp the mystery as a whole, comprising as it does the death, resurrection, and ascension of Christ, and the sending of the Spirit. That is the total mystery that the Church lives out in each of her members, and the only real purpose of the liturgy is to assure the actualization of it.

In his first sermon on Pentecost, St. Leo the Great speaks as follows:

> This day contains within itself the great mysteries of the old and new economies, showing clearly that the law had foretold grace and that grace brought the fulfillment of the law. It was on the fiftieth day after the sacrifice of the lamb that the law was given on Mount Sinai to the Hebrews who had been liberated from Egypt. So too, once Christ had suffered and the true Lamb of God had been slain, it was on the fiftieth day after his resurrection that the Holy Spirit came upon the apostles and the multitude of believers. The alert Christian will readily see that the initial events of the Old Testament served the gospel in its beginnings and that the second covenant had its origin in the same Spirit who had instituted the first.[198]

There is an interesting passage in the Saint's second sermon on Pentecost in which he insists that the gift given on Pentecost is not an absolute beginning but rather a new outpouring of grace:

> Let us not doubt that when on Pentecost the Holy Spirit filled the Lord's disciples, he was not giving his gift for the first time but was rather extending a gift already given. The patriarchs, the prophets, the priests, and all the saints of earlier times were

nourished by the same sanctifying spirit. No sacrament was ever instituted, no mystery ever celebrated, that did not involve his grace. The power of his gifts had ever been the same, though the gifts had not previously been given in so great a measure.[199]

The Spirit today

The sequence for Pentecost, though grandiose and perhaps even somewhat outmoded in style, sings compellingly of the Church's joy and of all that the world owes to the Holy Spirit. The Spirit's activity has not ceased. Pentecost was doubtless a climactic moment in which the Spirit showed how generous his gifts are, but, as St. Leo has just told us, the Spirit had acted in the world before Pentecost and he has not ceased to act since then. The constitutions and decrees of the Second Vatican Council are filled with references to the Holy Spirit; in fact, a study of the theology of the Holy Spirit as found in these documents would be most worthwhile.

We have the impression that the Catholics of our day restrict the activity of the Spirit to the elaboration of dogma and to the making of decisions with regard to the present circumstances of the Church's life. They too readily forget the constant activity of the Spirit in the sacraments. Every Christian lives his life under the influence of the Spirit given to him in baptism and confirmation. It is the Spirit who strengthens our faith and unity each time we receive the Eucharist. The epiclesis that has been made a part of the three new Eucharistic Prayers should remind us that the Spirit acts in the Eucharist not only to transform the bread and wine but also to intensify our faith and deepen our unity within the Church.

The Spirit also acts in priestly ordination to give the person called the power to actualize the mysteries of Christ. He is present in the sacrament of marriage to give the partners the strength and courage they need for fidelity to their mutual union in imitation of the union of Christ and his Church. At every moment, in fact, we are permeated by the Spirit. There is no prayer meeting and no liturgy of the word in which the Spirit is not actively enabling us to pray and converse with the Lord present among us by the power of the same Spirit, for it is the Spirit who brings the Scripture text to life. It is the Spirit who enables us to say, "Father!"

24. THE FERIAL READINGS OF THE EASTER SEASON

The readings for the weekdays of the Easter season are chosen according to a principle that allows little scope for a coherent commentary. As on the Sundays of Ordinary Time, one Gospel is read continuously. On these Sundays, however, the other reading suggests the viewpoint from which the Church reads each of the successive Gospel pericopes. But on the ferias of the Easter season the first reading cannot serve this purpose, since along with the continuous reading of St. John's Gospel, there is also a continuous reading of the Acts of the Apostles. The two series of readings advance side by side but without any intrinsic relation to each other.

This practice is the renewal of an ancient tradition that has been followed in almost all the other Liturgies. The reading of the Acts of the Apostles is quite suited to this period of the Church year, since it brings us into vivid contact with the Church of the risen Christ, who has now sent his Spirit upon it. Similarly, there is great profit to be drawn from the reading of the Fourth Gospel during this season. We must not, however, try to correlate the two readings; there is no specific connection between them. The spiritual fruit that we are offered consists of a global vision, and on this there is no point in trying to offer a commentary, since such a commentary would amount to commentaries on the Fourth Gospel and on the Acts of the Apostles.

Even if we were to attempt a commentary on these two books of the New Testament, it would contribute nothing as far as an understanding of the liturgical celebration goes, since the Fourth Gospel and the Acts of the Apostles are not related to each other on each successive day in accordance with some pattern that the liturgy intends to impose. All we can do here, then, is to refer the reader to good commentaries on the two books and to urge the reading of the texts in the light of Easter and the paschal mystery.

Octave of Easter

As we read the texts for the octave, we can at least note that while the Acts of the Apostles is read continuously, the texts from the Gospels are each chosen, not by reference to Acts, but by reference to the resurrection celebrated a few days before. To this extent the octave does form a whole and can be presented as such.

The Gospel pericopes [74–84] all relate various appearances of the risen Christ to such witnesses as the holy women, the disciples at Emmaus, and the disciples on the shore of the Sea of Tiberias. The fact of being chosen as a witness always requires of the one chosen the giving of testimony to others, since the resurrection is Good News that must be proclaimed to the world. The resurrection also looks to the past, inasmuch as it is the fulfillment of the prophecies relating to the history of salvation.

The readings from the Acts of the Apostles [73–83] emphasize the apostles' role as witnesses of the resurrection. They cannot remain silent about what they have seen [83] but must preach Christ dead and risen [79], in whom alone salvation is to be found [81]. It is in the name of this Jesus that Peter heals a paralytic [77]. Let everyone therefore be converted, begin to believe, and be baptized [75].

Second week

We may, in a similar way, attempt to pull together the teaching of each of the other weeks, as presented in the continuous reading of the Fourth Gospel and the Acts of the Apostles. We need not, however, expect any great unity of thought that would bind the two series of readings together, since the Church has not chosen the texts in view of a theme.

The Gospel pericopes of this week continue to show Christ to us: he comes from God and enables us to know God [88]; God sent him so that he might save the world [90], for the Father has now put everything into his hands [92]. It is the risen Christ who continues to secure the salvation of the world, and that is why he shows his disciples how real his resurrection was and and how real his risen body now is [94]; that is why he walks on the water [96]. If we too want to enter upon the way of salvation and reach the kingdom, we must be reborn of water and the Spirit [86].

The Acts of the Apostles shows us the new life of the young community. We see the community praying for the power the Spirit gives so that Christians may proclaim the Good News [85]. Deep love binds the community together; the faithful have but one mind and one heart [87]. The apostles, for their part, cannot but testify to what they have witnessed [91]; they may have to suffer imprisonment, but that will not prevent them from continuing their teaching [89]. The choice of seven men for stewardship functions assures the proper organization of the Church's life [95].

Third week

Each Christian's life comes from the risen Christ, but that life must then be focused on eternal life and the demands the Lord makes of us — such is the teaching of the Gospel pericopes during this week. We must look for the food that does not perish [98]; it comes from God our Father [100]. Christ's flesh is truly food [106], for he is the living Bread

that has come down from heaven [104]. Anyone who sees
the Son has eternal life [102]. Christ is thus the center of
our lives; to whom else shall we go? [108].

The Acts of the Apostles shows us the ongoing witnessing activity of the disciples: they proclaim the Good News
everywhere [101]. Philip baptizes an Ethiopian [103],
while Paul proves to be an instrument God has chosen for
the conversion of the Gentiles [105]. The Church is thus
continually growing under the guidance of the Spirit [107].
The obligation to preach the Good News may even bring a
man to martyrdom: the wisdom and the Spirit of God fill
Stephen [97], and he gives his life in testimony to the message entrusted to him [99].

Fourth week

The Gospel pericopes emphasize the fact that the person
of Jesus is our sole way to salvation. He and the Father are
one [112], so that whoever sees him sees the Father [120].
He is the Door [110], the Light that has come into the
world [114], the Way, the Truth, and the Life [118]. Those
whom he sends represent him [116].

The readings from Acts show us Jesus, who is of the race
of David [115], as risen from the dead [117]. This proclamation of the person of Jesus leads to conversions among the
pagans [109–119], even among the Greeks [111]. The
Church faces a continuing need to organize itself for its
missionary task, and Barnabas and Paul are chosen under
the inspiration of the Spirit [113].

Fifth week

During this week the Gospel pericopes emphasize the
special situation of the Christian: he is called upon to remain in Christ so that he may bear fruit [126] and find joy
[128], for Christ is the giver of true peace [124]. To remain
in Christ means loving one another [130]. The disciple, to
whom the Spirit now teaches everything [124], is so permeated by the life of Christ that, like the original disciples

whom Jesus chose, he no longer belongs to this world
[132].

The readings from the Acts of the Apostles continue the
story of the new Church's life. She is ever faithful to her
mission of preaching that men must abandon idols [121],
while the community also keeps constantly before it the
memory of what God has done for it [123]. The problem of
the conversion of the Gentiles is resolved, as is the problem
of circumcision [125]. Missioners are not to lay excessive
burdens on the pagans who are converted [127]; in fact,
nothing extra that is unnecessary is to be required of them
[129]. The Church continues to grow; Paul and Luke set off
on a missionary journey [131].

Sixth week

In the Gospel, Jesus announces his departure [140],
which is necessary if the Spirit is to come [136]. The Spirit
will bear witness to Jesus [134] and will guide the disciples
to the truth in its entirety [138]. The disciples have now
found their true way: The Father loves them because they
have loved Jesus and have believed in him [144]; no one
will be able to take their joy from them [142].

The community's life is focused chiefly on the mission of
witnessing. Thus Paul and Silas, while in prison, preach
conversion [135] and continue to proclaim Jesus [137]; each
Sabbath Paul addresses the congregation in the synagogue
[139]; the Lord also sends him to the Corinthians [141].
The witness of the apostles is so convincing that it leads
others likewise to bear witness, for example, the Jew Apol-
los, who preaches to his fellow Jews about Christ [143].
New members are constantly entering the community, for
example, Lydia and her household [133].

Seventh week

Jesus reaches the end of his time on earth and prepares to
sacrifice his life. His priestly prayer is broad in scope: May

the Father glorify him, now that his mission is accomplished, so that his disciples may be glorified in him [148]. His disciples must seek unity above and before all else [152] and be one as Jesus and his Father are one [150]. They must not be fearful or downcast, for Christ has conquered the world; this should fill them with courage [146]. To secure this unity and renew this courage, the disciples need a leader who will represent Jesus in this world and be the shepherd of his sheep [154]. John ends his Gospel by asserting his own apostleship: he is one who has seen the risen Jesus, and he bears witness to him [156].

The Acts of the Apostles continues the story of the community's missionary activities: Paul baptizes and bestows the Spirit at Ephesus [145], where he also preaches a sermon in which he asserts that God has the power to build up the community and give its members a share in his heritage [149]. Paul continues to bear witness to Christ and is ordered to go to Rome [151]. He never stops preaching the resurrection of Christ as the center of Christian faith [153], for his great desire is to carry out fully the ministry Christ gave him [147]. He will die at Rome after proclaiming the kingdom of God [155].

The two books that are thus continuously read during the weeks of the Easter season have the power to enable us to grasp vividly what the Lord did and is still continuing to do. When we read the Acts of the Apostles, we are reading our family history, but not simply as though it concerned only past events. The Gospel of John, with its many deeply moving passages, brings home to us the reality of what we are, for Jesus' words, addressed long ago to his first disciples, are addressed now to us.

25. MISSAL PRAYERS DURING THE EASTER SEASON

It will be worth our while to take a look, even a hurried and superficial one, at the various prayers said in the Masses of the Easter season. Our purpose is to discern the chief points of theology that the Church is emphasizing during the season.

The liturgical mystery

The paschal mystery is not simply a memory but a present, transforming reality. Each year, therefore, we must ask the Lord for the power to live the Easter season as we should:

> May we who relive this mystery each year
> come to share it in perpetual love.[200]

The Pasch is a present reality and not a mere memory. It is a continuation of redemption, and God must help us if we are to keep it present, not only at the moment when it is celebrated but throughout our Christian lives, which are meant to be paschal lives:

> Almighty Father,
> let the love we have celebrated in this Easter season
> be put into practice in our daily lives.[201]

The mystery thus present has transforming power and continues to work its effects in us:

> Ever-living God,
> help us to celebrate our joy
> in the resurrection of the Lord
> and to express in our lives
> the love we celebrate.[202]

> Lord,
> give us joy by these Easter mysteries.

> Let the continuous offering of this sacrifice
> by which we are renewed
> bring us to eternal happiness.[203]

The transformation we undergo is entirely the work of the Spirit; he it is who disposes us to do the Father's will:

> Father,
> let your Spirit come upon us with power
> to fill us with his gifts.
> May he make our hearts pleasing to you
> and ready to do your will.[204]

It is also the power of the Spirit that enables us to discern just what God's will for us is:

> Lord,
> send the power of your Spirit upon us
> that we may remain faithful
> and do your will in our daily lives.[205]

We have now passed from our former world and live among the signs of the new age:

> Father of mercy,
> hear our prayers
> that we may leave our former selves behind
> and serve you with holy and renewed hearts.[206]

Faith and baptism are the source of our rebirth and renewal:

> Lord, through faith and baptism
> we have become a new creation.
> Accept the offerings of your people
> and bring us to eternal happiness.[207]

Baptism purifies us, and the celebration of the paschal mystery reinvigorates our faith:

> God of mercy,
> you wash away our sins in water,
> you give us new birth in the Spirit,

and redeem us in the blood of Christ.
As we celebrate Christ's resurrection
increase our awareness of these blessings.
and renew your gift of life within us.[208]

The prayers of the Easter season call attention to the action in us of the paschal liturgy:

Father of love,
watch over your Church
and bring us to the glory of the resurrection
promised by this Easter sacrament.[209]

Those who have been initiated into the Christian mysteries are now capable of leading a transfigured life:

Merciful Father,
may these mysteries give us a new purpose
and bring us to a new life in you.[210]

The ultimate reason for this possibility is that we are nourished by the Easter sacraments; they are the foundation of our abiding transformation in Christ:

Lord,
you have nourished us with your Easter sacraments.
Fill us with your Spirit,
and make us one in peace and love.[211]

It is therefore not only at the moment of the celebration that we are touched by God's renewing grace; the effects of the Easter mystery are constantly being produced in us:

God of mercy,
may the Easter mystery we celebrate
be effective throughout our lives.[212]

Some of the postcommunion prayers take up this last theme but connect it specifically with the Eucharist:

Almighty and ever-living Lord,
you restored us to life
by raising Christ from death.

Strengthen us by this Easter sacrament;
may we feel its saving power in our daily life.[213]

Some prayers go even further in linking Easter and the sacraments by seeing the latter as the means of our redemption and our participation in the divine nature:

Lord, may this celebration of our redemption
help us in this life
and lead us to eternal happiness.[214]

Lord God,
by this holy exchange of gifts
you share with us your divine life.[215]

All this is not independent of us and our inner attitudes. On the contrary, our minds and hearts must be fully involved in the celebration and must truly participate in the paschal mystery:

Lord,
by this Easter mystery
prepare us for eternal life.
May our celebration of Christ's death and resurrection
guide us to salvation.[216]

Victory over sin and death

The prayers at times present the "negative" side of the paschal mystery, that is, the abandonment or elimination of a past situation so as to make possible the creation of a new being. The negative aspect (destruction of sin and death) and the positive aspect (rebirth, new life, glory) are not always brought together in the prayer. We shall therefore illustrate each aspect separately.

We are liberated from our errors and sins, from death and a corrupt world:

You have freed us from the darkness of error and sin.
Help us to cling to your truths with fidelity.[217]

His death is our ransom from death.[218]

Because Christ has conquered, we are freed and share in his conquest:

> Today the Lord Jesus, the king of glory,
> the conqueror of sin and death,
> ascended to heaven. . . .[219]

He has destroyed the corrupt world;[220] by being sacrificed he has conquered death,[221] that is, by dying, he has destroyed death itself.[222] Easter is for us, as it was for the Israelites, a night of liberation.[223]

A new being

Far more attention is given in the prayers to the positive side of the paschal mystery. We are a new creation; we are beings made new by the Lord's paschal mystery. Some prayers simply state the fact without giving the reasons for the renewal and without specifying its nature. They simply emphasize that we are now new men. Moreover, the renewal affects not man alone but the whole of creation:

> Lord,
> may this sharing in the sacrament of your Son
> free us from our old life of sin
> and make us your new creation.[224]

The paschal mystery is the source of our rebirth to a new life, and the Holy Spirit is the one who effects the transformation.[225] In a literal sense, we are made new creatures along with the rest of the created order.[226] Our being is wholly renewed.[227]

We experience a new birth[228] and become new men.[229]

Adoptive sonship

The goal of the whole history of salvation is to make us God's adopted sons and daughters. That is the viewpoint of the prayers during the Easter season; they contain many references to this adoption.

Sometimes the adoption is linked to faith, freedom, and eternal life:

> God our Father,
> look upon us with love.
> You redeem us and make us your children in Christ.
> Give us true freedom
> and bring us to the inheritance you promised.[230]

Other prayers remind us that mankind had at one time possessed the rank and dignity of God's sons but had lost it; God's action, then, was really one of restoration:

> God our Father. . . .
> you have made us your sons and daughters,
> and restored the joy of our youth.[231]

Sometimes our adoption is seen as a grace contributing to the growth of the Church:

> Almighty and eternal God,
> glorify your name by increasing your chosen
> people.[232]

Another prayer of the Easter Vigil touches on the same theme:

> Everywhere throughout the world you increase your
> chosen people.[233]

Adoption is given bolder expression in the alternate prayer for the beginning of the Good Friday service. Here the Church asks that we become like God's own Son:

> Lord,
> by the suffering of Christ your Son
> you have saved us all from the death
> we inherited from sinful Adam.
> By the law of nature
> we have borne the likeness of his manhood.
> May the sanctifying power of grace
> help us to put on the likeness of our Lord in
> heaven.[234]

Adoption is a gift already bestowed on us. If, however, we are to live as God's children should, then our own inner attitudes must progressively deepen and become more perfect:

> Increase your Spirit of love within us.[235]

The adoption means a sharing in the divine nature. The prayers that speak of it link this sharing with our sharing in the Eucharist:

> Lord God,
> by this holy exchange of gifts
> you share with us your divine life.[236]

In this context, the ascension of Christ into heaven has special meaning for the Christian, being a sign that he is already, in a measure, divinized:

> In his risen body he plainly showed himself to his disciples
> and was taken up to heaven in their sight
> to claim for us a share in his divine life.[237]

Through adoptive sonship, our human nature is not only restored to its pristine condition; it is even exalted beyond that:

> Father,
> in restoring human nature
> you have given us a greater dignity
> than we had in the beginning.[238]

One prayer looks even beyond mankind to the world at large when it speaks of the effects of redemption:

> Father,
> through the obedience of Jesus,
> your servant and your Son,
> you raised a fallen world.[239]

The paschal mystery, then, has truly wrought a change in us. It has sanctified us:

> Lord, by shedding his blood for us,
> your Son, Jesus Christ,
> established the paschal mystery.
> In your goodness, make us holy
> and watch over us always,[240]

and has made us so like to Christ that we have already been clothed in his immortality:

> Watch over your chosen family.
> Give undying life to all
> who have been born again in baptism.[241]

The baptized people

All these graces are not only given to men as individuals but are meant to form a people. The kingdom is open to those reborn of water and the Spirit:

> Father,
> you open the kingdom of heaven
> to those born again by water and the Spirit.[242]

The reference here is to the whole baptized people, who are renewed by the joy of the resurrection;[243] the whole Church is the subject of God's sanctifying action.[244] Christ, the Head, is now glorified, and the Church, his Body, shares his glory and is advancing toward the completion of that glorification:

> God our Savior,
> hear us,
> and through this holy mystery give us hope
> that the glory you have given Christ
> will be given to the Church, his body.[245]

In her celebration of the paschal mystery, the Church prays that God's people in its entirety may enter the glory of heaven:

> Almighty and ever-living God,
> give us new strength

from the courage of Christ our shepherd,
and lead us to join the saints in heaven.[246]

Created anew for resurrection and eternal life

We have been created anew, and the change that has been worked in us, making us adoptive sons and sharers in the divine life, is leading us to our own resurrection and to eternal life:

Almighty and ever-living Lord,
you restored us to life
by raising Christ from death.[247]

Christ's resurrection has thus become ours; for us individually, however, the resurrection is still an object of hope:

God our Father,
may we look forward with hope to our resurrection.[248]

The resurrection certainly lies ahead as an objective we can attain, but our weakness is also a fact, and the resurrection is a grace:

May we come to share the glory of his resurrection.[249]

Our victory

The resurrection, in which we became sharers through baptism when we passed from death to life,[250] is for us, as it was for Christ, a victory:

Today the Lord Jesus, the king of glory,
the conqueror of sin and death,
ascended to heaven. . . .[251]

Or again:

Christ is the victim who dies no more,
the Lamb, once slain, who lives for ever.[252]

We share this victory with Christ:

His ascension is our glory and our hope.[253]

It is a victory that should shine out in our lives and be visible to those around us because of our outlook and conduct:

> All-powerful God,
> help us to proclaim the power of the Lord's resurrection.[254]

The reason is that Christ's victory, which is the condition of ours, is a victory that opens the door to eternal life for us:

> God our Father,
> by raising Christ your Son
> you conquered the power of death
> and opened for us the way to eternal life.[255]

26. THE EASTER VIGIL IN OTHER LITURGIES

There is no point in printing a table of the readings found in the older Latin liturgies for the paschal triduum and for the Easter season. Such a table would show us little that is different in any significant way.

The Würzburg Lectionary[256] provides readings for nine Sundays after the octave Sunday of Easter; not all of these could have been used, since at no period was there ever so long an Easter season. The readings continue the reading from the Letters of Peter and the Gospel of John. The Murbach Lectionary[257] has almost exactly the same list of readings as are to be found in the epistolary and evangeliary of Würzburg. The Missal of 1570 in turn adopted almost without exception the readings proposed by the Murbach Lectionary.

On the Milanese and Gallican liturgies, it is quite difficult to express an opinion, since the readings are presented in various ways by a number of lectionaries and sacramentaries; on some days no readings are indicated. The same is true of the Spanish liturgy.

This is not the place for suggesting explanations of such phenomena as the one just mentioned; it is far better to point out what may be still useful and manifests some real originality. For this reason, we have decided to limit ourselves to a list of the readings used in the Roman liturgy of the Easter Vigil until the first of the recent reforms (1955); a list of the readings for the Vigil in the Byzantine liturgy; and, finally, a list of the Vigil readings in the Coptic liturgy.

The current reform has considerably enriched the lectionary for the Easter season. There is nothing to be gained by printing the far less substantial lists of readings from the Würzburg Lectionary and Evangeliary, especially since it is difficult to see what principle was at work. Why, for example, should the so-called Catholic Letters be read during the Easter season? It looks as if their introduction into this season was due to an early reform of the lectionary; the reformers realized that certain books of Scripture were not being read and decided to get them in on the Sundays of the Easter season. This would also explain why readings are provided for nine Sundays after Low Sunday in the Würzburg Lectionary.[258]

The Vigil readings in the Roman liturgy of 1570

1. Genesis 1:1-31; 2:1-2   Creation.
2. Genesis 5:32–8:21   The Deluge.
3. Genesis 22:1-19   The sacrifice of Isaac.
4. Exodus 14:24-31; 15:1   Crossing of the Red Sea.
5. Isaiah 54:17; 55:1-11   Come and draw water.
6. Baruch 3:9-38   Praise of wisdom.
7. Ezekiel 37:1-14   The dry bones come alive.
8. Isaiah 4:1-6   The remnant of Israel; the vine.
9. Exodus 12:1-11   The Passover lamb.
10. Jonas 3:1-10   Jonas at Nineveh.
11. Deuteronomy 31:22-30   Last words of Moses.
12. Daniel 3:1-24   The youths in the fiery furnace.

Byzantine liturgy[259]

1. Genesis 1   Creation.
2. Isaiah 60:1-16   The glory of the new Jerusalem.
3. Exodus 12:1-11   The Passover lamb.
4. Jonas 1–4   Story of Jonas.
5. Josue 5:10-16   Circumcision of the Hebrews.
6. Exodus 13:20–15:19   The pillar of cloud; the covenant.
7. Sophonias 3:8-15   Remnant of Israel.
8. 1 Kings 17:8-24   Raising of widow's son to life.
9. Isaiah 61:10–62:5   Resurrection of Jerusalem,
10. Genesis 22:1-18   Sacrifice of Isaac.
11. Isaiah 61:1-10   Mission of the redeemer.
12. 2 Kings 4:8-27   Eliseus revives a child.
13. Isaiah 63:11–64:5   Divine vengeance.
14. Jeremias 31   Restoration of Israel.
15. Daniel 3:1-56   The youths in the fiery furnace.

Coptic liturgy[260]

1. Gospel of John (entire).
2. Deuteronomy 32:39-43   Canticle of Moses.
3. Isaiah 60:1-7   Glory of the new Jerusalem.
4. Isaiah 42:5-17   Song of the suffering Servant.
5. Isaiah 49:13-23   Renewal of Jerusalem.
6. Jeremias 31:23-38   Restoration of Jerusalem.
7. Habakkuk 3   The prophet's prayer.
8. Zacharias 2:10-13   Liberation of Zion.
9. Isaiah 49:6-11   The Servant, light to the nations.
10. Wisdom 5:1-17   Remorse of the wicked who did not recognize the just man.
11. Psalm 7:7-9   The persecuted just man.
12. Psalm 11:6   The Lord saves the poor man.
13. Psalm 23:7-10   Triumphal entrance song of the Lord.
14. Psalm 46:6-9   The Lord, King of Israel and the world.
15. Psalm 75:9-10   Hymn to the awesome and conquering Lord.

16. Psalm 67:19-34　The glorious epic of Israel.
17. Psalm 77:65-66　History of the Chosen People.
18. Psalm 81:1-8　The Lord's judgment against wicked judges.
19. Psalm 95:1-2, 10　The glory of the Lord.

SOLEMNITIES OF THE LORD
IN ORDINARY TIME

27. FEAST OF THE BLESSED TRINITY

Two approaches to the Trinity

It may seem strange that a special feast of the Blessed Trinity should ever have been established, since such a feast may seem to be a celebration of an abstraction. Latin theology approaches the Trinity in a highly metaphysical way by analyzing the concepts of person and nature and speaking of the Trinity as consisting of three distinct Persons, each with its complete personality but with all three possessing a single divine nature. Try as we will, that is bound to remain rather abstract!

The liturgy, on the other hand, both Latin and Oriental, constantly shows us the three divine Persons engaged in the work of saving and rebuilding the world. Greek theology likewise takes a more vital approach to the Trinity. It speaks of the Father so loving the world that to save it he sends his Son, who gives his life for us, rises from the dead, ascends to heaven, and sends his Spirit. The Spirit forms the image of the Son in us, so that as the Father looks at us, he sees in us his own Son. This "economic" approach to the Trinity, as it is called, gives us a more concrete grasp of the Trinity and enables us to situate ourselves in relation to the divine Persons, for we are better able to understand how our baptism and our entire Christian activity is connected with the Trinity.[261] In this approach, the Trinity is no abstraction.

The liturgy thus takes the same approach as Greek theology: it shows us the activity of the divine Persons. The

liturgy of the sacraments and the various prayers of the
liturgy have from the very beginning emphasized either the
action of the Trinity or our response of praise. Think, for
example, of the various doxologies (the "Glory be to the
Father . . .", etc.) and ancient hymns such as the *Gloria* and
the *Te Deum*.

Establishment of the feast

By the ninth century there were churches dedicated to
the Trinity, for example, in the monastery of St. Benedict of
Aniane.[262] There was a votive Office composed by Stephen,
bishop of Liege (d. 920).[263] At that period, however, there
was no feast of the Trinity. Yet we do find a feast being
celebrated in 1030 on the first Sunday after Pentecost, and
it quickly became popular and widespread. We are in-
formed of the event because it roused opposition, including
that, later on, of Pope Alexander III (d. 1181). Nonetheless,
the feast continued to be celebrated and became increasingly popular, to the point where Pope John XXII approved
it in 1334 as a feast of the universal Church, to be celebrated on the first Sunday after Pentecost.

It is not easy to determine the reasons for placing the
feast on the Sunday after Pentecost. It may be that once
Pentecost had climaxed the Easter season by celebrating
the sending of the Spirit, and thus the cycle of activities of
the three Persons, there was a desire to sum up their work,
as it were, in a single celebration. However, not all the
churches celebrated the feast on the Sunday after Pentecost; in fact, some celebrated it on the last Sunday after
Pentecost.

It must be acknowledged that a celebration of this type
could become popular only at a time when the liturgical life
and the proper understanding of the Bible were on the
wane. Close contact with the Scriptures as proclaimed in
the Church and with a liturgy that expressed at every moment the activity of the three divine Persons would not
have roused a desire for such a feast. On the other hand, the
theological mentality of the age when the feast became

universal could only have been pleased by it. The feast has at least this advantage, that it draws our attention to the fact that the Trinity is active in every liturgical celebration throughout the entire Church year.

CYCLE A

Believe in the love of God (John 3:16-18)

The Gospel for this Sunday does not deal in abstractions but confronts us in a very concrete way with the activity of the Trinity. More accurately, it speaks of the Father and the Son, but it does so in the same manner that Greek theology was later to adopt: "God so loved the world that he gave his only Son" (John 3:16).

This passage has already been used on the fourth Sunday of Lent (Cycle B), but the perspective there was different. This twofold use of the same passage should remind us of a point we have emphasized several times before, namely, that the texts of the liturgy take on a coloration from their liturgical context. On the fourth Sunday of Lent, attention was focused on what Jesus had to say to Nicodemus about rebirth, since at that time the catechumens were being prepared for baptism and the Christian community as a whole was preparing for Easter and the commemoration of its baptism in water and the Spirit. Here, on Trinity Sunday, the emphasis is on our contact with the divine Persons who effect our salvation.

The work of salvation which the Son accomplishes (and of which the Scriptures tell us) is also a sign of the Father's love for us. We can glimpse something of the character of this fatherly love, for when Jesus tells us that the Father has sent his "only" Son, we cannot help thinking of Abraham and his unconditional surrender of his son Isaac. That is the kind of love the Father shows us in sending his only Son — not to condemn the world but to save it.

If the encounter with the divine Persons is to be authentic, we must have faith. Not to believe in the name of the only Son of God is already to be condemned; to believe in the Son and therefore in the Father's love for us is to possess eternal life.

The Trinity, then, is Love. It is entirely at the service of the world, which It intends to re-create and thereby save.

A God merciful and gracious (Exod. 34:4b-6, 8-9)

When God reveals himself to Moses, he presents himself as a merciful and gracious God: "The Lord, the Lord, a God merciful and gracious, slow to anger, and abounding in steadfast love and faithfulness" (Exod. 34:6). The inspired writers were awestruck by the graciousness of God and by the fact that God should reveal himself in this way and speak thus of himself. "Your God bore you, as a man bears his son" (Deut. 1:31). "I trust in the steadfast love of God for ever and ever" (Ps. 52:8). "My God in his steadfast love will meet me" (Ps. 58:10). "Thou, O God, art my fortress, the God who shows me steadfast love" (Ps. 58:17). "Let thy compassion come speedily to meet us" (Ps. 79:8). "I will recount . . . the great goodness to the house of Israel, which he has granted them according to his mercy, according to the abundance of his steadfast love" (Is. 63:7). There are many other passages that exalt the tender, gracious love of God for men.

It would be impossible to list all the passages in which the Old Testament praises the mercy of God. Here are a few of the themes. Mercy is identical with God: He is the God of mercy (Deut. 4:31; Ps. 86:15; Wis. 9:1); he always acts mercifully (Exod. 20:6; Deut. 5:10), and his mercy is immense and without limit (Pss. 51:3; 115:5; 17:2; Dan. 3:42); it is even eternal (1 Chr. 16:34, 41; 2 Chr. 5:13; 7:13; 20:21; Pss. 100:5; 103:17; 107:1; 118:1, 29).

This is the God who appeared to Moses and whom Moses asked to remain in our midst (Exod. 34:9). The encounter with the God who loves gave Moses confidence, so that he can ask with hope and without fear: "O Lord, let the Lord, I pray thee, go in the midst of us, although it is a stiffnecked people; and pardon our iniquity and our sin, and take us for thy inheritance" (Exod. 34:9).

The God of peace and love will be with you (2 Cor. 13:11-13)

The end of the second reading confronts us with the full mystery of the Trinity, but does so in the atmosphere of love that is already characteristic of God in the Old Testament when he decides to make himself known. This same ending provides one of the greetings the celebrant may use at the beginning of the Eucharistic celebration: "The grace of the Lord Jesus Christ and the love of God and the fellowship of the Holy Spirit be with you all" (2 Cor. 13:13).

St. Paul usually ends his Letters with the formula: "The grace of our Lord Jesus Christ be with you" (Rom. 16:20; 1 Cor. 16:23; 1 Thess. 5:28; etc.). This may explain why he begins his Letters with greetings from one who comes in the name of Jesus Christ. In any event, the "grace" of Christ is evidently the redemption he won for us. Christ's act of ransoming us and our resultant salvation have God the Father for their ultimate source; it is he who out of love sent us the only Son, in whom we find salvation (Rom. 5:1-11; 8:28, 39). Finally, the Spirit gives himself to us through the faith we receive in baptism; he transforms us into new creatures as adopted children of God and members of Christ's Body, the Church; he makes us his temples.

It is God's love, then, that bestows salvation upon us by handing over his Son to death for us and raising him to glorious life again. The Father also sends us the Spirit, who unceasingly gives us the salvation that Christ acquired for us once and for all and that we progressively make our own by means of the Church's sacraments.

It would be difficult to find a better expression of what the Trinity is than the ending of Second Corinthians. We are also told there that by living in permanent union with the divine Persons, the Christian is to seek perfection and to live in peaceful unity (2 Cor. 13:11).

In the Liturgy of the Hours, at the Office of Readings, St.

Athanasius describes the splendors of the Trinitarian life in a letter to Serapion, bishop of Thmuis in Egypt. Here are two sections from the reading:

> The Father does all things through the Word in the Spirit, and thus the unity of the Holy Trinity is safeguarded. In the Church, therefore, we proclaim one God, "above all and through all and in all. He is "above all" as Father, principle, and source; he acts "through all" through the Word; he is "in all" in the Holy Spirit. . . . The gifts that the Holy Spirit distributes to each person are those granted by the Father through the Word. . . . When the Spirit is in us, the Word who gives us the Spirit is also in us, and the Father is in the Word.[264]

Commenting on the final verse of Second Corinthians, the Saint writes:

> The grace and gift given in the Trinity are given by the Father through the Word in the Holy Spirit. Just as the grace given comes from the Father through the Son, so we can have no participation in the gift except in the Holy Spirit. For it is by participating in him that we have the love of the Father and the grace of the Son and the communication of the Holy Spirit himself.[265]

CYCLE B

Baptized in the Father and the Son and the Holy Spirit (Matthew 28:16-20)

What we might call the "proccupation" of the Trinity is that the nations of the world should become "disciples." This means the nations must heed the Trinity, observe the commandments, and because of this observance, be sure that the Lord is with them to the end of time.

All authority in heaven and earth has been given to Jesus, the Son. Now that he has risen and acquired the title *Kyrios*, that is, Lord of heaven and earth, Jesus has the authority to send his disciples on a mission that is of radical importance for the Church and for the world as a whole. The apostles are to "make disciples."

According to Mark 13:10; 14:9; 16:15) and Luke (24:47), the apostles are to "preach" the good news. Here the language is stronger: not only are they to present the message objectively, but they are also to forge a bond between the message and those who accept it so that the message will work a profound change in them. A Christian, after all, is not simply a person who listens to teaching, studies it, and contemplates it as something outside himself. A Christian absorbs the message into his life and becomes a disciple. This, however, supposes faith, a gift bestowed by the Spirit in baptism.

Are the words "baptizing them in the name of the Father and of the Son and of the Holy Spirit" a reflection of the baptismal formula? I personally do not think so, despite the commentaries which argue that they are. I do not think we can say that in the apostolic period baptism was administered with a Trinitarian formula, in the sense that the formula with which we are familiar was already in use: "I baptize you in the name of the Father and of the Son and of the Holy Spirit." If we study the ancient liturgical books, we will soon be convinced that this formula did not appear in the Roman liturgy before the end of the seventh or the beginning of the eighth century. It is true, however, that in the earlier period baptism involved a triple immersion, each immersion being accompanied by a question put to the candidate about his faith in the each of the three divine Persons successively, and by his response: "I do believe." Properly Trinitarian formulas did, of course, exist from a very early time, and we find a number of them in Paul; there is no evidence, however, that they were used in the conferring of baptism.

We may think that the words "baptizing them in the

name, etc." mean bringing them into union with the Father, the Son, and the Holy Spirit. When all is said and done, to be a disciple and a Christian is to live in union with the divine Persons. Baptism establishes a close bond between each of us and the Trinity. We have been baptized into a relationship with them; this was always true, even when the formula "in the name of the Father and of the Son and of the Holy Spirit" was not used, as in fact it was not until the eighth century in the Latin Church. The very meaning of the sacrament is, in part, that it makes men share the life of the Trinity.

A God who took a nation for himself from the midst of another nation (Deut. 4:32-34, 39-40)

Concrete deeds manifest love. That principle holds for the Lord and all he did for his people. His preoccupation was to unite that people to himself. Thus the order given to the apostles to make disciples means that Christ wants to unite the nations to himself and thereby make them sharers in God's Trinitarian life.

The passage from the Book of Deuteronomy focuses attention on this desire of God to encounter a people and make it his own. "Did any people ever hear the voice of a god speaking out of the midst of the fire, as you have heard, and still live? Or has any god ever attempted to go and take a nation for himself from the midst of another nation . . . by a mighty hand and an outstretched arm . . . ?" Because of God's actions, history itself becomes an ongoing revelation of the Divinity.

The concrete conclusion to be drawn from this revelation of God through his actions is that we must obey the commandments. Today's passages from the Gospel and from the Old Testament thus reach the same conclusion. Because the triune God has revealed himself and because we are now really incorporated into the mystery, an attitude becomes obligatory and indeed increasingly urgent: We must heed God's commands and follow in his paths.

The Spirit makes us sons (Rom. 8:14-17)

The theme of union with God is also developed in the second reading. We are children of God and heirs of God along with Christ. God's promise to us is the promise of an inheritance (cf. Eph. 3:6; 2 Tim. 1:1; Titus 1:2). The Spirit who makes us children of God also leads us to our promised inheritance.

What is it that is promised us? In what does the inheritance consist? St. Paul speaks frequently on this subject. For him, the heritage that God intends for his children is his own kingdom and glory (1 Thess. 2:12). If we study the vocabulary of Paul a little more closely, we will find him saying the same thing in various other ways: the heritage is the kingdom (1 Cor. 6:9-10; Gal. 5:21; Eph. 5:5), or it is glory (Rom. 5:2; 8:18; Eph. 1:18); it is also eternal life (Rom. 6:22-23; Gal. 6:8; Titus 1:2), or glory and eternal life (Rom. 2:7). And this heritage is ours because we are God's children.

We must therefore allow ourselves to be "led" by the Spirit who is constantly active within us. He wishes to lead us, and we must let ourselves be led. That is what Paul means by saying that we should not "grieve the Holy Spirit" (Eph. 4:30).

All this amounts to saying that the Spirit radically transforms us, making us children of God and heirs to the promise with Christ. The Spirit makes the Christian so like Christ that the Father finds in the Christian the very image of the Son whom, out of love for us, he sent to save us.

Paul's language renders almost sensible to us the Trinity to which we are bound through baptism. Once again, all this supposes faith, but faith itself is something the Spirit constantly strengthens in us. If the beginning of faith leads us finally to the Trinity, it is the Trinity that bestows upon us, through the sacraments, the faith that leads us to It. Thus we are the constant object of the Trinity's action in our lives.

CYCLE C

The Spirit will guide us into all the truth (John 16:12-15)

The Gospel passage is part of the discourse after the Last Supper and contains words spoken by Jesus shortly before his earthly links with the apostles would be at an end.

The statement at the beginning of the passage is important: Jesus tells us he cannot teach us everything he would like to. The reason is not any indisposition on his part to do so or any failure to have used his time well while he was with the disciples; the reason is that his hearers were not yet capable of entering into the necessary dialogue with him.

To understand this, we must realize that Christ's teaching is not primarily a matter of doctrine; his teaching is indistinguishable from his person, and it is his person we must receive and accept. As John says in his Prologue, the message of Jesus takes the form of a gift of himself (John 1:4, 10), so that we must enter into dialogue with him rather than simply discuss a doctrine. However, despite the time he had spent with his disciples, they had not advanced far enough in this dialogue to be able to understand everything.

John had frequently been struck with the disciples' inability to enter into a true dialogue with Christ and to understand his mystery. Recall, for example, Thomas's question when Jesus says he is going away in order to prepare a place for them: "Lord, we do not know where you are going; how can we know the way?" (John 14:5). In reply, Jesus asserts that they can indeed know him and that they now do know him: "If you had known me, you would have known my Father also; henceforth you know him and have seen him" (14:7). At this point, it is Philip who shows his lack of understanding: "Lord, show us the Father, and we shall be satisfied." Jesus replies: "Have I been with you so long, and yet you do not know me, Philip? He who has seen me has seen the Father; how can you say, 'Show us the Father'? Do you not believe that I am in the Father and the Father in me?" (14:8-10).

In the same chapter, Judas asks, "Lord, how is it that you will manifest yourself to us, and not to the world?" Jesus answers, "If a man loves me, he will keep my word, and my Father will love him, and we will come to him and make our home with him" (14:22-23). Still later, immediately after today's passage, we see the disciples wondering what Jesus could mean by his words about going to the Father (John 16:16-17).

It is evident, then, that the Spirit will have to continue Christ's work and help the disciples understand the truth. Jesus seems here to be thinking of the Spirit's work in guiding the entire Church of the future; the Spirit will have to help the Church understand all that happens and give it meaning.

The passage thus shows us the relations between Father, Son, and Spirit. Jesus is sent by the Father; the Spirit, too, is sent by the Father to continue the Son's work in the Church. It is because of Jesus' prayer that the Father sends the Spirit (14:16). But Jesus himself also sends the Spirit from the Father (15:26).

Our whole lives as Christians in the Church are guided by the Spirit toward the full grasp of the truth. The Church's entire life is Trinitarian, for it is a sign of the Father's love that gives us the Son through whom we touch the Father, and does so in the Spirit, who is constantly leading us more fully to the truth in its whole extent.

The work of God is revealed as God's by its wisdom (Prov. 8:22-31)

We may be struck by the poetic beauty of this passage from the Book of Proverbs and be tempted, at a first reading, to see in it a hymn to the Person of the Son or the Person of the Spirit. And as a matter of fact, the New Testament identifies Christ as Wisdom that has become incar-

nate (Col. 1:15, 18; Apoc. 3:14); the Fathers, too, often identify Christ with Wisdom, or if they do not, they identify the
Spirit and Wisdom. And yet the passage does not allow the
exegete to say that wisdom is here a person; it is rather a
personification, used in order to exalt God's work, which in
its entirety is a manifestation of divine wisdom. We should
not therefore exaggerate the importance of the text as
though it contained a theology of Christ himself or of the
Spirit.

In the passage, Wisdom steps forward and describes herself. She was created by God, and this before anything else
was created; she exists, therefore, before the world was
made.

How is the passage to be understood in its liturgical context, that is, as part of the celebration of the Blessed Trinity? We shall not undertake a detailed interpretation of the
verses, but this much can be said: We should see expressed
in the passage the Church's intention of showing how God
had from the beginning prepared the mystery of love that
he would later reveal in his Son through the Spirit. The
passage in its context is thus an invitation to marvel at the
entire great work of God that ultimately leads us to share in
the life of the Trinity.

That, certainly, is how the responsorial psalm interprets
the passage, for it bids us say, as a refrain, "O Lord, our
God, how wonderful your name in all the earth!" (Ps. 8:1a).

Sharing the glory of God (Rom. 5:1-5)

"Our hope of sharing the glory of God" (Rom. 5:2) is a
hope that is already being fulfilled.

A very ancient prayer of exorcism that is still used in
the baptismal ritual tells us that we already possess the
rudimenta gloriae, that is, the beginnings of our future
glory.[266] We already live with the Trinity in the "love [that]
has been poured into our hearts through the Holy Spirit
which has been given to us" (5:5). We are already justified
by faith (5:1) and "have obtained access to this grace in

which we stand" (5:2). In other words, we are experiencing God's love for us.

This does not mean that all problems are solved; no, we are still in the stage of struggle and testing. But because we have faith and the assurance that we are united to the triune God, the trials and struggles take on a meaning they can have only for someone who has received the Spirit: "We rejoice in our sufferings, knowing that suffering produces endurance, and endurance produces character, and character produces hope" (5:3-4).

Life in the Spirit thus brings us peace with God through Christ in the Spirit, who pours out the love of God in our hearts.

28. FEAST OF CORPUS CHRISTI

Cultus of the reserved Sacrament

The twelfth century saw the rise of a desire for a more intense devotion to the Eucharist, but in a specialized form. Although it was not forgotten that the Eucharist is a sacrifice, the devotional impulse was focused especially on the real presence and on the need of paying Christ thus present the tribute of adoration and splendid surroundings. This new devotion to the Blessed Sacrament came into existence particularly in Belgium.

Hitherto the reserved Sacrament had, of course, been treated with great respect, but the Latin Church did not develop a special cultus of it, any more than had the Oriental Churches. The reasons for the growth of the new devotion were complex. It may have initially been a by-product of canon law; apologetic needs and theological developments then played a part. The end result, however, was a mysticism that eventually gave birth to religious congregations dedicated to the cultus and adoration of the Blessed Sacrament.

Motives

The penitential discipline continued to be quite severe, and many Catholics could not readily approach the Eucharistic table and communicate. At this same time there developed a widespread desire to look upon the Host; so intense was this wish that in some places the faithful would go from church to church, arriving at each just in time for the elevation of the Host at the consecration. For some classes of sinners, the only way they could participate in the Eucharistic celebration was to gaze at the Host.

At this period the Church was also busy defending the faithful against doubts about the reality of Christ's Eucharistic presence. These were the years when a number of miracles took place in which blood was seen to flow from the Host; we meet these phenomena in Belgium, Italy, and elsewhere. Meanwhile, in the theological schools, there had been a shift of emphasis in the treatment of the Eucharist. The Mass was always regarded as a sacrifice, but the aspect of sacrificial meal receded very much into the background, and attention was focused rather on the idea of God's majestic descent to the altar at the consecration. As a result, celebration of the Mass came to be characterized by profound reverence; increasingly monumental and majestic altars were built; the ritual became ever more solemn.

Development of the feast

Juliana of Retinnes (1192–1258), a nun in the Augustinian convent of Mont Cornillon near Liège (Belgium) and later prioress, revealed a series of visions that had been granted her, the first of them occurring in 1208. She saw a lunar disk surrounded by rays of dazzling white light; on one side of the disk, however, there was a dark spot that spoiled the beauty of the whole. The Lord explained to her that the dark spot meant that the Church still lacked a solemn feast in honor of the Blessed Sacrament.

Such a feast was introduced at Liège in 1246 and celebrated on the Thursday within the octave of Trinity Sunday. James Pantaléon, archdeacon of Liège and a confidant of Julian's, later became Pope Urban IV (1261–64) and extended the feast to the universal Church. While living as Pope at Orvieto, he was overwhelmed at the news of a Eucharistic miracle in nearby Bolsena: a priest tormented by doubts about the real presence saw a host change before his eyes into a bit of bloody flesh that left stains on the corporal.

The procession in honor of the Blessed Sacrament was not prescribed in the papal bull promulgating the feast, but the practice arose spontaneously and quickly spread.

CYCLE A

His flesh is food indeed and his blood is drink indeed (John 6:51-58)

The pericope is from the end of the discourse on the bread of life. Using different language, John often refers throughout the discourse to what we know elsewhere as the account of institution (Matthew 26:26-29; Mark 14:22-25; Luke 22:15-20; 1 Cor. 11:23-25). The whole of chapter 6, after the story of the multiplication of the loaves, is really a discourse on the Eucharist. The exegetes raise problems concerning the discourse, however, and some have even denied that it alludes to the Eucharist at all. We shall not enter into these discussions; what is of interest to us is the spiritual value of the passage on this feast when the Church reads it as the word of the Lord who, in the final analysis, is therein proclaiming himself.

It has been maintained that the verses in today's pericope were a later addition, because they show a certain lack of coherence. In any case, the whole discourse bears the marks of being the result of reflection by St. John long after the actual events. This is not to challenge the authenticity of the discourse; it is simply to indicate that the Savior's original words have been meditated on and recast for catechetical purposes.

Despite a superficial lack of unity, chapter 6 is in fact an excellent example of how John went about writing his Gospel. The procedure here can be paralleled elsewhere: Christ presents a truth in such a way that it can be interpreted in at least two different senses; the reactions of the hearers then lead him to correct misunderstandings and to explain more fully the truth he wants to teach. Other passages in which he follows the same pattern are the conversations with Nicodemus (chapter 3) and with the Samaritan woman (chapter 4).

In the discourse of chapter 6, the starting point is the exhortation: "Do not labour for the food which perishes, but for the food which endures to eternal life" (6:27). The language is such as to permit the hearers to mistake the true meaning, so that Christ then has the opportunity to specify his thought and lead the hearers more deeply into the mystery. The explanations finally become so clear that they provoke among the disciples a crisis that Jesus has been expecting. Their faith is tested, and some of them leave him.

Jesus' explanation proceeds by contrasting the manna in the desert with the bread of life, which is the true bread for man. Before identifying himself as the true Bread of life, the true Manna, Jesus must first show who he is. He does so by presenting himself as the Son of Man who is to come on the clouds of heaven; to the great scandal of the Jews, he speaks of himself as coming from heaven and as of divine origin (6:32-33). He can then go on to assert that he is the true Manna or Bread from heaven, and to compare it with the manna that Moses obtained from God: those who ate the manna in the desert are now dead, whereas the food Jesus offers gives unending life (6:30-35). Jesus is himself the Bread of life, and his hearers must seek this bread that does not become corrupted. He is the Eucharistic Bread; those who eat his body and drink his blood will abide in him and he in them (6:56). Jesus is here asserting the union that exists between himself and his disciples; in chapter 15 he will use the same language to teach the same truth.

He fed you with manna (Deut. 8:2-3, 14-16a)

We know how fond the Jews were of remembering the past in their prayers. It was natural that they should do so, for the experience of the deliverance from Egypt had left a permanent mark on Jewish life. We also know that for the Hebrew mind, "remembering" meant not simply recalling but actualizing the past, that is, making it present and operative. To recall the past was to make it present and thereby give the present the power it needed to face the future. Past events were therefore recalled with love; the great crises of the journey in the desert were a source of glory for Israel's God, and Israel shared the glory. The forty long years of wandering in the wilderness taught the people lessons they would never forget. It was a time when God could test his people's hearts and learn whether or not they would obey his commandments.

The time of testing did not end when the desert journey was over. It was an ongoing thing, and the people of later generations had to make their own the experiences their forefathers had undergone at a time when they were cast down and yet were also sure of God's presence and his gift of life.

In the passage read in today's Mass, the manna is the focus of attention. The passage makes the point that the later generations had to learn, like their fathers before them: their life depended not on material bread alone but on every word that came from the mouth of God. What did this statement mean? It meant that God gives life through his word, as he did first at creation. The word of God was given, for example, through the prophets, and the Hebrews looked upon it as truly a form of food. The manna was food also, a material food, but it was also a sensible sign, a kind of materialization, of God's life-giving and nourishing word. At a later point in the Book of Deuteronomy (30:15, 20, etc.), we are told again that God gives his people life through his word. He is the God who saves, and it is as Savior that he was the object of the people's remembrance and praise.

All this holds true for us, the new people of God. The Gospel tells us that Christ, the Word of God, is the true Bread of life. He is also the Bread of the covenant, but now of a new and everlasting covenant, the covenant that achieves its purpose.

The responsorial psalm, Psalm 147, sings of the Lord who "declares his word to Jacob, his statutes and ordinances to Israel" (v. 19). Proudly and jealously it adds: "He has not dealt thus with any other nation; they do not know his ordinances" (v. 20).

The Bread that makes us one: One Bread, one Body (1 Cor. 10:16-17)

While the manna helped the people's physical life, the word of God sustained and united and refreshed them. These last words describe the role of the Eucharist.

Jewish rites were no longer practiced by those who had converted to Christianity, but the apostles were fully cognizant of the Jewish context in which the Lord had instituted the Eucharist. The language that the apostles use reflect that context and background, as do the accounts of institution. Speaking a blessing and breaking bread — that is what happened at the Passover meal, and that is what Christ likewise did. For the Jews, the Passover meal was a commemorative meal that actualized the "passage" of the people from slavery to freedom. Christ took the rite and made it his own, but the bread broken was now the true Bread, his body, and the cup of the covenant was the cup of his blood. The Bread broken, the one Bread that is shared by many, is the sign that effects community: one Bread, one Body.

The Eucharistic meal is a sacrificial meal that unites the faithful to Christ their Head. As the theologians put it, the Eucharist builds the Church. We are "one thing" (cf. John 17:21): the Lord and we, each of us with all the others.

The well-known sequence for Corpus Christi is really not poetic in character, but rather takes a metaphysical approach to the Eucharist. In its own way, however, it expresses all aspects of the mystery by which the Church has lived through the centuries and by which we continue to live today: God's word and God's bread.

CYCLE B

This is my body, this is my blood of the new covenant (Mark 14:12-16, 22-26)

This is a text we already met when we were meditating on the readings for Holy Thursday. However, as we shall see, the accompanying Old Testament reading here puts the New Testament text in a special light, emphasizing the "new covenant" aspect of it. This is to say that the passage from Mark was chosen for Corpus Christi, not so much to glorify the real presence (though this presence is certainly presupposed) as to underline the fact that the Eucharist is the sacrifice of the new covenant. It is for this reason that the Gospel passage includes so much detail about the preparation for the Passover and about the room where the meal will be eaten.

"The blood of the covenant" is thus the main reason why the pericope is used on this day. In the New Testament, blood acquires great importance because of Christ's death. References to the blood of Christ occur quite often (1 Cor. 10:16; 11:27; Eph. 2:13; Heb. 9:14; 10:9; 1 John 1:7; 1 Peter 1:2; Apoc. 7:14; 12:11). These references, with their explicit or implicit allusion to the sacrifice of the Cross, are a way of emphasizing the saving power of Christ's death, by which the new covenant was concluded. As the old covenant of Sinai was sealed by blood (Exod. 24:8), so the new covenant is sealed in an incomparably more perfect way by the blood of Christ (Heb. 9:18). The effect of the new covenant is the forgiveness of sins, as foretold by the prophets (Jer. 31:31-34).

We may ask whether, in the thinking of Jesus, this covenant blood, like the covenant blood of Sinai, is connected with the Book of Isaiah (42:6; 49:8) and the Servant of Yahweh, who gives his life for his people. In any case, the new covenant represents a new stage in the history of salvation. Henceforth the relations between God and men will concern the effective fulfillment of the divine plan of salva-

tion. It was God who took the initiative in the earlier covenants; it is he who has now brought into being the new,
definitive, everlasting covenant.

The new covenant is an anticipation of the end of time.
The reference to drinking the wine new in the kingdom
shows that the messianic age has begun and that participation in the Eucharist is already a participation in the eschatological banquet.

The blood of the covenant which the Lord has made with us (Exod. 24:3-8)

The choice of this passage from the Book of Exodus as a
first reading justifies us, as we have already pointed out, in
concentrating, in the Gospel reading, on the new covenant
that is renewed and actualized in the Eucharistic celebration.

The text from the Book of Exodus does not, however,
simply detail the rites in which the covenant is concluded
by means of the blood of animals. The passage also emphasizes the concrete commitment on the part of the people
that the conclusion of this divinely initiated covenant supposes. The outward rite and its bloodshed will not save; the
people must live by the words the Lord has spoken.

What is God's will as expressed in his words here? It is
clear that he wants to bring men together into a people that
will worship him and be devoted to his service; he, for his
part, will keep the promises he has made. On Sinai, then,
God links himself to a people. We may think that the juridical manner in which the covenant is concluded renders it
too exclusive and that salvation is too much connected with
the existence of a nation and with its temporal prosperity.
We may also ask whether salvation is not turned too much
into a reward for obedience, so that its character as a free
gift is diminished.

Whatever be the validity of these objections, the new
covenant eliminates all such ambiguities. It is addressed to
all the peoples of the earth, and it involves first and

foremost a changing of men's heart through the power of Christ's blood and the sending of the Spirit. Participation in the Eucharist draws the Christian ever more fully into the covenant and assures its concrete fulfillment both in him individually and in the world at large.

The responsorial psalm, Psalm 116, is a thanksgiving for the covenant and an expression of the desire to offer sacrifice while invoking the Lord's name: "I will lift up the cup of salvation and call on the name of the Lord" (v. 13).

Christ, Mediator of a new covenant (Heb. 9:11-15)

The Letter to the Hebrews looks at the new covenant from a cultic and priestly point of view. In the opening lines of the pericope, Christ is seen as the High Priest of the new covenant, and the temple that is his own body is said to be more perfect than the temple of the former covenant, because Christ's temple was not built by men and therefore does not belong to this world.

The passage continues the comparison of the two covenants by giving a theological description of Christ's priestly activity. The blood of the covenant is no longer that of an animal but the blood of Christ himself. There is no longer a mere sprinkling with blood that purifies men only outwardly so that they can legally engage in worship; in the new covenant, the blood of Christ, who has offered himself as a spotless victim, purifies the very consciences of men.

The passage thus provides several profound ideas: Christ as the High Priest who enters once and for all into the sanctuary and there offers his own blood; the sacrifice of Christ, who offers himself to God as a holy victim; the blood of Christ that purifies men's consciences; the new covenant.

To begin with, Christ is the High Priest of the good things to come, for he is Mediator between God and men (Heb. 5:1). He gives men the objective possibility of entering into a covenant with God and of receiving superior blessings and the good things to come. "To come," because while on God's part the offering of a covenant is complete and unreserved, our acceptance of it is still imperfect. In the covenant, God made his plan of salvation fully available, but we must respond to it with a completeness as yet unrealized. Nonetheless, Christ, prefigured by the Jewish priesthood, has now supplanted that priesthood, because the covenant promises are totally fulfilled in his person.

Christ needed to enter the sanctuary only once (Heb. 9:12). He did so by passing from this world to his Father. Consequently, his entry into the heavenly sanctuary was not merely symbolic, as it was in Old Testament ritual, but fully real. Moreover, he made his offering in the temple of his own body, which, though it was a truly human body, was not man-made and now is no longer part of the present creation.

The victim that Christ offers is himself. Here the Letter to the Hebrews shows how the theology of Christ's sacrifice differs from the theology of Old Testament sacrifice. In the latter, the important thing was the sprinkling of blood; in the former, death and bloodshed are symbols of the inner attitude of Christ. What redeems us is not, strictly speaking, the shedding of his blood and his death, but what these signify, namely, his perfect self-giving to the Father by doing the Father's will. This inner attitude of Christ was and continues to be a permanent reality; consequently, he offers once and for all, yet his intercession is ongoing.

The blood of Christ, that is, the interior offering of himself that is signified by the shedding of his blood, purifies our consciences. This is to say that Christ's self-giving has a purifying power that produces its effect in us whenever we have recourse to it. Christ did not offer a victim distinct from himself; he offered his very self. Consequently, once our consciences are purified, we can offer worship to the Father in union with Christ the Priest.

The covenant is now objectively, fully, definitively in existence. The task set before us is to enter as perfectly as we can upon the way opened to us by this covenant.

In the Office of Readings, a reading from St. Thomas Aquinas explicates the thought of the Letter to the Hebrews. Here are a few lines from this reading:

> The only-begotten Son of God determined to make us sharers of his divinity. To this end, he took our nature to himself in order that, having become a man, he might make men divine. Moreover, everything of ours that he took to himself, he bestowed upon us for our salvation. Thus he offered his body to God the Father as a victim on the altar of the Cross in order to reconcile us with the Father. He poured out his blood as both a ransom and a purifying stream so that we might be freed from our wretched slavery and be cleansed of all our sins.[267]

CYCLE C

Jesus took the loaves, blessed them, broke them, and gave them to his disciples (Luke 9:11b-17)

The mystery of the bread is the central focus of the Gospel pericope in Cycle C. The first reading recalls the prefigurative sacrifice of Melchisedech, which consists of an offering of bread and wine (Gen. 14:18-20). The second reading records the actions and words of Jesus at the institution of the Eucharist (1 Cor. 11:23-26). In proper sequence, then, we move from Melchisedech's sacrifice, through the multiplication of the loaves as told by Luke, to the Eucharistic meal as described by Paul.

There is no denying that the Gospel pericope reflects a concern of the early Church: to show how its sacramental life was continuous with the actions of Jesus during his earthly life. To put it another way, we have here a typical example of a catechesis that uses an action of the earthly Jesus in order to teach the meaning of the sacrament. The

Fourth Gospel, which is the most catechetically oriented of the four Gospels, makes frequent use of the method, and the Fathers would later adopt it in their turn.

The earliest teaching method used by the Church, then, was to bring the sacraments and their meaning alive by seeing them in the light of the Old Testament types and of events in the life of Christ. The pericope from Luke applies the method even in the style chosen for the account. A historical context is given: the wilderness, and the hunger of the people who followed Jesus there in order to hear him. From a literary point of view, however, it is as though we were already at the Last Supper, for the language used at the multiplication is the language to be used later in describing the institution of the Eucharist. Evidently the intention is to present the multiplication of the loaves as a "type," prefiguration, anticipation, and implicit announcement of the Eucharist. For this reason nothing is said of the wonder that the crowd felt at the event. The whole is presented rather as an introduction to an infinite mystery: the mystery of the Eucharist, which fulfills man's need and desire abundantly.

At the same time, however, we should not forget that every meal in the Bible functions as an anticipation of the messianic banquet. This is why the ancient liturgies, and ours today, make use of the account of the multiplication of the loaves during Advent.

Melchisedech offered bread and wine (Gen. 14:18-20)

As is well known, the Roman Canon mentions the sacrifice of Melchisedech, along with those of Abel and Abraham, as prefigurations of the Christian sacrifice. In a similar manner, today's liturgy links Melchisedech's sacrifice with that of the Eucharist (second reading).

The fact that Melchisedech's ancestry was unknown ("He is without father or mother or genealogy": Heb. 7:3) and that he was a priest gave him considerable prestige in the Old Testament and the New as well. So special was his priesthood that men could speak of a priesthood "after the order of Melchisedech" (a phrase of Psalm 110:4, which is repeated in Hebrews 5:6). Melchisedech was not a priest like other priests; his priesthood was not governed by the Law but was in the prophetic line. For that reason he is a type or figure of Christ; Psalm 110 foresees the Messiah as being a priest not in the line of Aaron but in the line of Melchisedech.

While the priesthood of Melchisedech is extremely important, since it prefigures that of the Messiah, in the present context the passage from the Book of Genesis is chosen for the offering of bread and wine, which is seen in the liturgy as a prefiguration of the Eucharistic offering. The passage also gives an example of the Hebrew "blessing" that will leave its imprint on the Eucharistic Prayers of the Church.

The liturgy showed an early awareness of the significance of Melchisedech's sacrifice for the sacrifice of the Mass. That is why the Roman Canon mentions him. The reader will readily recall the passage: "Look with mercy and gladness on them [the Eucharistic bread and cup], and accept them as you deigned to accept the gifts of your just servant Abel, the sacrifice of our father Abraham, and that which your high priest Melchisedech offered you, a holy sacrifice, a spotless victim." In this prayer we pass from prefigurations to fulfillment.

The responsorial psalm, Psalm 110, sings of the supreme kingship of Christ, who is Messiah and Priest par excellence. As we know, there is only one priesthood, that of Christ, and there are two fully real but essentially different participations in it: priesthood through ordination and priesthood through baptism. Both of these priesthoods, like that of Christ himself, are prefigured by the sacrifice of Melchisedech.

Bread and wine proclaim the Lord's death (1 Cor. 11:23-26)

This passage from St. Paul parallels the accounts of institution that we find in the Synoptic Gospels. St. Paul's points of reference are the Jewish Passover and its meal, which signified covenant and liberation. The death and resurrection of the Lord are seen by Paul as the foundation of the definitive covenant, and this covenant is actualized in the Eucharistic celebration.

This passage has been chosen for the feast, not so much because it enunciates the theme of covenant as because the covenant is concluded under the signs of bread and wine. This is what puts the Supper in continuity with the sacrifice of Melchisedech.

The celebration as a whole, then, calls to mind the sacrifice of Melchisedech, who offered bread and wine and gave a blessing to Abraham; that is the theme of the first reading (we should not overlook the presence of Abraham, father of all who believe and father of the covenant as well). In the third reading, Christ gives men bread to eat, a sign both of the Eucharist and of the messianic banquet. He is the eternal High Priest, and the Eucharist perpetuates the exercise of his priesthood under the signs of bread and wine. The second reading explicitly describes the Eucharist.

29. FEAST OF THE SACRED HEART

The earlier approach to Christ

It is impossible, of course, that no one in the course of Church history down to the last few centuries should have focused his attention on the love of Christ's Heart for us. On the contrary, we need but read St. Paul's Letter to the Romans (8:28, 39) and especially the Gospel of St. John to see how close to the Christian mind was the image of Christ's loving Heart.

Down to the Scholastic period, however, the Christian mentality was very biblical. This means that Christians attended more to the global mystery of salvation than to the precise details by which the mystery was implemented in time. In the earlier ages of the Church, worship was addressed to the person and not to particular attitudes or actions of his. Consequently, the love of God and the love of Christ, though always present in Christian thinking, were not expressed in a specialized way and in a special feast. The death of Christ and, more generally, the whole mystery of Christ were a constant and sufficient reminder of the Lord's love for us. No one would have dreamed of celebrating a special feast in honor of his love, still less a feast that concentrated on the Heart of God.

A shift in theological outlook

The development of theology and its methodology, together with the growing desire of the theologians to enter into details and to systematize, led to the contemplation (first private, then publicized) of the Lord's love as seen in the popular image of the heart, the seat of love.

The Franciscans, and especially St. Bonaventure with his fervent style, contributed greatly to spreading this special devotion to the Heart of Christ. The pierced Heart became the object of intense contemplation. At almost the same time, various holy nuns in Germany and Italy, in their intimate colloquies with the Lord, were struck by the love manifested in the Heart of Jesus. In Italy there were St. Margaret of Cortona (1247–97) and Blessed Angela of Foligno (1248–1309), the latter of whom wrote an account of her visions. In Germany, St. Mechtild of Magdeburg (1210–80) and St. Gertrude of Helfta (1256–1302) spread the devotion by their visions and revelations, though the devotion was already known in Flanders and practiced there by two nuns, Blessed Mary of Oignies (1177–1213) and St. Luitgard of Tongern (1182–1246). However, the devotion, which initially spread rather rapidly, eventually declined somewhat.

The sixteenth century on

From the sixteenth century on, the devotion gained ground again. In France, St. John Eudes (1601–80) based his devotion to the Sacred Heart on the theology of St. John and gained permission for his congregation to celebrate the feast of the Sacred Heart on August 30, using a Mass and Office that he himself had composed. The experiment was initially limited to the diocese of Rennes but was soon adopted in other dioceses. It is worth noting that St. John Eudes won recognition of the devotion in his diocese in 1670.

The appearances of the Lord to St. Margaret Mary Alacoque (1647–90) at Paray-le-Monial occurred some years after the cultus proposed by St. John Eudes had been allowed. These visions roused such enthusiasm that fervent petitions were submitted to Rome to make the celebration of the feast universal. It was only in 1856, however, that Pius IX took this step, assigning the feast to the Friday after the octave of Corpus Christi. Later on, additions were made to the celebration: the consecration of the human race to the Sacred Heart, and then, under Pius XI, the act of reparation to the Sacred Heart.

CYCLE A

The Heart gentle and lowly (Matthew 11:25-30)

The passage from the Gospel of Matthew has been chosen because of the qualities Jesus there ascribes to his own Heart: "I am gentle and lowly in heart" (v. 29). The meaning of the words is not so obvious, and to grasp it we must read them in their context. Jesus is urging his hearers to become his disciples, and he tells them that any demands he makes can be met. His attitude is thus in contrast to that of the scribes and Pharisees, whom he accuses elsewhere because "they bind heavy burdens, hard to bear, and lay them on men's shoulders" (Matthew 23:4). Jesus addresses himself precisely to those who "labour and are heavy laden" (Matthew 11:28); that is, he is solicitous about those who are crushed by the heavy burden of Jewish observances. The yoke Jesus lays on his disciples is easy to carry, and the burden light. He himself is gentle and lowly in heart, and will not crush those who entrust themselves to him as their master.

All this does not mean that the life to which he summons his disciples is not a demanding one. They must after all carry a yoke, the very same one Christ carries; but the yoke, though it remains a yoke, is easy to carry because it is not a yoke made up of outward observances but a yoke consisting of the service of others out of love.

We must not draw hasty conclusions from this passage, as though Christ did not take seriously the life of the community he founded or as though he were tricking his disciples into an undertaking by describing it as easy when in fact it is difficult. There are demands that can be crushing because they are demands for meticulous, legalistic observances that do not foster love and concern for others. Such are not the demands Jesus makes. He is gentle and humble of heart; he does not break the bruised reed or quench the still smouldering wick (Matthew 12:19-20). The God he brings to men is a God who desires mercy, not sacrifice (Matthew 9:13; 12:7). Jesus offers those who wish to be his disciples the opportunity to follow him along the way of love. If they accept, they will find rest.

Redeemed from the house of bondage (Deut. 7:6-11)

In his love, God has gathered a small people whom he himself has chosen and freed from the yoke of slavery. We are therefore invited to contemplate God's love for his people, a love shown in the fact that he freely chose them. This love that redeems is, however, also a love that demands fidelity. God liberates, but he also requires that men keep his covenant and obey his commandments.

God himself is a faithful God, and gives himself to his people to the point of freeing them from captivity and creating them anew. He is not now proposing to enslave them all over again! The observance of his commandments is not meant as a crushing burden but as a way of continuing to draw down God's fidelity. If man commits himself to God, God pledges himself to man in return. The issue here is not a juridical contract, but the mutual self-giving in fidelity that is the very heart of love.

The responsorial psalm, Psalm 103, captures perfectly the meaning of the first reading and also prepares the community for the Gospel. "The Lord is merciful and gracious, slow to anger and abounding in steadfast love. . . . He does not deal with us according to our sins, nor requite us according to our iniquities" (vv. 8, 10).

Unity in love (1 John 4:7-16)

The statement made early on in this reading, "God is love," is not a kind of theological declaration. St. John is concerned not with concepts but with history, with the experience that the world, and especially the Jewish people, has had of God's concern to preserve, deliver, and lead onward.

In John's case, it is evidently the Christian experience of God's incarnation that enables him to say, not as a theological abstraction but as a historical fact, that "God is love."

The number of passages in the Old Testament that speak of God's love for his people is quite impressive. At least thirty times the Old Testament books tell in one way or another of this faithful love on God's part. The prophet Osee boldly uses the image of husband and wife to describe the relation of love that God desires should exist between himself and his people; because that love truly exists in him, he pardons his people's infidelity over and over (Osee 2:18-25). This theme will be picked up by other books and by various prophets (e.g. Jer. 2:2).

St. John is heir to this tradition, but he goes further. He bases his assertion that God is love on the fact that the Father has sent his only Son into the world so that we might have life through him. To convince us of God's love, he gives us, not a definition, but the sign by which we can discern that love. The sign is this: "In this is love, not that we loved God but that he loved us and sent his Son to be the expiation for our sins" (1 John 4:10).

The love of God for us and the love of his Son for the world entail consequences for us, and not simply moral consequences imposed on us from outside. Rather, since God has so loved us and since we are his children, we must love one another. Here again John seeks to be very concrete. After all, no one has ever seen God. But if we love one another, God dwells in us and his love is perfected in us. By faith we know God's love to be present among us. He is love; therefore, anyone who abides in love abides in God and God in him.

This feast of God's love for us will normally influence our

behavior toward others, and this behavior will be a sign to
the world that God has loved us and continues to love us.

CYCLE B

They shall look on him whom they have pierced and they shall believe (John 19:31-37)

Exegetes have seen in chapter 19 of the Fourth Gospel
and especially in verses 34-35, on the blood and water that
flow from the lance-pierced side of Jesus, an allusion to
chapters 6 and 7 of the same Gospel. In chapter 6 Jesus
spoke of the gift of his own flesh and blood that he would
give to his disciples; verses 51-58 gave a hint as to the form
the gift would take. Now, in chapter 19, seeing the blood
flow from the side of the dead Christ, we realize that the
food spoken of in chapter 6 is closely connected with the
death of Christ and with the sacrifice of himself that he offered by doing the Father's will.

Verse 38 of chapter 7: "Out of his heart shall flow rivers
of living water," likewise yields its full meaning now. We
cannot but observe that in the account of the Passion every
detail is a sign. In fact, every event of Christ's life has its
permanent consequences.

We must keep our attention focused not so much on the
event as on the abiding reality that it signifies. In this case,
however, the event is one that is a turning point of universal history. In fact, we must say that the Cross is not only a
sign; it is itself also the thing signified. Water flows from
the body of Jesus; the water is the life he gives to those
who believe in him (John 7:38-39). If anyone drinks this
water, he will never thirst again (John 4:14). The blood of
Jesus is man's true drink (John 6:55).

In short, it makes little difference whether the fact related by John is historical or simply a symbolic way of relat-

ing Jesus to the prophecies. At the same time, however, John does appeal to what he has seen with his own eyes, that is, to historical facts. It would be imprudent to refuse him credence.

We are here confronted with a sign of Christ's love and of the love of the Father who accepts the sacrifice Christ offers in our name. The sign refers to the grace that is bestowed through water and the Spirit and that truly quenches our thirst. The Father wants to rebuild the world; the Son offers himself for the work and communicates to us the life that flows from his death and resurrection as from a wellspring. In Jesus who sacrificed himself for us we find both love and reconciliation. This is the point made in the second of the Alleluia verses before the Gospel.

Believe in the love that forgives (Osee 11:1, 3-4, 8c-9)

God does not come to destroy. He may in the past have been "forced" to punish Israel, but now he "repents" of that. What he did, he did for the sake of his people: he saved them from Egypt, called them his children, taught them to walk in his ways. But he will not execute his anger, for he is the Holy One who does not come to destroy. As the Gospel account tells us, the blood and water that flow from the side of the crucified Christ are signs that God is a loving and forgiving God.

The responsorial psalm, taken from the Book of Isaiah, reminds us of the water flowing from Christ's side: "With joy you will draw water from the wells of salvation" (Is. 12:3). It also reminds us of Christ's words: "If any one thirst, let him come to me and drink" (John 7:37).

You will know the love of Christ (Eph. 3:8-12, 14-19)

Unless we are rooted and grounded in love, we cannot comprehend the breadth and length and height and depth of Christ's love, which surpasses knowledge. This is Paul's enthusiastic outburst in the Letter to the Ephesians. As a matter of fact, any contact with the Cross of Christ, and the quenching of our thirst by drinking his blood, after having been washed by the water from his side and having become one body in the Church — that too is too much for our imaginations to grasp.

God's plan, hidden through the ages within his bosom, has now been revealed through his Son, and all of us are commissioned to proclaim it and help it transform other lives. We must make all men see that we approach God with confidence, because we trust in the pierced Christ, to whom we raise our eyes and who is the wellspring and fountainhead of our life.

The religion we are to proclaim is not primarily an institution. Its characteristic trait is that it is a religion of love in which God and man are intimately united and in which the chief preoccupation is that the community should be a sign of love at work. That is how we achieve our fulfillment and can enter into the fullness of God himself.

CYCLE C

We have been sought and found (Luke 15:3-7)

God's love for men finds expression here in a parable that is well known to us yet never fails to move us deeply: the parable of the lost sheep, which the shepherd anxiously searches out and carries home on his shoulder and for which he then celebrates a joyful feast: "I have found my sheep which was lost" (v. 6). How could the Lord's attentive love for us be better expressed?

The parable reminds us of other passages, especially in St. John, where Jesus speaks of himself as a shepherd. "This is the will of him who sent me, that I should lose nothing of all that he has given me" (John 6:39). "My sheep hear my voice, and I know them, and they follow me; and I give them eternal life, and they shall never perish, and no one shall snatch them out of my hand" (John 10:27-28). "I lay down my life for the sheep" (John 10:15). We know how the Synoptic Gospels describe the shepherd's role: he gathers his sheep together (Matthew 15:24); he gives his life for them and then returns to life again for them (Matthew 26:31; Mark 14:27). To this St. John adds the intimacy created by the reciprocal knowledge of the good shepherd and his sheep: "I know my own and my own know me" (John 10:14). The image of the shepherd becomes an authentic revelation of love.

God will feed his flock (Ezek. 34:11-16)

The New Testament revelation of God as the loving Shepherd fulfills the promise God made through Ezekiel: "I myself will search for my sheep, and will seek them out" (34:11). The image of the shepherd is much used in the Old Testament, where it is applied to earthly kings and to God himself, who is called the "Shepherd of Israel" (Ps. 80:1). The image is especially popular in the psalms. Psalm 23, for example, reflects the experience of God's people, whom he had led as a shepherd leads his flock and to whom he had given peace and joy. In the present passage, Ezekiel adopts a wholly unpolitical perspective; the God whom he sees as a shepherd will lead all the nations of the earth to good pasture. "I will seek the lost and I will bring back the strayed, and I will bind up the crippled, and I will strengthen the weak, and the fat and the strong I will watch over; I will feed them in justice" (Ezek. 34:16).

The Gospel parable and Ezekiel's prophecy give a true and permanently valid picture of God. In fact, it is God himself who presents himself to us under this image.

The proof that he is a shepherd and loves us (Rom. 5:5-11)

Both the prophecy of Ezekiel and the parable of Luke might well be simply literary dressing. In his Letter to the

Romans, St. Paul shows us that the image points to a reality. "God shows his love for us in that while we were yet sinners Christ died for us" (Rom. 5:8). Christ's death reconciled us to God when we were still in sin; now that we have been reconciled by his blood, we shall surely be saved by him in his risen life. We are sure because, as Paul says at the beginning of the pericope, "God's love has been poured into our hearts through the Holy Spirit which has been given to us" (v. 5).

Today's celebration does not specify the response we are to make to God's love. Each of us must respond as God wishes us to do in our daily lives.

In a passage read in the Office of Readings, St. Bonaventure writes: "From you flows the river . . . that gladdens the city of God . . . so that with joy and thanksgiving we may sing you songs of praise, knowing as we do from our own experience that with you is the source of life and that in your light we shall see light." [268]

NOTES

[1] *Egeria: Diary of a Pilgrimage*, trans. G. E. Gingras (Ancient Christian Writers 38; New York, 1970).

[2] A. Camus, *L'homme révolté* (Paris, 1951), pp. 50–51. The passage is not in the abridged English translation published as *The Rebel* (London, 1953) and is here taken from J. Moltmann, *The Crucified God: The Cross of Christ as the Foundation and Criticism of Christian Theology*, trans. R. A. Wilson and J. Bowden (New York, 1974), p. 226.

[3] Moltmann, *op. cit.*, p. 226.

[4] *Ibid.*

[5] On St. John, see L. Bouyer, *The Fourth Gospel*, trans. P. Byrne (Westminster, Md., 1964); C. H. Dodd, *The Interpretation of the Fourth Gospel* (Cambridge, 1953).

[6] On all this, see L. Cerfaux, *Christ in the Theology of St. Paul*, trans. G. Webb and A. Walker (New York, 1959), pp. 131–39. We have sometimes followed this book step by step.

[7] Moltmann, *op. cit.*, p. 201.

[8] B. Steffen, *Das Dogma vom Kreuz* (1920), quoted in Moltmann, *op. cit.*, p. 241.

[9] Elie Wiesel, *Night* (1969), pp. 75–76, quoted in Moltmann, *op. cit.*, pp. 273–74.

[10] G. Martelet, *The Risen Christ and the Eucharistic World*, trans. R. Hague (New York, 1976), p. 91.

[11] *Ibid.*

[12] See A. Festugière, *L'idéal religieux des Grecs et l'Evangile* (Paris, 1932), pp. 143–69; reference given in Cerfaux, *op. cit.*, p. 78.

[13] See P. de Surgy *et al.*, *The Resurrection and Modern Biblical Thought*, trans. C. U. Quinn (New York, 1970).

[14] On all this, see E. Schillebeeckx, *Christ the Sacrament of the Encounter with God*, trans. P. Barrett, M. Schoof, and L. Bright (New York, 1963); Martelet, *op. cit.*

[15] *Epist.* 23, 12–13 (*PL* 16:1030).

[16] P.-M. Gy, "Semaine sainte et triduum pascal," *La Maison-Dieu*, no. 41 (1955), p. 9. The article gives an excellent sketch of the history of the paschal triduum.

[17] *De consensu Evangeliorum* III, 66 (*PL* 34:1199).

[18] *Epist.* 55, 24 (*PL* 33:215).

[19] J. Gaillard, "Le mystère pascal dans le renouveau liturgique: Essai de bilan doctrinal," *La Maison-Dieu*, no. 67 (1961), p. 85.

[20] See the Capua Epistolary (ca. 545), edited by G. Morin, "Lectiones ex epistolis paulinis excerptae quae in Ecclesia Capuana

saec. VI legebantur," *Anecdota Maredsolana* 1 (Maredsous, 1893), pp. 436–44.

²¹ *Epist.* 25: *Ad Decentium*, cap. 7, no. 10 (*PL* 20:559).

²² *Epist.* 77 (*OL* 22:692–93), cited in P. Jounel, "Le jeudi saint: La tradition de l'Eglise," *La Maison-Dieu* 68 (1961), pp. 15–16.

²³ H. Bruns, *Canones Apostolorum et Conciliorum* 1 (Berlin, 1839), p. 127.

²⁴ *Epist.* 54, 5 (*PL* 33:202).

²⁵ *Egeria: Diary of a Pilgrimage*, ch. 35, pp. 107–8. The Martyrium is the church enclosing the place where Jesus was crucified or, more accurately, the place where the Cross was found.

²⁶ A short exposition of the various interpretations is given in H.A.P. Schmidt, *Hebdomada Sancta* (2 vols.; Rome, 1956–57), 2:733–36.

²⁷ *Apologia I*, ch. 35 (*PG* 6:427).

²⁸ *La Tradition Apostolique de saint Hippolyte: Essai de reconstitution*, ed. B. Botte (Liturgiewissenschaftliche Quellen und Forschungen 39; Münster, 1963), cc. 4 and 21, pp. 11 and 55.

²⁹ See E. Lanne, "Textes et rites de la liturgie pascale dans l'ancienne Eglise Copte," *Orient syrien* 6 (1961), p. 291.

³⁰ See *Le pontifical Romano-Germanique du dixième siècle*, ed. C. Vogel with R. Elze (Studi e testi 226–27; Vatican City, 1962), 2:71–75 and 77–85.

³¹ See Nathan Goldberg, *Passover Haggadah* (rev. ed.; New York, 1966). The prayers quoted in this outline will be found on pp. 7, 8, 25, 27, 42–43.

³² See A. Jaubert, *La date de la Cène* (Paris, 1967), a book that has occasioned further essays. Its thesis is that the Supper was celebrated on Monday evening; this would clarify certain passages in the Gospels and would also make the Synoptics and John more coherent. The possibility that two different calendars, an ancient and a more modern, were in use would explain how the Lord's Supper could be located on either Monday or Thursday, but the thesis is far from having convinced all the exegetes.

³³ See M. Thurian, *The Eucharistic Memorial*, trans. J. G. Davies (2 vols.; Ecumenical Studies in Worship 7–8; Richmond, Va., 1960–61).

³⁴ R. Aron, "La liturgie juive et le temps," *La Maison-Dieu*, no. 65 (1961), p. 19.

³⁵ St. John (18:28; 19:14) says that the Jews had not yet eaten the Passover when Jesus was put to death. The problem this statement raises is simplified if John is following a different calendar than the Synoptics (see n. 2 above). Recent exegetes (e.g., J. Jeremias), have insisted that in any case the atmosphere of the Last Supper is clearly that of the Passover. In Luke 22:15 Jesus says he wishes to eat this Passover with his disciples before he suffers. Cf. J.

Jeremias, *The Eucharistic Words of Jesus*, trans. N. Perrin (London, 1966), pp. 41–62.

[36] "Anamnesis" is a technical term meaning "remembrance" or "memorial." In the present context it means a reminder of what Yahweh has done for his people.

[37] *Didache* 10, 1–5. Text in *Prex Eucharistica: Textus e variis liturgiis antiquioribus selecti*, eds. A. Hänggi and I. Pahl (Spicilegium Friburgense 12; Fribourg, 1968), pp. 66–68; or in J.-P. Audet, *La Didachè: Instructions des Apôtres* (Paris, 1958), pp. 234–36.

[38] *Epist.* 55, 18–24 (*PL* 33:212–16).

[39] *Rule of St. Benedict*, ch. 53.

[40] *Ibid.*, ch. 35.

[41] See A. Chavasse, "A Rome, le jeudi saint au VIIᵉ siècle d'après un vieil Ordo romain," *Revue d'histoire ecclésiastique* 50 (1955), pp. 21–35.

[42] See Lanne, *art. cit.*, p. 291.

[43] *De sacramentis* III, 5 (*SC* 25bis:94).

[44] P.-M. Gy, "Les origines liturgiques du lavement des pieds," *La Maison-Dieu* no. 49 (1957), p. 52.

[45] See G. Khouri-Sarkis, "La semaine sainte dans l'Eglise syrienne," *La Maison-Dieu*, no. 41 (1955), pp. 105–9; F. Mercenier and F. Paris, *La prière des Eglises du rit byzantin* (2 vols.; Amay, 1937–39), 2:161–66.

[46] See Abul'l Barakat, *La lampe des ténèbres*, cited in Lanne, *art. cit.*, p. 291, n. 28. On all this development, see Schmidt, *op. cit.*, 2:763–76; Th. Schäfer, *Die Fusswaschung im monastischen Brauchtum und in der lateinischen Liturgie* (Texte und Arbeiten 47; Beuron, 1956).

[47] A wide black cloak which, in the case of a monk, is unadorned.

[48] A white apron.

[49] Mercenier and Paris, *op. cit.*, 2:164–65.

[50] See B. Fischer, "Formes de la commémoration du baptême en Occident," *La Maison-Dieu*, no. 58 (1959), p. 120.

[51] *Ibid.*

[52] *Didascalia Apostolorum*, trans. R. H. Connolly (Oxford, 1929), pp. 122, 124.

[53] *Sermo* 26, 2 (*SC* 22bis:138; *CCL* 138:126).

[54] *Sermo* 53, 6 (*SC* 74:82; *CCL* 138:386).

[55] *La Tradition Apostolique de saint Hippolyte*, ch. 4, p. 11.

[56] Even if strict exegesis does not enable us to say that Christ celebrated the Eucharist on this occasion, surely there are Eucharistic overtones to the language.

[57] See M. Andrieu, *Les Ordine Romani du Haut Moyen Age* 2 (Spicilegium Sacrum Lovaniense 23; Louvain, 1948), p. 82.

[58] *Epist.* 23, 12–13 (*PL* 16:1030).

[59] *Epist.* 55, 24 *(PL* 33:215).

[60] *Apologia I*, ch. 67 *(PG* 6:430).

[61] See, for examples, *Ordines* 16, 17, 23, 24, and 30B (all in Andrieu, *op. cit.*, vol. 3 [Spicilegium Sacrum Lovaniense 24; Louvain, 1951]), which date from the end of the eighth century, as well as some of the sacramentaries of the same period. See also Schmidt, *op. cit.*, 2:778–84.

[62] Several sacramentaries (the Gelasian, for example) showed this pattern.

[63] *Egeria: Diary of a Pilgrimage*, ch. 24, p. 90.

[64] The Council of Vaison (Provence, France; 529) speaks of the Italian custom of saying the *Kyrie*.

[65] See B. Capelle, "Le Kyrie de la Messe et le pape Gélase," *Revue bénédictine* 34 (1924), pp. 126–44; reprinted in his *Travaux Liturgiques* 2 (Louvain, 1962), pp. 116–34.

[66] Andrieu, *op. cit.*, 2:413, thinks that the *Ordines* began to be composed in the seventh century and even in the second half of the sixth. A. Chavasse, *Le sacramentaire gélasien* (Tournai, 1968), p. 171, refuses to date their appearance before the seventh century and considers the first *Ordo* to be dependent on the Gelasian Sacramentary.

[67] *Egeria: Diary of a Pilgrimage*, ch. 37, pp. 110–11.

[68] See H. Grisar, "Il 'Sancta Sanctorum' in Roma e il suo tesoro novamente aperto," *Civiltà Cattolica* 57 (1906), pp. 513–44, 708–30. On the iconography, see J. Wilpert, "Le due più antiche rappresentazioni della 'Adoratio crucis,'" *Atti della Pontificia Accademia Romana de Archeologia* (1927).

[69] See M. Férotin (ed.), *Le Liber Ordinum en usage dans l'Eglise Wisogothique et Mozarabe d'Espagne du cinquième au onzième siècle* (Monumenta Ecclesiae Liturgica 5; Paris, 1904), pp. 193ff.

[70] See *Ordo* 23, nos. 9–22, in Andrieu, *op. cit.*, 3:270–72.

[71] See Schmidt, *op. cit.*, 2:791.

[72] *Egeria: Diary of a Pilgrimage*, ch. 37, p. 112.

[73] See *Ordo* 24, no. 35, in Andrieu, *op. cit.*, 3:294–95.

[74] See A. Baumstark, "Der Orient und die Gesänge des Adoratio crucis," *Jahrbuch für Liturgiewissenschaft* 2 (1922), pp. 1–17.

[75] *Liber officialis* 1, 14, ed. J. M. Hanssens, *Amalarii Episcopi opera liturgica omnia* 2 (Vatican City, 1948), p. 101.

[76] *Ordo* 31, nos. 45–46, in Andrieu, *op. cit.*, 3:498.

[77] See J. M. Hanssens, *Institutiones liturgicae de ritibus orientalibus* (Rome, 1932), 3:108–56; I.-H. Dalmais, "L'adoration de la croix," *La Maison-Dieu*, no. 45 (1956), pp. 76–86; H. Engberding, "Zum formgeschichtlichen Verständnis des *hagios ho theos, hagios ischuros, hagios athanatos, eleison hemas*," *Jahrbuch für Liturgiewissenschaft* 10 (1930), pp. 168–74.

[78] M. Andrieu, *Le Pontifical Romain au Moyen Age* 1: *Le Pon-*

tifical Romain du XIIe siècle (Studi e testi 86; Vatican City, 1938), p. 236. Schmidt, *op. cit.*, 2:796, cites *Ordo* 31 as prescribing the unveiling of the cross; Andrieu thinks, however, that this *Ordo* was a purely literary composition and was not used in fact for conducting a service.

79 Andrieu, *Le Pontifical Romain . . .* 1:237.

80 In the Antiphonary of Senlis (880); an antiphonary is a book containing the various antiphons and hymns for Mass or other services. The practice is also to be found in the Romano-Germanic Pontifical of the tenth century.

81 *Epist.* 25: *Ad Decentium*, cap. 4, no. 7 (*PL* 20:555–56). See G. Malchiodi, *La lettera di S. Innocenzio I a Decentio vescovo di Gubbio: Breve studio esegetico-storico* (Rome, 1921), p. 11.

82 *Ordo* 23, no. 22, in Andrieu, *Les Ordines Romani* 3:272.

83 *Liber officialis*, in Hanssens, *Amalarii Episcopi opera liturgica omnia*, 2:107–8.

84 C. Vogel, *Le Pontifical Romano-Germanique du dixième siècle* 2:92–93.

85 *Ordo* 31, no. 11, in Andrieu, *Le Pontifical Romain . . .* 1:237.

86 Andrieu, *Le Pontifical Romain au Moyen Age* 2: *Le pontifical de la Curie Romaine au XIIIe siècle* (Studi e testi 87; Vatican City, 1940), pp. 469, 541–78.

87 J. Lécuyer, *Le sacrifice de la Nouvelle Alliance* (Lyons, 1962), p. 17.

88 L. Moraldi, *Espiazione sacrificale e riti espiatori nel ambiente biblico e nell'Antico Testamento* (Rome, 1956), pp. 237–38, quoted in Lécuyer, *op. cit.*, p. 117.

89 See Lécuyer, *op. cit.*, p. 17.

90 On this subject, see L. Cerfaux, *Christ in the Theology of St. Paul*, trans. G. Webb and A. Walker (New York, 1959), pp. 122, 143. The reader will find the references to St. Paul's Letters that show the link between blood and sacrifice (Rom. 3:25; 5:6-11; Eph. 1:7; 2:13; Col. 1:20).

91 *Catecheses* 3, 13–19 (*SC* 50bis:174–77).

92 *Sermo* 61, 4–5 (*SC* 74:71; *CCL* 138A:372).

93 See volume two of this series, page 195, "The glorious Passion for the sake of the covenant."

91 *Sermo* 53, 3 (*SC* 74:29–30; *CCL* 138A:315).

95 Edited by M. Férotin (see n. 69, above).

96 See L. C. Mohlberg (ed.), *Liber sacramentorum romanae aeclesiae ordinis anni circuli (Sacramentarium Gelasianum)* (Rerum ecclesiasticarum documenta, Series maior: Fontes 4; Rome, 1960), nos. 419–24 (henceforth cited as Gel. with number of text, e.g., Gel. 419–24); *Ordo* 11, in Andrieu, *Les Ordines Romani . . .* , 2:83–88.

97 *Rite of Christian Initiation of Adults* (Washington, D.C., 1974), no. 259.

[98] *Historia Ecclesiastica* V, 24, 6.

[99] *Commentaria in Evangelium Matthaei* IV, 25 (*PL* 26:192).

[100] H. M. Féret, "La Messe, rassemblement de la communauté," in *La Messe et sa catéchèse* (Lex orandi 7; Paris, 1947), pp. 220–21.

[101] Aron, *art. cit.*, p. 19.

[102] On this subject, see Eusebius of Caesarea, *Historia Ecclesiastica* V, 23–25; O. Casel, *La Fête de Pâques dans l'Eglise des Pères*, French translation by J. C. Didier (Lex orandi 37; Paris, 1963), p. 29 (a translation of "Art und Sinn der ältesten christlichen Osterfeier," *Jahrbuch für Liturgiewissenschaft* 14 [1934], pp. 1–78); M. Richard, "La question pascale au IIe siècle," *Orient syrien* 6 (1961), pp. 179–212.

[103] The *Didascalia Apostolorum* is a third-century Syrian document. It was edited by F. X. Funk, *Didascalia et Constitutiones Apostolorum* (Paderborn, 1905); see nos. 18–19, p. 288. English translation by R. H. Connolly (see n. 52, above).

[104] *La Tradition Apostolique de saint Hippolyte*, cc. 20–21, pp. 43–55.

[105] *De baptismo* 19, 1 (*SC* 35:93; *CCL* 1:293).

[106] *La Tradition Apostolique de saint Hippolyte*, ch. 25, p. 65.

[107] See *Ordo* 24, no. 41, in Andrieu, *Les Ordines Romani . . .*, 3:295 and 321.

[108] See *Ordo* 32, nos. 1–7, in Andrieu, *Le Pontifical Romain au Moyen Age* 1:238–40.

[109] See *Ordo* 23, no. 24, in Andrieu, *Les Ordines Romani . . .* 3:272.

[110] See Schmidt, *op. cit.*, 2:809–12.

[111] *Ordo* 50, no. 17, in Andrieu, *op. cit.*, 5 (Spicilegium Sacrum Lovaniense 29; Louvain, 1961), p. 267; text of hymn on pp. 396–98.

[112] Andrieu, *Le Pontifical Romain au Moyen Age* 2:565.

[113] See F. C. Conybeare (ed.), *Rituale Armenorum* (Oxford, 1905); H. Leclercq, "Semaine sainte," *Dictionnaire d'archéologie chrétienne et de liturgie* 15:1177–78.

[114] *Ordo* 17, nos. 102–4, in Andrieu, *Les Ordines Romani . . .* 3:190.

[115] Complete text in Schmidt, *op. cit.*, 2:629–34.

[116] J. Deshusses (ed.), *Le sacramentaire gélasien* (Spicilegium Friburgense 16; Fribourg, 1971), p. 183.

[117] Gel. 431–43.

[118] *Ordo* 23, no. 26, in Andrieu, *op. cit.*, 2:27. On this whole matter, see Schmidt, *op. cit.*, 2:827–47; B. Botte, "Le choix des lectures dans la veillée pascale," *Questions liturgiques et paroissiales* 33 (1952), pp. 65–70; A. Chavasse, "Leçons et oraisons des Vigiles de Pâques et de la Pentecôte dans le sacramentaire gélasien," *Ephemerides Liturgicae* 69 (1955), pp. 209–26, and his *Le sacramentaire gélasien*, p. 113.

119 In his *Euchologion*; text in Funk, *Didascalia et Constitutiones Apostolorum* 2:181–83.

120 *Contra Parmenianum Donatistam* VII, 6 (*CSEL* 26:153).

121 *Constitutiones Apostolorum* VII, 43; text in J. Quasten, *Monumenta eucharistica et liturgica vetustissima* (Florilegium Patristicum 7; Bonn, 1936), pp. 192–94.

122 L. C. Mohlberg (ed.), *Sacramentarium Veronense* (Rerum ecclesiasticarum documenta, Series maior: Fontes 1; Rome, 1956), no. 1331 (henceforth, Ver. with number of text, e.g., Ver. 1331).

123 *De sacramentis* II, 14 (*SC* 25bis:80).

124 *Ordo* 17, no. 102, in Andrieu, *op. cit.*, 3:190.

125 *Ordo* 23, no. 28, in Andrieu, *op. cit.*, 3:273.

126 *Ordo* 16, nos. 43–44, in Andrieu, *op. cit.*, 3:153. Other *Ordines* say the same.

127 *Ordo* 31, nos. 91–95, in Andrieu, *op. cit.*, 3:503–4.

128 *Ordo* 30A, no. 21, in Andrieu, *op. cit.*, 3:457–58.

129 First antiphon, Vespers, Holy Saturday. [The Latin text, "O mors, ero mors tua; morsus tuus ero, inferne," represents the Hebrew text rather than the Greek and Syriac readings that are reflected in the usual English translation (for example: "O Death, where are your plagues? O Sheol, where is your destruction?" [RSV]). — Tr.]

130 These words used to be part of the prayer of blessing but have now been omitted; see. e.g., *The Maryknoll Missal* (New York, 1964), p. 329, which is quoted here.

131 Blessing of the fire.

132 See B. Capelle, "L'Exultet pascal, oeuvre de saint Ambroise," in *Miscellanea Giovanni Mercati* 1 (Vatican City, 1946), pp. 214–46.

133 The Vigil at Rome originally had six readings; later, there were twelve, and even twenty-four in the period when both Greeks and Latins attended the liturgy in the Lateran Basilica and the pericopes were read in both languages.

B. Botte, "Le choix des lectures de la veillée pascale," *Questións liturgiques et paroissiales* 33 (1952), pp. 65–70, establishes that the traditional number of readings in the Church of Rome was six; the four readings in the Gregorian Sacramentary represent a later usage.

134 See Volume one of this series, "The presence of the Lord," page 21.

135 Exod. 14:15–15:1; third reading of the Vigil.

136 Exod. 15:1–6, 17–18, provides the responsorial psalm for the third reading.

137 See J. Delorme, "The Resurrection and Jesus' Tomb," in P. de Surgy *et al.*, *The Resurrection and Modern Biblical Thought*, trans. C. U. Quinn (New York, 1970), p. 74.

138 See the bibliography given by Delorme, *op. cit.*, pp. 147–48.

139 On this and the preceding four paragraphs, see Delorme's essay, pp. 95–100.

[140] *De sacramentis* II, 1, 1 (*SC* 25bis:74).

[141] *De baptismo* 8, 4 (*SC* 35:77–78; *CCL* 1:283).

[142] Complete Latin text in Schmidt, *op. cit.*, 2:854–55.

[143] *Apologia I*, ch. 61 (*PG* 6:420).

[144] *Sermo* 24, 3 (*SC* 22bis:114; *CCL* 138:112–13).

[145] *De sacramentis* II, 4, 12–13 (*SC* 25bis:80).

[146] *De sacramentis* II, 7, 20 (*SC* 25bis:84, 86).

[147] *De sacramentis* II, 6, 19 (*SC* 25bis:84).

[148] *De sacramentis* II, 7, 23 (*SC* 25bis:86, 88).

[149] *De mysteriis* 7, 34–35 (*SC* 25bis:175).

[150] *De sacramentis* V, 3, 12–13 (*SC* 25bis:124).

[151] *De mysteriis* 8, 43 (*SC* 25bis:181).

[152] *Explanatio in Psalmum* 22 (*PG* 69:841).

[153] *Catecheses mystagogicae* 4, 7 (*SC* 126:140).

[154] *Catecheses mystagogicae* 4, 7 (*SC* 126:142).

[155] See page xxx on "Three sacramental stages."

[156] *La Tradition Apostolique de saint Hippolyte*, ch. 21, p. 55.

[157] See the title of J. M.-R. Tillard's excellent book on the Eucharist: *The Eucharist, Pasch of God's People*, trans. D. L. Wienk (Staten Island, N.Y., 1967).

[158] G. Martelet, *op. cit.*, has provided a remarkably good discussion of the complex but essential aspects of the Eucharistic celebration.

[159] P. Nautin (ed.), *Homélies pascales* 1 (*SC* 27:158).

[160] On the discourse, see J. Dupont, *Etudes sur les Actes des Apôtres* (Lectio divina 45; Paris, 1967).

[161] The Gospel of the Easter Vigil (three-year cycle) may be read instead.

[162] See Casel, *op. cit.*, p. 103.

[163] See *Sur la Pâque*, ed. O. Perler (*SC* 123; Paris, 1966). Melito was probably a bishop.

[164] *On the Pasch* 1–6 (*SC* 123:60, 62).

[165] *On the Pasch* 40 (*SC* 123:80).

[166] *On the Pasch* 46 (*SC* 123:84).

[167] See C. Mohrmann, "Pascha, Passio, Transitus," *Ephemerides Liturgicae* 66 (1952), pp. 37–52; reprinted in her *Etudes sur le latin des chrétiens* 1 (Rome, 1961), pp. 205–22.

[168] *Catecheses mystagogicae* 3, 13–19 (*SC* 50bis:158–62).

[169] *Explanatio symboli* 5 (*SC* 25bis:52).

[170] *Sermo* 63, 1 and 3 (*SC* 74:78, 80; *CCL* 138A:382).

[171] *Sermo* 63, 4 (*SC* 74:80–81; *CCL* 138A:384).

[172] *Sermo* 63, 5 (*SC* 74:81; *CCL* 138A:385).

[173] *Sermo* 63, 6 (*SC* 74:82–83; *CCL* 138A:386).

[174] *Sermo* 65, 4 (*SC* 74:93; *CCL* 138A:399).

[175] *Sermo* 71, 3–4 (*SC* 74:125–26; *CCL* 138A:436–37).

[176] *Sermo* 72, 1 (*SC* 74:129; *CCL* 138A:441).

[177] *Sermo* 72, 7 (*SC* 74:135; *CCL* 138A:447).

[178] *Apologia I*, ch. 67 (*PG* 6:430).

[179] See M.-E. Boismard, *Quatre hymnes baptismales dans le premier épître de saint Pierre* (Lectio divina 30; Paris, 1961).

[180] See L. Bouyer, *Eucharist: Theology and Spirituality of the Eucharistic Prayer*, trans. C. U. Quinn (Notre Dame, 1968).

[181] The French text gives a more direct translation of the Latin original. In English: "God of everlasting mercy, through the recurring celebration of the paschal feast you inflame the faith of your holy people. Intensify the grace you have given them so that all may rightly understand the baptism that has purified them, the Spirit that has given them rebirth, and the blood that has redeemed them" ("Deus misericordiae sempiternae, qui in ipso paschalis festi recursu fidem sacratae tibi plebis accendis, auge gratiam quam dedisti, ut digna omnes intelligentia comprehendent, quo lavacro abluti, quo spiritu regenerati, quo sanguine sunt redempti").

[182] See, e.g., B. Botte's preface (with its notes) to Casel, *op. cit.*, pp. 7–10.

[183] *Dogmatic Constitution on the Church*, no. 10 (Flannery, pp. 360–61). See also nos. 3, 9, 11, 31, 32.

[184] *Didache* 9, 1; text in Hänggi-Pahl, *op. cit.*, p. 66, and Audet, *op. cit.*, p. 372.

[185] See volume one of this series, page 31, "Let the mirror be broken!"

[186] *Sermo* 73, 4 (*SC* 74:138; *CCL* 138A:453).

[187] *Sermo* 74, 1 (*SC* 74:139; *CCL* 138A:455–56).

[188] *Sermo* 74, 2 (*SC* 74:140; *CCL* 138A:465–57).

[189] E. Schillebeeckx, *op. cit.*, develops such a theology on the basis of the ascension.

[190] Ver. 176.

[191] C. H. Dodd, *The Interpretation of the Fourth Gospel* (Cambridge, 1953), p. 177.

[192] *Ibid.*

[193] *De resurrectione mortuorum* (*PL* 2:837; *CCL* 2:959).

[194] *Commentaria in Ezechielem prophetam* (*PL* 25:349; *CCL* 75:515).

[195] See J. van Goudoever, *Fêtes et calendriers bibliques* (Théologie historique 7; Paris, 1967), pp. 30ff.; G. F. Moore, *Judaism in the First Centuries of the Christian Era* (3 vols.; Cambridge, 1927–30), 2:43–47.

[196] On this problem, see M.-E. Boismard, "De son ventre couleront des fleuves d'eau," *Revue biblique* 65 (1958), pp. 522–46; A. Feuillet, "Les fleuves d'eau vive de Jean 7, 38," in *Parole de Dieu et sacerdoce (Mélanges Weber)* (Paris, 1962), pp. 107–20; idem, "Eau du rocher ou source de temple?" *Revue biblique* 70 (1953), pp. 43–51.

[197] See A. George, "The Accounts of the Appearances to the

Eleven from Luke 24, 36–53," in P. de Surgy *et al.*, *op. cit.*, pp. 62–64.

[198] *Sermo* 75, 1 (*SC* 74:144–45; *CCL* 138A:465–66).

[199] *Sermo* 76, 3 (*SC* 74:151; *CCL* 138A:476).

[200] Wednesday of second week, opening prayer.

[201] Saturday of seventh week, opening prayer.

[202] Sixth Sunday, opening prayer.

[203] Tuesday of second week, prayer over the gifts; Saturday in octave of Easter, prayer over the gifts.

[204] Thursday of seventh week, opening prayer.

[205] Monday of seventh week, opening prayer. [The French Sacramentary has "discerner ta volonté" for "voluntatem tuam fideli mente retinere." The English Sacramentary is more accurate; the French is an adaptation. — Tr.]

[206] Saturday of seventh week, prayer after communion. [The English Sacramentary omits some words of the Latin: "that, *just as we have passed from the Old Testament signs to those of the New (sicut de praeteritis ad nova sumus sacramenta translati)*, we may leave . . ." — Tr.]

[207] Second Sunday, prayer over the gifts.

[208] Second Sunday, opening prayer.

[209] Easter Sunday, prayer after Communion. [A more literal translation of the final words would be: "now that she [the Church] has been renewed by the paschal mystery ("paschalibus renovata mysteriis)." — Tr.]

[210] Thursday of third week, prayer after Communion.

[211] Easter Vigil, prayer after Communion.

[212] Thursday of second week, opening prayer.

[213] Thursday of second week, prayer after Communion; Thursday of sixth week, prayer after Communion.

[214] Wednesday of third week, prayer after Communion. ["Celebration of our redemption" translates "redemptionis nostrae sacrosancta commercia"; a more literal translation would be "the holy exchange that effects our redemption." — Tr.]

[215] Thursday of third week, prayer over the gifts.

[216] Friday of fifth week, opening prayer. [Nocent's comment corresponds to the French version of the original Latin: "Tribue nobis, quaesumus, Domine, mysteriis paschalibus convenienter aptari, ut quae laetanter exsequimur, perpetua virtute nos tueantur et salvant." A literal translation: "Lord, conform us to the paschal mystery so that while we celebrate it joyfully, its abiding power may protect and save us." — Tr.]

[217] Thursday of third week, opening prayer.

[218] Second preface of Easter.

[219] First preface of the ascension.

[220] Fourth preface of Easter.

221 Third preface of Easter.

222 First preface of Easter; Good Friday, alternate opening prayer.

223 *Exsultet*.

224 Wednesday in octave of Easter, prayer after Communion.

225 Easter Vigil, alternate prayer after third reading.

226 Easter Vigil, prayer after first reading.

227 Easter Vigil, prayer after seventh reading; Monday of second week, prayer after Communion.

228 Blessing of baptismal water; Easter Vigil, alternate prayer after third reading.

229 Good Friday, alternate opening prayer.

230 Fifth Sunday, opening prayer. [The English omits the element of faith. A literal translation of the Latin: "God, you redeem us and make us your adopted children. Look with mercy on the children you love, and grant to those who believe in Christ true freedom and an eternal inheritance" ("Deus, per quem nobis et redemptio venit et praestatur adoptio, filios dilectionis tuae benignus intende, ut in Christo credentibus et vera tribuatur libertas et hereditas aeterna"). — Tr.]

231 Third Sunday, opening prayer.

232 Easter Vigil, prayer after fourth reading.

233 Easter Vigil, prayer after second reading.

234 Good Friday, alternate opening prayer.

235 Monday of second week, opening prayer. ["Spirit of love" here translates "spiritum adoptionis filiorum" (spirit of adoptive sonship"). — Tr.]

236 Thursday of third week, prayer over the gifts.

237 Second preface of the Ascension.

238 Thursday of fourth week, opening prayer.

239 Monday of fourth week, opening prayer.

240 Good Friday, opening prayer.

241 Saturday in octave of Easter, opening prayer.

242 Tuesday of third week, opening prayer.

243 Preface of Pentecost.

244 See Pentecost Sunday, opening prayer. [In a more literal translation of the Latin, this prayer would begin: "God, through the mystery we celebrate today you sanctify your entire Church in every race and nation. . ." ("Deus, qui sacramento festivitatis hodiernae Ecclesiam tuam in omni gente et natione sanctificas. . ."). — Tr.]

245 Seventh Sunday, prayer over the gifts.

246 Fourth Sunday, opening prayer.

247 Thursday of sixth week, prayer after Communion; Thursday of fourth week, prayer after Communion; Monday of third week, prayer after Communion.

248 Third Sunday, opening prayer; see also the prayer after Communion.

249 Friday of second week, opening prayer. [The Latin text has "ut resurrectionis gratiam consequamur" ("that we may win the grace of resurrection"). — Tr.]

250 Tuesday in octave of Easter, opening prayer.

251 First preface of the ascension.

252 Second preface of Easter.

253 Ascension, opening prayer.

254 Tuesday of second week, opening prayer.

255 Easter Day, opening prayer.

256 Edited by G. Morin, "Le plus ancient lectionnaire de l'Eglise romaine," *Revue bénédictine* 27 (1910), pp. 41–74. For its history, see C. Vogel, *Introduction aux sources de l'histoire du culte chrétien au Moyen Age* (Biblioteca degli "Studi Medievali" 1; Spoleto, n.d. [1965]), pp. 309–10, 313–14, 322–23.

257 Edited by A. Wilmart, "Le comes de Murbach," *Revue bénédictine* 30 (1913), pp. 26–59. See Vogel, *op. cit.*, pp. 318–19.

258 See A. Chavasse, "Le lectionnaire et l'antiphonaire romains," *Revue bénédictine* 62 (1952), pp. 74–76.

259 Mercenier and Paris, *op. cit.*, 2:210–61.

260 O. H. E. Burmester, *Le lectionnaire de la semaine sainte* in *Patrologia Orientalis* 25:433ff.

261 [In Christian usage, the Greek word *oikonomia* means "administration," and then "arrangement, order, plan." The "economy" of salvation is the working out of God's plan of salvation. An "economic" interpretation of the Trinity analyzes, not the relation of each of the three Persons to the others within the Godhead, but the relation of each to the work of salvation. — Tr.]

262 See *Vita S. Benedicti Anianensis* 26 (*PL* 103:364).

263 See P. Browe, "Zur Geschichte des Dreifaltigkeitsfestes," *Archiv für Liturgiewissenschaft* 1 (1950) 69.

264 St. Athanasius of Alexandria, *First Letter to Serapion* 28 and 30 (*SC* 15:134, 138).

265 *Ibid.*, no. 30 (*SC* 15:138–39).

266 See L. C. Mohlberg (ed.), *Liber sacramentorum romanae aeclesiae ordinis circuli (Sacramentarium Gelasianum)* (Rerum ecclesiasticarum documenta, Series maior: Fontes 4; Rome, 1963), no. 286. [N.B.: In the older baptismal ritual and in the revised rite, the Latin text has *gloriae tuae rudimenta* (see *Ordo Initiationis Christianae Adultorum* [editio typica; Rome, 1972], p. 30, no. 87). This is translated in the official English version as "your initial teachings" (*Rite of Christian Initiation of Adults* [Washington, D.C., 1974], no. 87). Mohlberg's critical edition of the Gelasian Sacramentary, from which this prayer is taken, has *magnitudinis gloriae rudimenta*, which Nocent interprets as meaning "the beginning of his [the catechumen's] future great glory." — Tr.]

267 St. Thomas Aquinas, *Opusculum* 57: *Officium de Festo Cor-*

poris Christi, In primo nocturno lectio 1. Text in *Opuscula theologica*, ed. R. A. Verardo, O.P., and R. M. Spiazzi, O.P. (Turin, 1954), 2:276.

[268] *Opusculum* 3: *Lignum vitae* 47 (*Opera Omnia*, ed. Quaracchi, 8:79).

ABBREVIATIONS

AAS	*Acta Apostolicae Sedis*
CCL	*Corpus Christianorum, Series Latina.* Turnhout, 1953–.
CL	*Constitution on the Sacred Liturgy*
CSEL	*Corpus Scriptorum Ecclesiasticorum Latinorum.* Vienna, 1866–
Flannery	*Vatican Council II: The Conciliar and Post Conciliar Documents*, Austin Flannery, O.P., General Editor. Collegeville, Minn., 1975
LH	*Liturgy of the Hours*
PG	*Patrologia Graeca*, ed. J. P. Migne. Paris, 1857–66
PL	*Patrologia Latina*, ed. J. P. Migne. Paris, 1844–64
SC	*Sources Chrétiennes.* Paris, 1942–
TPS	*The Pope Speaks.* Washington, 1954–
TDNT	*Theological Dictionary of the New Testament.* Grand Rapids, 1964–74